Philip Shelley is a producer and script editor who has been working with screenwriters for the last thirty years.

He has run the Channel 4 screenwriting course since 2010, and also runs the Greenlight Screenwriting Lab for new writers in Ireland. Many of the UK's most successful screenwriters and script editors have come through the Channel 4 course, including Charlie Covell, Cat Jones, Anna Symon, Vinay Patel, Nida Manzoor, Theresa Ikoko, Nathaniel Price and Grace Ofori-Attah.

Philip has run many screenwriting and script-editing courses through his own script consultancy and with BBC Studios, ITV Studios, thinkBIGGER! Channel 4 Production Trainee Scheme, Screen Ireland, BBC Writers, Northern Ireland Screen, Screenskills, University of the Arts London, De Montfort University, Filmnation UK, Baby Cow Productions, and many others.

He has extensive experience as a script editor on series like *Waking the Dead* (BBC), *Inspector Morse*, *Kavanagh QC*, *The Knock*, *Staying Alive*, *Cider With Rosie*, *Medics* (all ITV), and produced *First Sign of Madness* (which won awards at the New York TV Festival, Worldfest Houston, and the Columbus Ohio TV Festival), *Margery and Gladys* and *Making Waves* (all ITV).

He was Head of Development for Carlton TV Drama for seven years, where he also ran the Carlton New Writers' Course, and has worked in script development for BBC TV Drama and several independent production companies.

Philip runs his own script consultancy (www.script-consultant.co.uk) and works with writers of all levels of experience, as well as production companies and broadcasters.

'For writers and script editors looking for help and guidance, there is no better resource than Philip Shelley and this book!' Nathaniel Price (*Mr Loverman, Noughts + Crosses*)

'Getting a place on Philip Shelley's 4Screenwriting course was one of the most important things to ever happen to me. It taught me so much, and gave me a great start in the industry. Philip's knowledge and guidance is unparalleled: this book is wise, practical, and brilliantly helpful.' Charlie Covell (*The End of the F***ing World, Kaos*)

'This brilliantly executed, comprehensive book is the definitive guide to screenwriting. Packed with invaluable information, personal insights, practical tasks, and references from across the TV landscape, it is essential reading for newcomers to the art form, as well as anyone who wants to work with screenwriters.' Grace Ofori-Attah (*Malpractice, In the Long Run*)

'An indispensable book for anyone who writes TV, who's thinking of writing TV, or is simply interested in how creativity works. Philip writes with passion, knowledge and sensitivity.' Laurence Bowen, CEO of Dancing Ledge Productions (*The Responder, Wedding Season*)

'This brilliant, highly informative guide to screenwriting demonstrates, step by step, how to create a dramatic story from scratch, as well as the key components that are needed to make a script both original and compelling. Drawing on his own vast experience of working with writers, Phillip Shelley illustrates in real detail how to radically improve screenwriting craft and build a successful career in the industry. I wish it had been published when I was starting out.' Anna Symon (*The Essex Serpent, Joan*)

Philip Shelley

Screen-writing

The Craft and The Career

NICK HERN BOOKS
London
www.nickhernbooks.co.uk

A Nick Hern Book

Screenwriting: The Craft and The Career
first published in Great Britain in 2025
by Nick Hern Books Limited
The Glasshouse, 49a Goldhawk Road, London W12 8QP

Copyright © 2025 Philip Shelley

Cover image: Shutterstock.com/Plasteed
Designed and typeset by Nick Hern Books, London
Printed and bound in Great Britain by Ashford Colour Ltd, Gosport, Hampshire

A CIP catalogue record for this book is available from the British Library

ISBN 978 1 83904 409 0

*For my darling wife Cindy,
who is everything to me.
I love you.*

Contents

Preface	xvii
Introduction: The Inspiration of Story	xxiii
PART ONE: THE CRAFT	1
I. **Creativity and Screenwriting: Getting Started**	3
Where We're At	4
Your 'Spec' or 'Calling Card' Script	4
Voice	6
UK screenwriters and what defines their voice	8
II. **Story Ideas**	11
Ideas that Inspire Dramatic Stories	11
Testing your ideas	13
Dreaming and Creativity	17
Collaboration and discussion	18
Dreams	18
Don't create?	21
Generating Ideas from Other Media	25
Documentaries: the lessons for screenwriters	30
What is Your Story About?	34
Story Ideas: Conclusion	37

III. Storytelling for the Screen — 40

The Basis of Your Story — 40
    The logline — 40
    The story premise — 41
    The dramatic proposition — 42

Genre — 48

Tone — 53

Form — 54

Principles of Dramatic Storytelling — 56
    Introduction — 56
    Research: know what you write — 57
    The essential dramatic events of your story should happen on, not off screen — 59
    Withhold exposition until the moment of maximum dramatic impact — 61
    The hook: posing questions is at the heart of effective storytelling — 62
    Generate suspense — 64
    Make a virtue of context — 65
    Subtext and counterpoint are essential elements in dramatic storytelling — 65
    Humour and humanity are the bedrock of story — 66
    Good writing is about accessing an emotional response to an event — 67
    Acknowledge and subvert tropes and clichés — 69
    Think carefully about what to include and what to leave out — 71
    Every single scene needs to change the status quo of your story — 72
    Make use of the infinite potential variety in the nature and character of scenes — 72
    Tell the story through the cut — 75
    Pay attention to the rhythm of how your story plays — 76
    Hit the ground running — 77

Key Storytelling Elements	78
Stakes	78
Narrative clarity and connections	79
Story gaps	80
Point of view	81
Set-ups and pay-offs	85
Signposts	86
Metaphors, imagery and motifs	87
Movement	88
Story world	90
Things to Consider Carefully	90
Random events and *deus ex machina*	90
Politics and preaching to the converted	92
Character-driven versus plot-driven	93
Two Further Thoughts	94
Be specific	94
Get your story onto the page	94
Aspects of Exposition	95
Disguise or dramatise exposition	95
Reveal exposition through action rather than dialogue	96
Exposition and evoking an emotional response through the use of objects	97
Who knows what, when?	98
Familiar expositional devices and tropes	100
Stylised Storytelling Devices	101
Voice-over	102
Flashback	103
Direct address to camera	103
Mockumentary	104
Montage	105
Captions	106
Treatment of Time	106
Condensing time	108
The ticking clock	109

CONTENTS

Structure — 109
  Introduction: what is 'structure' and how can it be useful to us? — 109
  The units of storytelling for the screen — 115
    Shots — 115
    Beats — 115
    Scenes — 116
    Acts — 116
    Sequences — 116
  The beginning and end of your story — 117
  Aspects of structure — 118
    Time structures — 118
    Form structures — 118
    Societal structures — 119
    Physical structures — 119
  Creative approaches to story structure — 120
    Football matches — 120
    Other media — 121
  Structure ≠ story — 121
Structure: Conclusions — 123

IV. Character — 126

Introduction — 126
Elements of Characterisation — 127
  Empathy — 127
  Character choices — 127
  The character journey — 129
  Distinctive characters — 130
  Internal conflict and contradiction — 130
  Subtext — 133
  Character 'intelligence' — 133
  Heightened but identifiable — 135
  Conjunctions of character and story world — 135
  Throw stones at your characters — 137

Character and risk	137
Character and tone	138
Active versus passive	138
Character arcs	139
Real people	140
Self-awareness	147
Character agenda	149
Character detail	150
Appearance and physicality	151
Character status	151
Characters and communities	153
Relationships	153
Non-human relationships	154
Relationship units	154
The family unit	155
Stereotypes	156
Character history and backstory	157
Audience perception of character	158
Characters who are engaged by their own story	158
Engaging characters, characters we care about	162

v. Dialogue   175

Introduction   175

Dialogue Considerations   176

Dialogue and exposition	176
Reality versus economy	177
Articulate versus inarticulate	178
Subtext in dialogue	180
Dialogue and genre	181
Dialogue and story	181
Dialogue and the intention of the scene	182
Dialogue is speaking and listening	182
Dialogue and research	183
Distinctive dialogue	183

Dialogue as 'voice'	185
Dialogue and dialect	186
Foreign language	186
Subtitles	188
Texting, messaging, WhatsApp, etc.	188
Dialogue: Conclusions	189
VI. Presentation	195
Introduction: Getting Your Story onto the Page	195
Read screenplays	196
Use screenwriting software	197
Presentation Considerations	197
Tell your story with clarity and simplicity	197
The reader experience should be as close as possible to the audience experience	198
Introducing characters	199
Imagine your script from the reader's perspective	199
Open your script on the protagonist	200
Distinguish between what the writer and director brings to the film	200
Guiding the reader	201
Don't cheat!	202
Writer's commentary	203
Some principles for directions	204
Elements of the Screenplay	206
Scene headings	206
Action	207
Character names	208
Parentheticals	209
Dialogue	210
Dual dialogue	210
Transitions	210

Once You've Finished Writing	211
Proofread on paper, not on screen	211
The objective read	211
Titles	213
VII. Supplementary Screenwriting Documents	218
Pre-script Documents: Treatments, Outlines, Beat Sheets	218
They're important!	219
Pitching: Verbal and Written	220
Don't 'perform' your pitch!	221
The context of the pitch	222
The quality of the idea	223
Meetings and written pitches	224
Copyright and ownership	224
Trust	225
Pitching: essential elements?	226
The incomplete pitch	228
Pre-meeting research	228
What's your story?	229
Know what genre your story is	229
The form of the written pitch	230
Deliver content	231
Pitch decks	231
Visual details	232
References and comparisons	232
Writer's agenda, and theme	233
Character biographies	233
Loglines	233
Pitching – sealing the deal	234
Story Documents: Outlines, Beat Sheets, or Scene-by-Scenes	239
Developing an idea	239
Learning from the best…	240
Visual, dramatic storytelling	240

PART TWO: THE CAREER   243

Introduction   245

1. Breaking In   248

Screenwriting Training   248
- Longer university courses – BAs and MAs   249
- Shorter courses   251
- Competitions   253

CVs and Interviews   255
- CVs   255
- Interviews   258

Your Network: Writing Groups, Peers and Support, Community   261
- Networking   262
- Selling yourself and your work   264
- Events   265
- Champions   266
- Readings and showcases   267
- Do your research   268
- Friend of a friend of a friend   268

Other Media   269
- Podcasts   269
- Theatre   269
- Audio and radio   270
- Short films   271
- Other writing   271
  - Journalism   272
  - Novels   272
  - Graphic novels and comics   272
  - Blogs   272
  - Documentary film-making   273
  - Poetry and songs   273

Social Media   274
- X (Twitter)   274
- Facebook/Meta   275

WhatsApp	275
LinkedIn	276
TikTok	276
Instagram	277

II. Sustaining a Career — 278

Strategy: Making the Most of the Opportunities — 278

General Meetings — 279
    What are general meetings for? — 280
    Come prepared — 281
    A two-way relationship — 282

Literary Agents — 283
    The writer and literary agent relationship — 283
    Finding the right agent — 284
    Approaching agents — 287
    What should you expect from your agent? — 288
    What should your agent expect from you? — 291

Notes, Feedback and Collaboration: Working with Script Editors — 291
    Notes — 291
    The fragility of story — 296
    Writers' rooms — 296
    Love the craft — 297
    Process, longevity and sustainability — 297
    Vomiters versus plotters — 298

Career: Conclusions — 300

Afterword — 303

Further Reading and Resources — 306

Acknowledgements — 311

Glossary — 313

Index of Names and Titles — 317

Index of Subjects — 322

Preface

I have been working with writers and on scripts for over twenty-five years – and this book is a response to that hugely enjoyable experience. Through my teenage years, I had always been passionately interested in dramatic writing through television, cinema and theatre and then, as a struggling actor, I started writing myself. A screenplay, then a stage play which I submitted to Paines Plough theatre company. The literary manager at the time, the excellent Robin Hooper, let me down gently and with great kindness and took me on as a script reader and occasional dramaturg. It was reading my first script professionally and then beginning to talk to writers face to-face about their work that introduced me to the possibility of script-editing as a career.

Trying to balance the dying days of my thirteen years as a professional actor with an ever-increasing pile of script-reading work eventually led to my first two-week contract in the Granada TV drama department offices in Golden Square, London.

The bridge from life as an actor into script-editing was through this reading work for theatre, TV and film. One of the most interesting jobs I had was for Anthony Hopkins' acting agent, reading and assessing the scripts he had been sent as job offers. One script I read for this was Dennis Potter's adaptation of Dickens' *The Mystery of Edwin Drood*, which I remember to this day as a dark, brilliant, inspiring piece of writing (sadly a film that never got made). Among many other companies, I read for David Puttnam's Enigma Films, Film 4, Paramount Pictures and the First Film Foundation.

This was pre-internet days and script-reading work often meant coming into London for meetings in which you hand-delivered your (paper) script reports, returned the (paper) scripts and discussed your feedback with the (flesh and blood) development person at the company in question who had hired you. This face-to-face time with such industry luminaries as Laurence Bowen (I remember Laurence talking to me about what 'structure' in dramatic storytelling was all about!), Kate Leys, Allon Reich and Tony Dinner at the old BBC Script Unit – the less publicised forerunner of the current BBC Writers – was invaluable. (Tony, for instance, was a brilliant supporter of new writers and budding script editors, one of those people that the industry relies upon.)

I sat at home, between acting jobs, reading scripts – of variable quality – for the best part of two years; and it was the most brilliant grounding in scripts and story, particularly having to write a report on each script – synopsis, comment, verdict – trying to make sense of the pros and cons of every story, and thinking about why the good ones were good and the other ones not so good.

It made me realise that you learn at least as much from the bad as the good scripts. It also made me appreciate the power of genuinely excellent dramatic writing. There are scripts I read in those two years that I remember to this day – or I remember at least the thrill I felt in reading work that was outstanding.

On arrival for my two weeks at Granada to research a drama series idea about missing people written by Paul Abbott (another show that never got made) I remember what seemed like the extraordinary novelty of having my own office. It was a great first job to have as my introduction to the world of TV drama. My wonderful, eccentric bosses, Sally Head and Gwenda Bagshaw, ran a department that created and produced such seminal shows as *Cracker* (Jimmy McGovern), *Prime Suspect* (Lynda La Plante) and *Band of Gold* (Kay Mellor). My first script-editing job was on a long-running 9 p.m. medical drama series, *Medics*, working with many outstanding writers including Neil McKay and Sarah Daniels.

The world of the drama departments at ITV companies, Granada TV and after that London Weekend Television (again with Sally and Gwenda) was incredibly exciting but, in retrospect, something of an emotional whirlwind. Although people probably behave with greater circumspection and courtesy now than they did when I first started, I think this is still to some extent true of a lot of film and TV drama development and production in the UK.

Most producers get to where they are more often for their creative than their organisational skills. To this day, there is too rarely in the production of TV drama a really well-organised system to support the creative endeavours of writer, director, actors, etc., but that's a whole other story.

I still remember (at this distance, with a smile) some of the more emotionally jagged moments. For instance – the first ever script meeting I attended as junior, observing script editor (after the script editor I was replacing had fallen out with the producer and been summarily sacked), consisted of a writer declining – politely but firmly and with no real creative explanation – to address every single note the script editor suggested in a two-hour meeting. After the writer left, this script editor (understandably) burst into tears. The following day the meeting was reconvened with writer, script editor and – this time – executive producer present and giving the notes. On this occasion the writer enthusiastically agreed to address the exact same notes they had declined the previous day. I can see no evidence that this writer ever worked in TV drama again! (Not that there was a witch-hunt, just that this writer must have decided collaboration was not for them.)

I remember a meeting in which a head of department threw a very weighty script at a producer in some argument over a minor story point; a stand-up row between head of department and producer at a read-through in front of the assembled cast; leaving the office at 8 p.m. one evening and returning next morning to discover my fellow script editor and producer were still in the meeting I had left and had been working on the script through the whole night; and an 11 p.m. meeting with a (drunk) executive producer who praised my work and promised to pay me a substantial financial bonus (which was never mentioned again, let alone paid, in the sober light of day).

It can be an intense, difficult process – but it can also be incredibly exciting, creatively rewarding and a lot of fun.

The lesson from all of this is that creating a TV show or film is an emotive business, particularly in production where all the deadlines are locked in and there can be no stopping (or leaping off) the runaway train that is production. When a lot of egos come together in a creative undertaking, there are bound to be occasional clashes and disagreements; creative decisions are personal. It's sometimes hard to find that distinction between the story you're trying to tell and your own personal feelings.

I think it's true of all of the best writers that there is a huge amount of themselves in their work. Writing and delivering any script is a personal act of courage. As a writer, even if you're not intending it to, your writing will reveal a huge amount about you. Writing is very exposing in what you reveal about yourself and even more so in the way you open yourself up to instant judgement. To put yourself through this, you have to *need* to be a writer, it needs to be a huge part of who you are as a person. Writing – and screenwriting in particular – is for the brave and the resilient.

The other side of that coin is that there is of course enormous fulfilment in writing a script of which you're proud and seeing it being launched into the world; of seeing people responding positively to it; and sometimes through your script, changing entrenched attitudes and the world around you (campaigning TV films like Jimmy McGovern's *Hillsborough*, Nicole Taylor's *Three Girls* and Jack Thorne's *Help* are outstanding examples of what can be achieved socially and politically through great screenwriting).

But, in trying to sustain your morale and your career, you need to have some method, technique and storytelling principles to call on. Much of writing is instinctive but instinct needs to be supported by craft and guiding principles.

★ ★ ★

Part of the purpose of this preface is to make the distinction that I am not a screenwriter (a lot of my professional life is spent writing – but not screenwriting), but that what I can bring to the table for you as screenwriters/dramatic writers is the fact that, for such a long time, and continuing right now and into the future, I am one of those industry people to whom you will be submitting your script. And through years of thinking about story and observing and working with many successful writers, I have developed strong views as to what it takes to gain success as a professional dramatic writer, both in terms of the craft of dramatic storytelling and the more pragmatic areas of building and sustaining a career – and this, I hope, is how I can be helpful to you.

In both regards, my last fifteen years as a freelancer, running my own independent script consultancy and the Channel 4 screenwriting course, have been particularly valuable.

In my work as a script consultant, I have now fed-back on over 2,000 different projects.

The Channel 4 screenwriting course is now in its fourteenth year. More than a hundred and fifty writers have come through the course and many of the course alumni are among the hottest properties in UK screenwriting.

Writers need to write – every day. For professional and budding professional writers, writing is more than a habit or a hobby, it's a compulsion, it's unthinking. It's important that script editors like me recognise that big distinction between the script editors, producers and executives on one side of the table and the writer on the other (more of which later) – although it should be noted that there are also many people who successfully move between working as script editors or development executives and screenwriting themselves.

What I can bring you is the perspective of someone who has worked with writers for more than twenty-five years, who has read and assessed many thousands of scripts, and worked face-to-face with hundreds of writers.

Introduction:
The Inspiration of Story

The real inspiration for this book is a life lived enjoying story in all its forms. Storytelling is an inextricable part of all our lives. The way we think about our own lives is often the same way we think about fictional stories. The way journalists work is to select information and work it into the coherent shape of a 'story'.

Life is fundamentally mysterious and we all have a deep need to create and/or experience fictional stories – or fictionalised dramatisations of 'true' stories – to inform and impose order on the ordinary and extraordinary, strange and often unfathomable events of our real lives.

Story helps to make sense of the confusion, mystery and messiness of real life. Story in all its forms addresses the primal mysteries of birth, death, procreation, individuality, fate, time, disease, natural disasters, love – and all the other multifarious aspects of life that defy rational explanation.

Story goes some way to providing both an intellectual – but more importantly emotional – response to the Great Uncertainties of Life.

At its epic, large-scale best, the way we experience story is akin to a religious experience. (What is the New Testament if not a series of artfully constructed, character-driven, human stories?)

We all have an intimate, personal connection to those televisual and cinematic stories that we first experienced and enjoyed at a formative, impressionable age. For me those stories were films like *The Godfather, Apocalypse Now, One*

Flew Over the Cuckoo's Nest, Butch Cassidy and the Sundance Kid, Annie Hall, Manhattan, A Hard Day's Night, Harold and Maude, The Graduate, Kramer vs. Kramer, American Graffiti, Jaws... I could go on. Those films that still say something fresh to you every time you see them, while at the same time giving you that repeated appreciation of those story moments that make your heart jump, that send a chill down your spine. *The Godfather* is packed full of those – images and moments that are imprinted on my retina.

The first time I saw *The Godfather* I was in the US, where we lived for two years in the 1970s. The film had just come out and was already a big hit. I can't remember exactly where we saw it but it was in a packed movie theatre somewhere in the suburbs of Philadelphia. As well as being struck by my first experience of a US movie audience – and how vocal and raucous they were in their expressions of excitement at the film – I remember being taken by what I saw as some of the explicit sexual moments; and simultaneously by the uncomfortable awareness that the most explicit sex scenes I had ever seen in a film (it had been a sheltered upbringing) were experienced sitting next to my dad.

But also I remember being incredibly excited by the visceral power of the story, the images and moments that felt so powerfully dramatic and have stayed with me to this day. *The Godfather* is one of those seminal films where virtually every scene and sequence feels like a 'greatest hits' moment.

I have seen the film many times since and every time I watch it, I marvel at some other scene or sequence that strikes me anew as brilliant screen storytelling.

Among other formative cinema-going memories is one of the very first films I ever saw in a cinema (by which I mean one of the first films I saw, full stop, as films on TV weren't a thing back in the mid-1960s). This was The Beatles' Richard Lester-directed *A Hard Day's Night*. I still recall the joyful rush that film and The Beatles' music gave (and still gives) me. Many years later I had two stints working as drama script editor for Sally Head Productions at Twickenham Studios. There was one small office on our corridor that belonged not to SHP but to the great man himself, a film-maker with a key role in the history of British Cinema – Richard Lester – a gentle presence who would quietly and politely greet you on his way to and from his office.

Two John Wayne films also come to mind: firstly, *The Alamo*, to which my mother took me as a desperate displacement activity on the last miserable day of the school holidays before I was packed off to boarding school. This was actually one instance when a film story didn't work its magic – the memory of the whole experience of this visit to an empty-ish matinee in a cinema in Canterbury, Kent, is one of misery.

And then another Wayne film, *True Grit*. There is a scene where a character falls into a pit of snakes. The woman in the row in front was so lost in the film that she started hitting her rolled-up newspaper on the back of the seat in front of her, yelling and warding off the imagined snakes. A wonderful and funny example of the power of cinema to enable you to inhabit a story so completely.

Cinema continues to this day to be one of the hugely positive aspects of my life. Nothing compares to the escape and joy of being pulled into a compelling story in the comforting isolation of a cinema.

★ ★ ★

In my youth, television fiction soon became as big a joy as cinema – from the comedy genius of Monty Python and Morecambe and Wise to wonderful TV dramas – the riches of BBC drama in the 1970s and '80s – *Play for Today*, and so many other brilliant writer-led strands (*The Wednesday Play*, *Screen One*, *Screen Two*, *Second City Firsts*, etc.). In fact it was this sort of wonderful TV drama – strands that highlighted the creative primacy of the writer – that first alerted me to the exciting world of dramatic writing in general and screenwriting in particular – exceptional writers like Jack Rosenthal, Dennis Potter, Mike Leigh, Peter Nichols, Stephen Poliakoff, Howard Schuman, Ken Loach, Alan Clarke, G. F. Newman, Jim Allen and Alan Bennett, all starting to make their mark as dramatists for the screen. (Not a lot of gender or racial diversity in the profile of TV writers of that period!)

Each generation form their beliefs, passions and identities at least partly around the films, plays, books and music they experience at that formative age.

One of the real strengths and virtues of screenwriting is in the narrative possibilities, the range and richness, of series TV – multi-stranded, ensemble series like *Call My Agent!* (Fanny Herrero), *Euphoria* (Sam Levinson), *Orange Is the New Black* (Jenji Kohan) and *Last Tango in Halifax* (Sally Wainwright).

Series TV at its best is about our emotional investment in character and how this investment deepens and grows with every passing episode and season. Of course, it's also about story and the situations in which these characters find themselves. But without character, story can soon wear thin. *Money Heist* is an example of brilliant storytelling but with characters who don't, in my opinion, have the requisite texture of the very best TV series. I stuck with this for ten episodes, but my interest waned as the writing revealed the limits of the character definition.

On the other hand, the pilot episode of *Succession* is a wonderful example of the most brilliantly flawed and fascinating characters arriving fully formed on screen the moment you meet them. The way characters enter the story in this opening episode is memorable; inspiring examples of how to introduce your characters – Kendall on the way to his meeting in the chauffeur-driven limo, psyching himself up to rap music on his earphones, cousin Greg being humiliated in an animal costume at one of the Waystar theme parks; Logan waking confused in the night and pissing on the carpet. All of these opening character moments are utterly distinctive, idiosyncratic and dynamic; and they instantly get us to the heart of each of these characters' internal conflicts.

The shows that first really excited me in the way they exploited the series format were US productions like *Homicide: Life on the Street* (Paul Attanasio), *Oz* (Tom Fontana) and *Thirtysomething* (Marshall Herskovitz, Edward Zwick).

All the best series make a necessary virtue of their limitations, of containing their stories in particular settings (precincts). In this way, series set in prisons, hospitals and police stations have spawned so many brilliant formats over the years.

★ ★ ★

My experiences running the Channel 4 screenwriting course feel like a wonderful mirroring of my first experience of TV dramatists. Remembering the joy and education (above all, a political education, for which I am eternally grateful) those writers above mentioned gave me, it's now deeply pleasing to be part of a course that introduces new dramatists to TV drama – brilliant, innovative, original writers like Charlie Covell, Anna Symon, Vinay Patel, Theresa Ikoko, Inua Ellams, and so many more, who I feel confident will be among the groundbreaking screenwriters of the next decade and beyond: the

2020s equivalents of current star TV dramatists like Sally Wainwright, Russell T Davies, Jack Thorne, James Graham, etc.

I'm in the privileged position of being at the cutting edge of trends in new dramatic writing. Above all, over the last ten years, it's been a privilege to see the blossoming of increased racial diversity in UK screenwriting. The range and quality of dramatic writing by new voices from the Black and Asian communities in particular has been a joy to behold and be a part of – writers like the aforementioned Inua Ellams (writer of acclaimed stage play *Barber Shop Chronicles* – a National Theatre production), Theresa Ikoko (*Rocks*), Vinay Patel (*Murdered by My Father*) and Abraham Adeyemi, Dipo Baruwa-Etti, Archie Maddocks, Nathaniel Price, Chandni Lakhani, Matthew Jacobs Morgan, Matilda Feyiṣayọ Ibini, Anna Ssemuyaba, Shyam Popat, Jenny Takahashi Stark, Kirsty Rider and many others – these are all writers who are starting to make a real impact and about whom you will hear much more in the coming years.

★ ★ ★

Screenwriting is hard. There are a lot of screenplays, a lot of films and TV shows, and not many of them are outstanding. Not only that, not many of the initial *ideas* for films and TV shows are outstanding. So it's something to strive for – to write a seriously good screenplay is a real achievement. Perversely this doesn't necessarily mean you have to suffer, that it will be a hard, painful, stressful process. Sometimes the best scripts will come easily, will pour out of you. Equally, sometimes a good script will take months and years of dead ends, strife and rethinks. There is no rhyme or reason to the process, to what clicks. There are some brilliant writers who have written some poor scripts; and some writers who have written one brilliant script and are then never able to repeat it. Not only is it difficult, it's mysterious and mercurial. So this book doesn't attempt to offer artificial short cuts. Trying to reduce the process and the template for stories to a single, reductive formula is simplistic, unrealistic and, frankly, insulting to the real writers who strive endlessly, coming at story from so many different angles, constantly learning, over a career of writing good scripts.

PART ONE
THE CRAFT

I
Creativity and Screenwriting: Getting Started

Creativity is where craft begins. As writers you need to be constantly returning to the well of invention and imagination. If you're very unlucky, your career will go like this: you will write one or two excellent 'spec' (as in 'speculative' – unpaid) scripts that will attract industry interest. This will lead to you being hired to write episodes on existing TV drama series. Your work on these episodes will lead to more of this work. This will (at first) be demanding but exciting, creatively satisfying, and financially rewarding work. But as the years go by and you are continuing to write these series episodes on other people's shows, as the demands of this work begin to sap your creative energy, you may lose your excitement and enthusiasm, the episodes you write will begin to lose their sparkle. You will start to feel used, overworked, and the originality of your voice will become tarnished and stale. You will forget the excitement and inspiration that first made you want to write; it will become just a job.

Gradually this regular series work will begin to dry up as you are replaced by younger, hungrier, fresher writers.

The industry can be brutal like this and it's so important that you do all you can to avoid this cycle by constantly refreshing your work and your voice.

This is where the 'spec' or 'calling card' script comes in.

Where We're At

The film and TV drama industry in the UK – but I think globally too – is in a fascinating place at the moment. When I first started working in the world of scripts back in the 1990s, in TV drama, genre was very much the staple – a lot of one-hour, 9 p.m. dramas were being made by the BBC and ITV, most of which were returnable crime, medical or legal shows. Variety came in the shape of longer-form episodes of shorter-run mini-series – but most of these were also crime – or adaptations of famous books (Dickens, Austen, Christie, etc.) that had been adapted several times before.

Now though, with the proliferation of broadcasters and platforms looking for scripted content, everyone is trying to cut through and make their mark – and conventional genre shows have become the exception rather than the rule. There are far more opportunities and openings now for genuinely innovative, authored work – often, the more outlandish and unexpected the better. In short, there has never been a better time for new writers to find their place in the industry and to make a mark by announcing themselves through the uniqueness of their work. (Much more about this in Part 2, the 'Career' section of this book.)

Your 'Spec' or 'Calling Card' Script

At the start of your career it's your spec script that is going to open doors for you and get you work. New writers sometimes tell me they have a great idea and ask if I can introduce them to potential employers and help them to try to interest producers in this idea. But this is putting the cart before the horse. No producer worth their salt will hire you as a writer – no matter how wonderful the idea – if they don't know your work as a writer, if they haven't read a script or scripts by you. As I will go on to discuss, good, exciting ideas will be the cornerstone and starting point of your script – but there is obviously a huge leap from brilliant idea to brilliantly executed, full-length script.

Writers get on to the Channel 4 screenwriting course principally through the script they write (and partly through the interview, more on which later) but these scripts, sadly and frustratingly, don't generally get made.

In the US there is a thriving spec market. Such a thing doesn't exist in the UK in the same way. To date, of the 150+ scripts written in the first fourteen years of the Channel 4 course, while literally dozens of these scripts have been 'optioned' by production companies – and many are still in active development – only one has been made: a script by Tom Wells that was made in the Channel 4 *Coming Up* series of films.

Your first few spec scripts, even though they probably won't get made, may well be the most important scripts you will ever write. I know of countless examples of writers for whom one or two of the first ever scripts they've written (or at least the first scripts they've shown to the world) have opened countless industry doors for them and sustained their writing careers for many years.

If you're not going to fall into the trap I laid out above, of the writer who gradually gets used up and spat out by the system (writers who become 'hacks'?), it's important that you keep writing spec scripts. As your career develops, as you get older, as the world changes and as you change, so will your outlook on the world, and what you have to say as a writer and how you say it.

It's therefore vital that you try to find the time to keep writing spec scripts, those scripts that highlight your unique talents and sensibilities as a writer. I have often heard agents talking about how they encourage their clients to write fresh spec scripts that they (the agents) can use to showcase their clients. After a few years your original spec script may not seem as relevant and impactful as it once did. For a writer, this process is about keeping working at developing and showcasing your particular strengths and passions as a writer, and letting the wider industry know that you're still relevant, still writing about the things that matter, and are still remaining creative and prolific.

One of the things an uncommissioned, spec script allows you is the freedom to write about whatever you like: a rare opportunity (if you are so inclined) to write a screenplay of real scale. Maybe the sort of script that – because of its potential budget or controversial subject matter – will never get made but that is about something utterly distinctive to you and your personal passions.

Voice

Writing is individual. No two writers are the same just as no two people are the same. How your work as a writer, as an individual, comes across to reader and audience can be identified as your unique writer's voice.

'Voice' is something that is talked about a lot in the industry. It's that hard-to-define quality, the thing that makes a writer stand out. 'A new, exciting, distinctive voice' is the quality that producers, script editors, development executives and literary agents are looking for in new writers. But what does this mean?

There are certain stories that you as writers were born to tell. The stories that come from your guts, the stories that you can't *not* tell. The more you write, the clearer your voice will become to you – even if you have to get through a lot of hours of writing before you start to get a strong sense of this. Your voice is the ability to tap into and write about your own truths. We all feel strongly about something (and if we don't, we have no business being writers). Voice is about finding those ideas, stories and characters that stir you up, that ignite your passion and enable you to produce stories that feel natural and important to you. But persevere. If writing is one thing, it is hugely time-consuming. You have to put in the hours.

So, without getting too hung up and unhelpfully self-conscious about it, you need to work at finding your individual voice as a writer. If we think about successful, high-profile writers, with some it's easy to identify their unique voice, with others less so.

I suppose one of the ultimate examples of a screenwriter who has become absolutely identified with a very particular style of storytelling that feels utterly distinctive to them is Quentin Tarantino. Of the few genuinely well-known screenwriters (don't go into screenwriting if it's fame you're after!), Tarantino is arguably the most imitated and influential (even if he's known more as a director than a writer). It's telling that so many writers who don't yet have the confidence of knowing their own voice fall back on Tarantino-esque dialogue and style. It's interesting to observe that Tarantino's voice developed from his own deep obsession with cinema. Often his 'voice' is itself one of homage or imitation of other screenwriters who came before him.

CREATIVITY AND SCREENWRITING: GETTING STARTED

Sarfraz Manzoor is a journalist and writer, whose book *Greetings from Bury Park* is the inspiration for the film *Blinded by the Light* (2019, screenplay by Paul Mayeda Berges, Gurinder Chadha and Sarfraz Manzoor). Growing up the son of Pakistani immigrants in 1980s Luton, Manzoor's guiding light and inspiration as a writer was Bruce Springsteen. It's hard to think of a story that is more specific than a British-Pakistani growing up in Luton in 1987 and falling in love with the music and philosophy of Bruce Springsteen. Here is Sarfraz Manzoor, writing in the *Guardian* (29 August 2019):

> *The film is uncompromising in its cultural specificity… What I had not appreciated was the power of storytelling to engender empathy. The feeling that you don't fit in – discovering your identity through music (or film, writing). In telling a very specific story, it turned out, I was actually telling a universal one… Perhaps I should not have been surprised. After all, I was deeply moved and affected by* This Is England, Wild Rose *and* Annie Hall, *even though I am neither a young white English skinhead, a Scottish country-music-loving single mum, nor a neurotic middle-aged American-Jewish comedian.*

★ ★ ★

Nina Stibbe's first novel was published in 2014 – thirty years after she'd started writing. Another excellent *Guardian* article, 'How Nina Stibbe found her voice' (Sam Jordison, 21 April 2020), talks about how Stibbe had a series of unsuccessful writing ventures because she was writing in a style that was too self-consciously literary. It was only when, years later, her sister Victoria found the letters the younger Nina had written to her when Nina was working as a nanny in the 1980s and Nina reread them, that she realised where her strengths as a writer lay, how her 'voice' had been there all along. As the article says:

> *It's to Stibbe's credit that she realised where the appeal lay and applied her rediscovered voice to her novels. Those sharp observations, period details and cheeky moments of insight and open-hearted affection are all present and correct in Stibbe's other novels.*

> There are clear lessons from the work and experience of these two writers: in telling the truths of their own stories, in finding the detail, minutiae and specifics of their own stories, their stories become universal. To quote Sarfraz Mansoor, '*In a time when politicians seem intent on defining us by our differences, my film may remind them that all of us are characters in a larger human story.*'

As audiences, we value the magic of spending time with characters and in worlds we wouldn't encounter in real life – but that feel utterly personal and distinctive to the writer – and therefore somehow relatable.

Write the stories you want or need to write. First and foremost, write for yourself.

UK screenwriters and what defines their voice

Of contemporary UK TV dramatists, Sally Wainwright's hallmarks as a writer are numerous – her brilliance at dramatising character and story, her dark sense of humour and underlying well of humanity. She writes about social injustice but always as an integrated part of a human story; and her stories are (almost) exclusively rooted in the communities of Northern England where she's from.

Jimmy McGovern has a clear, distinctive and powerful voice as a writer. His work is very much rooted in his Liverpool background. The stories he tells are mainly about injustices perpetrated on working-class (often Catholic) communities and individuals. The brilliance of his craft as a storyteller is characterised by dramatising knotty character dilemmas, telling stories of emotional intensity that feel rooted in an everyday, working-class reality.

Russell T Davies is another outstanding UK screenwriter with a highly distinctive voice. His stories are always full of colour, imagination, almost operatic passion; and a real narrative flair for telling stories in unexpected and exciting ways. He is also, like McGovern, a pioneering, campaigning writer; many of the stories RTD chooses to tell are in celebration of queer characters and communities; of under-represented characters swimming against the tide of the conventional mainstream.

Charlie Brooker's wonderful *Black Mirror* series was foreshadowed by *Dead Set*, and the brilliance of his writing – which is darkly comic, usually set in a dystopian future and subversively political – is also evident in his comedy shows like *Screenwipe*, taking eviscerating, satirical swipes at the absurdities of modern political life.

On the other side of the pond, Aaron Sorkin has a huge body of work that is always recognisable as his – from *The West Wing* to *The Social Network*, *The Newsroom* to *Steve Jobs*, among many, many others. Sorkin's screenplays are characterised by their liberal politics, by the intelligence and articulacy of the dialogue and characters. His scripts are slick, sentimental, but full of formal flair and brilliant, playful cut-and-thrust dialogue. As with Tarantino, the term 'Sorkin-esque' has become part of the screenwriting lexicon.

What so many of these writers have in common in their voice is a sense of passion, a burning need to tell the particular stories they tell, to dramatise the lives of the people they are writing about. Drama driven by righteous, humanitarian anger – but all dramatised through detailed, layered, grounded characterisation. Above all, their voice is defined by their choice of story material. All the stories these writers tell, the subjects they choose, seem to have factors common to these individual writers.

Ultimately a writer's voice comes down to a writer's conviction and integrity – filtered through their own unique personal circumstances and experiences. We should all be trying to tell the stories that mean something to us on a deep emotional level. We don't need to analyse exactly what that is – but we need to recognise and connect with that passion that compels us to tell particular stories.

Voice is about finding universal themes and emotional lines in stories and characters that feel rooted in a very distinctive story world.

In exploring the concept of voice, and as a screenwriting education in its own right, it's really valuable to focus on the work of writers whose work you admire, and to watch (and more importantly read) as much of their back catalogue as you can. It's so interesting to see how their work and voice have developed and changed over the years; to see what elements their work always has, what never changes in the way they tell stories; to consider what is unique about them as writers.

What you absolutely shouldn't do is try to copy the way these writers write. What you should do is learn from their experience and from the way they craft their stories, and the example of how all of these writers have achieved success by finding a way to tell the stories they want to tell in the way they want to tell them; to see that one of the strengths of all of these writers is the specificity and individuality of their take on the world. A Jimmy McGovern story is a million miles from a Charlie Brooker story – but in their completely different and unique ways, they are equally brilliant.

Most of the best writers are not chameleons. They aren't equally adept at telling stories on screen across all sorts of different genres. To say they have their particular strengths means that they write to these strengths; this also means that they know where their strengths lie and what their limitations are.

There are the brilliant 'freaks', like Jack Thorne and Jesse Armstrong, whose voices (arguably) don't feel as strongly distinctive or identifiable as a writer like Jimmy McGovern; but Jack Thorne is a freak because he does, unlike most outstanding writers, seem equally adept at telling stories in so many different genres and styles – from a high-concept, family-adventure film like *The Aeronauts* to the gritty realism of *This Is England* (written with Shane Meadows) and *Help*.

Shane Meadows is the other side of the coin to Jack Thorne – a writer whose work is usually utterly distinctive to him, his voice instantly recognisable (in tone, style, character and story world).

II
Story Ideas

Ideas that Inspire Dramatic Stories

The ideas that you come up with as a writer, the starting point for each project – the one-sentence pitch, the logline – are such a vital part of the process.

I'd go as far as to say: get this right and it's hard to go wrong with the development of the idea; but get this wrong and, no matter how strong the quality of your writing, it will be really hard to bring this project to life.

Working with screenwriters through my script consultancy, I sometimes wish that they had come to me at pitch or outline stage rather than with a completed script. Too often my questions are about the starting point of the script – the idea that sparked their interest and imagination in the first place. Too many scripts (even scripts that get made) just do not contain this kernel of something genuinely exciting and inherently dramatic.

Your initial story starting point needs to contain a seemingly insoluble dilemma and to have conflict as one of its defining characteristics.

The other issue I too often see is a lack of scale and ambition in writers' choice of story material. At times, the stories newer writers in particular choose to tell don't seem to address those huge, fundamental questions that keep us all awake at night – the fact that time is running out for us to save our planet from destruction; the depth of corruption and inequality in today's social and political life; the prevalence of incurable disease and epidemics; and on the less gloomy side, how love can change lives; how certain people have transformed their society and the wider world for the better against enormous odds; celebrations of people who are outstanding and extraordinary in their particular fields. You might argue that all of the above suggestions feel unmanageably huge and uncontainable as stories – and this is a danger, an issue that needs to be confronted. But it's possible to tell all of these sorts of stories in a way that makes them relatable and engaging – through the perspective of particular individuals and characters, finding the 'macro' through the 'micro'. *The Road* (written by Joe Penhall, based on the novel by Cormac McCarthy) and *Station Eleven* (created by Patrick Somerville, based on the novel by Emily St. John Mandel) are two specifically post-apocalyptic examples of dramatising the macro through the micro – a film and series respectively, both adapted from novels, both about the end of the world as we know it, both told through the prism of minutely observed and relatable characters and relationships.

Note This is not to say there isn't also a place for those smaller, human stories. Two random examples – the wonderful *Detectorists* (Mackenzie Crook) and *Somebody Somewhere* (Hannah Bos and Paul Thureen). It's just that in my experience newer screenwriters overwhelmingly seem to go for these smaller-scale types of stories as opposed to more ambitious and epic stories – when they may not, as working, professional screenwriters, have the opportunity to tell stories of such scale and ambition again, until they have achieved considerable success.

Events in the real world, day to day, are endlessly fascinating and awe-inspiring, a constant stream of extraordinary stories such that there is no way you can keep up with everything interesting that is happening.

What you should be aiming for is that idea that causes the reader to respond: 'Yes, that's great. Why didn't I think of that? That is disarmingly simple [many of the better ideas are] but brilliant!'

If you can get your reader or audience excited in this distillation of the narrative premise, that is a great starting point for any story.

Testing your ideas

Test the story you want to tell against the stories that are appearing in the news at the moment. Is the story you want to tell as powerfully dramatic? Are the characters you have created as compelling as the people who make the news? If not, why are you writing these smaller fictional stories when you could be dramatising (and if necessary fictionalising) stories from the news to make them your own? Test your one-line logline pitches on other people. Often, you don't have to wait for a verbal response: you will see an instinctive response in their facial expression – does their face light up?

If you're choosing in your calling-card script to write a medical or police drama, you need to be absolutely clear that you are bringing something unique and utterly individual to the genre – that the specifics of the story and/or the way you are telling it is completely distinctive to you as a writer.

> Jed Mercurio – one of the most successful, high-profile and excellent screenwriters in the UK – first made his name as a TV dramatist with two medical shows: *Cardiac Arrest* (1994) and *Bodies* (2004). Although both shows sprang from this very familiar genre of medical drama, they punched though because of the boldness and passion of the writing, and because of the strength and particularity of the writer's agenda. Mercurio came from a medical background and his anger about various aspects of the NHS and the practice of medicine shines through in those two shows. Both shows are brutally honest, shocking, impassioned – but also deeply humanitarian, caring and powerfully dramatic.
>
> A later Mercurio medical drama, *Critical*, made for Sky in 2015, was perhaps less striking in terms of content (although still, by the standard of UK medical drama, powerfully visceral), but more striking in terms of its form – the way each episode took place almost entirely in the operating theatre in real time – a storytelling approach that gave the series an intensity almost unprecedented in UK TV medical drama series.

And the emotional and political commitment in Mercurio's writing in those early shows reminds me of a more recent example of an 'authored' medical drama that has really cut through – Adam Kay's *This Is Going to Hurt* (2022).

> **The Newspaper Exercise**
>
> A practical exercise to relieve the inhibiting burden of creating something from nothing.
>
> Get a paper copy of a broadsheet newspaper (it doesn't need to be current but somehow it comes more easily when you have a hard copy of a newspaper rather than scrolling through a news website). At random, choose two sheets of newspaper. Take five minutes to look through these two pages (time yourself, make sure you take no longer than five minutes – the pressure of time will helpfully force you into making story decisions!) to come up with a TV drama series idea (or a feature film, a sitcom, a stage play – but the more specific you make this artificial parameter, the easier you will find it to come up with a specific, clear idea), either taken directly from an article or headline, or suggested more indirectly from an article, a photograph, an advert, or a sentence. Distil this idea into a compelling one-sentence logline as a starting point.

The person who springs to mind when thinking about dramatic writers who consistently write stories that have their basis in attention-grabbing, headline ideas, is James Graham.

Graham forged his reputation in theatre and has since gone on to great success in screenwriting. There is a boldness to his choice of story material. Among his stand-out TV projects are two factual political dramas for Channel 4 – *Coalition* (2015) and *Brexit* (2019, a brilliant examination of the campaign that led to the Brexit vote), and then *Quiz* (2020, for ITV), about the *Who Wants to Be a Millionaire?*, 'coughing Major' scandal. These are big, attention-grabbing drama ideas plucked from newspaper headlines, and feel like stories that demanded to be told. What I particularly enjoyed about *Quiz* was that, although it was superficially about the *WWTBAM?* scandal, it was ultimately about much more than this – about 'Middle England', about class, almost a State of the Nation/Brexit piece. It's interesting to note also that *Quiz* was adapted by Graham from his own very successful stage play. (Some of the most successful screenwriters write in more than one dramatic narrative medium.)

James Graham's writing CV is almost unique in that it is characterised predominantly by dramatisations of real headline stories, usually about UK politics or with fictionalised stories inspired by real events (his more recent TV drama series, *Sherwood*, is another excellent illustration of this). But I think it is true of his work that almost every single project he has written is a stand-out pitch inspired by a real news story.

Jeff Pope and Neil McKay are comparable in having written many 'factual dramas' – projects characterised by the drama and conflict inherent in the true stories on which they are based.

I am of course not saying that this method of creating and writing dramatic stories is right and any other way is wrong – just that this plucking of stories from the headlines of the day seems to be strangely uncommon in (up-and-coming) screenwriters.

One of the reasons it does work is that journalists have often done so much of the important work for you as dramatists. They have identified that these are stories that deserve to be told, that they are important, noteworthy and will attract a readership.

Incidentally, a journalistic background is very useful for screenwriting (for example Nora Ephron, Nicholas Pileggi). And, as above, part of a journalist's strength as a writer is often their choice of stories to tell – big stories that really make a splash.

The work of journalists is predicated on research. The best journalists – and screenwriters – develop an instinct for how to use research to inform their stories, to give their stories a feeling of authenticity and persuasive detail.

> **Aspects to Consider When Choosing Story Ideas**
>
> **Scale** – think about the range of your story – not just the physical scale but the emotional scale and scope. A sense of scale so often equates to a sense of the dramatic.
>
> **Universality through specificity** – stories that tap into the mysteries of life, death, creation, oblivion. At its most fundamental, the reason we all have such a hunger for stories is to address those massive questions around the mysteries and meaning of life.
>
> As with all of these principles, this isn't something that you *have* to have as part of your story – but so many of the best scripts have this element of exploring the human condition, e.g. *Normal People* is all about love and what that means (while absolutely not being a story of scale – very much exploring the macro through the micro).
>
> Even with the best low-key character stories, there is often something being said that is fundamental and important about the human condition.
>
> *The Salisbury Poisonings* (2020, written by – ex-journalists! – Declan Lawn and Adam Patterson) was an interesting example of a story of scale, a huge news story, told through the prism of a few key individuals. It was told largely from the point of view of the director of public health in Salisbury and a relatively junior CID officer on the case, not from the more obvious point of view of the police chiefs, politicians and Russian poisoners. In this way, a huge political story was made to feel personal, emotive and involving. This grounded the show and made it engaging and relatable.
>
> **Inherently dramatic** – *Money Heist*, for instance, is a show that feels inherently dramatic because there is so much at stake. I wanted to invest in the characters because of the situation in which the writer places them.

> **Passion/agenda** – why have you as the writer chosen a particular story? Does it excite and compel you?

Dreaming and Creativity

Indulging Yourself

There is a time in your writing process – right at the start, before considerations of voice, story, character, the industry or anything else – when it is important that you are completely indulgent, allowing yourself to be alone and trying to enter a dream-state of consciousness. Lying on the grass looking at the sky and the shapes of the clouds; closing your eyes and looking at the inside of your eyelids, trying to turn the shapes that present themselves to you into images that have meaning; images of shapes and faces that appear to you as you drift towards sleep. Look for ideas in the most unlikely of places, get yourself into a state of being where you are utterly receptive to any ideas or images that float into your consciousness.

At this stage, you need to forget the clock, forget your personal responsibilities and the day-to-day minutiae of your life – and disappear into your own head.

The worst place to do this is in your normal working space – your own home or office, and in particular in front of your computer. Leave the house, leave your phone behind (you don't want anyone calling you, you don't want to be able to access your emails and messages) – but take a notebook!

Indulge yourself in flights of fancy that deliberately have no set purpose other than to get you to apply your consciousness in a way that you normally don't. Shut down your inner critic, take all creative pressure off yourself. Give yourself permission to fail – if you return home four hours later and have produced nothing of worth, that's okay! Be receptive

> without being self-critical and self-judgemental. You should enter into this process with no set agenda or preconceptions.

This habit of daydreaming needs to be structured into the ongoing disciplines of your writing process. You need to keep coming back to this exercise of creative indulgence and unstructured daydreaming – to the well of inspiration.

Collaboration and discussion

Find other people to talk to and to join in (more about finding your community of writing peers in the Career section of this book, from page 243). If you have a germ of an idea, an image, an incomplete thought, find a fellow creative to whom you can articulate these half-formed thoughts and see what it triggers for them. Knock these ideas and images back and forth between you and see what it generates.

Note Collaboration and discussion with your fellow creatives is an important part of a screenwriter's work. Particularly in the world of TV drama, so much of the work and creativity is generated through conversation, through riffing, bouncing ideas off each other. A career in screenwriting makes demands of very different sides of your personality. You need to be equally adept at the introspective part of writing – living inside your own head, the solitary hours of writing – and the more social and extrovert part of the job – discussing story, bouncing ideas off other people, whether in a pitch meeting, a writers' room or with family or writing friends.

Dreams

Dreams so often have a filmic quality to them. I am a firm believer that we should take note of our dreams and what they're telling us, the glimpses they give us into our subconscious mind. So often moments, images and feelings from dreams feel like a creative gift. Dreams speak of journeys, they tell us about deep-seated fears and feelings. Dreams rarely give us fully formed stories but they can give shafts of light and insight. Asleep, our brains will present us with rich, strange, complex (and occasionally) compelling and fascinating story starting points, situations and ideas.

The best storytelling creates tension and narrative energy from the gap between the text and subtext of a scene, and dreams can give us that sense of subtext – what the subconscious mind is telling the waking, conscious mind; and the tension between the two.

An example: I wake from a dream in which I am having a panic attack about having to climb down a ladder on the outside of a tall building. I am pleading with someone in the building to please let me use the lift inside the building to descend, but they are refusing. This may or may not be a scene in itself but it occurs to me that vertigo,* a fear of heights, would be an interesting and different way to dramatise anxiety and a personal mental health crisis (that is ultimately about something else altogether).

And reading this back now, I have no memory whatsoever of this dream – dreams are so delicate and transitory – which is why it's important to record them immediately before they slip away and are lost.

My dreams are often about dealing with hostility and a feeling of inadequacy. They are very often about going on long, complicated, difficult, physical journeys. Sometimes I dream conversations and exchanges with my mother, now dead. I seem to have dreamt more about my mother in the years since her death than I did when she was alive.

Dreams often seem to generate ideas about insecurity, thwarted ambition, inability to communicate, a need to travel – or is this just me? But these feel like useful ways in to trying to define a character's internal conflict.

Think about your dreams and their connection to more conventional story. Often they have some of the elements – but with strange gaps and leaps.

---

* Okay, so Hitchcock beat us to this – but there is more than one story to be told about vertigo! Everything has been done before – and recognising that *nothing is 100 per cent original* is creatively freeing. You must feel free to take a familiar starting point like this and make it your own. If you give ten different writers exactly the same creative prompt or story premise, they will all write it in their own unique way – you will have ten completely different stories.

Think about how dreams equate to cinematic narrative, how much of how we dream consists of visual images and cuts between 'scenes' or 'shots'.

Dreams allow us a fascinating insight into our subconscious. During the coronavirus lockdown period, for instance, it was common for people living in isolation to dream about crowds and gatherings. Dreams often address our most primal fears and emotions – which is what we need to access in the stories we tell.

Thoughts that come to us unbidden, involuntarily – with no conscious, intellectual filter – are in their way even more valuable than the ideas that come to us consciously.

Sometimes you will feel driven to tell your nearest and dearest particular dreams in the same way you will feel driven to pitch them certain story ideas. In my experience the recounting of dreams is far less welcome than properly thought-out stories! What unedited dreams lack is a sense of narrative purpose or of something being at stake – but many of the random elements of narrative from dreams can be usefully isolated and re-contextualised.

Tracking Your Dreams

Keep your phone or a notebook by your bed, and when you wake, make a note of dreams that feel important or cinematic. A lot of the time they may seem much less interesting or relevant when you come back to them later. But enough of them will be sufficiently valuable to make this practice thoroughly worthwhile. And at this stage, you should be recording them without overly assessing or editing them. Once you have built a fund of dream descriptions, try this five-minute exercise (as with others, limit yourself to this self-imposed deadline):

Take the main thrust or image from three dreams – and from them create a character and their story.

One thing all of these techniques and exercises are aiming to do is to divert around the inner critic, the destructive, self-censoring part of your ego. It is not what you want at this stage of the creative process. You want the ideas to flow unfiltered. There will be a time when that inner, critical voice is of value – but it's not now when you're trying to create original, exciting and meaningful ideas from nothing.

Don't create?

Perhaps perversely, an effective way to enable creativity is by saying to yourself, 'I will create nothing. Instead, everything that goes into my story will be taken from real life: research, stories I've been told, real people and the details of their lives, real conversations overheard and noted, real places used and described, etc.'

Weirdly, this deliberate approach of non-creativity can be richly creative, can produce the richest, most original, credible dramatic stories, and can feel freeing.

'Creativity' does not mean plucking an idea fully formed from the ether, or that you must struggle to invent a moment, character or story that is unique. Disabuse yourself of the notion that any story is 100 per cent unique. Everything is inspired or suggested by something else. As a random example (but also arguably the pinnacle of twentieth-century creative achievement), many of The Beatles' songs are clearly inspired by other songs, from talking to other artists, experimenting with other people's styles. *The White Album*, for instance, pastiches many musical genres and styles.

Art leads to more art – and when we are consciously striving for something unique, even this urge is a response to specific artistic expression that has come before us. Once we recognise and acknowledge this, a big part of the terrifying and inhibiting burden of creativity is lifted from our shoulders.

As mentioned on page 17, one of the most important principles for creative endeavours is to spend some time away from your computer screen. Getting the words onto the page is obviously vital, but there is a law of diminishing returns. The process of creating story costs you psychologically. You need to keep refreshing your creative energy. Keep looking outside of yourself.

> **Character Observation Exercise**
>
> Find a public space where a lot of people congregate – a big railway station is ideal. When I am running courses nearby, I send writers into the Euston Station concourse in London. Alternatively, find a busy, central shopping area, a transport hub or terminus, a big supermarket. Or any town centre. Take your phone (or a notebook) to make notes.
>
> Then all you do is observe people. Identify and choose a person or people that intrigue you – whether it's because of the way they carry themselves, what they're wearing, who they're with, or what you overhear them saying, either to someone else in person or on their phone.
>
> Make a note of this person or people and of a snatch of dialogue that you overhear. Come home. Write out a description of what you observed. Think about what it was about them that drew your attention to this person, what it was that intrigued you.
>
> Now take this basis, this external appearance, the quirks that drew your attention, and begin to fictionalise this real person from the clues you picked up. Invent their lives – think about why they were out and about today, what they were doing, where they'd come from. Think about different aspects of their life, the things that suggest themselves to you from what you observed about them. Did they seem lonely, solitary, or sociable and at ease? Were they on a mission, going about their activity purposefully? Or did they seem aimless and somewhat lost? Did you see them doing their job?
>
> Start to build a character, a life, inspired and suggested by the real external details you observed.
>
> As you do this, focus on character, rather than trying to impose a weight of plot onto them. I think it's more effective to look first at all the minute

details of this character's life, rather than going straight to high-concept plot (building from in to out rather than the other way round). For instance, resist the urge to immediately imagine this person is planting a bomb or is about to murder someone. Try to start from a basis of creating a vivid, three-dimensional character. So that, once fleshed out and clear in your mind's eye, this person and their very particular qualities will start to suggest their own unique story.

Find a location that is crowded with a mix of people – so, for instance, at Euston, you get such a rich mix: stationary (excuse the pun) people looking up at the massive information screens, people moving between the stationary people, either arriving off a train or (usually more hurriedly) walking towards their soon-to-be-departing train. And then there's the moment when a platform number comes up on the board and two hundred people simultaneously start moving towards their train (*just* not running, although the speed at which they're moving suggests there are more people waiting than there are seats on the train). And then there are the people just loitering around the station without intent – browsing the shops, drinking in the bars, pickpocketing, whatever.

What this combination of competing intentions in a confined space gives you is a wonderful microcosm of the subconscious, physical (mainly) and verbal negotiations we all enter into in our interactions with our fellow humans on a daily basis. When you think about it, it's amazing that, every day, so many thousands of people in urban centres manage to pass each other, avoid conflict and coexist peaceably in such intense proximity. The way people move around each other in places like this strikes me as a wonderful story metaphor in its own right.

So there's that – but, if you're struggling for characters, there is also just the wealth of humanity to be observed in public spaces like this.

To my mind, there is no better basis for building character than in the observation of real people. Building characters from their external appearance – their clothes, hairstyle, physical bearing, the way they walk –

> can be a great starting point that removes some of the burden of creating characters from scratch, of overcoming the tyranny of the blank page.
>
> Once you have developed more than one character in this way, you can then begin to construct fictional relationships between them.
>
> A huge part of the definition of your voice is in the storytelling choices you make – and every writer will make different choices, will find different people interesting and will turn these people into fictional characters through the prism of their own taste, agenda and outlook.

Above all, you need to keep surprising yourself with new ways to approach story, different angles into story. There is value in studying different narrative forms – and of trying to impose narrative ideas on real or random events.

For instance, try thinking about your story in terms of colour. What colours feel connected to your story? Is this a story of rural greens or urban greys? Is this a story of warm summer blues or of winter whites and greys?

And in writing that sentence I have given myself another story cue – in what season or climate does your story exist? Is this a summer story, an autumn story, etc.?

Sometimes these specific questions won't have strong resonance for the story you're telling. But you need to find the particular questions that unlock, inform and enrich the story you're creating.

The more restrictive and artificial the limits you give yourself, the easier you will find it to release your imagination and creativity. The formal parameters will free your creativity.

Where, when and how you write is important. I feel my creativity is released on a train with views flying by, something good to read as an inspirational prompt, and earphones with good music; and my phone notes. A significant minority of this book has been written like this (or on the London Underground). Somehow, the vibrations of movement, the fact of travel, energises my creative urges. Or my creativity is unleashed by a stimulating conversation that then motivates writing.

For so many of us, brought up with a British, self-denying, protestant work ethic, this is hard! It feels transgressively self-indulgent and airy-fairy. But it's a really important and necessary part of writing. Be prepared for doing this for an hour and it producing nothing of worth. But keep at it and it will.

Generating Ideas from Other Media

I am a great believer in methods that involve lateral thinking to help you come up with strong, exciting, original story ideas. When trying to create and generate ideas, it's always helpful to come at it from an unexpected, oblique angle.

So I think it can be really valuable to look for story ideas in all sorts of different areas of life and, as a writer, to be in 'writer mode' for as much of the time as you can manage without losing your sanity (and the sanity of those close to you!).

Above all, think about the importance of images and tableaux for film storytelling. Visual or physical images are so often more compelling and persuasive than reams of explanatory text. Think particularly about images suggested in other media, as the following examples: two song lyrics and a poem that strike me as potential inspirations for screen drama or stories (issues of copyright and ownership notwithstanding!).

'Stolen Car' by Bruce Springsteen

The lyrics to this song can be found in full online.

I love how visual this song is – how the idea of a love that has gone wrong is dramatised through the imagery of this young man, lost in his life, driving a stolen car aimlessly (and, tellingly, at night), waiting to be caught, as a way of escaping the personal difficulties of his life. It feels poignant, melancholic but, above all, cinematic.

And although I don't know Eldridge Avenue, somehow the specificity of the name draws you even further into the story.

The way the images are ordered within the lyrics heightens the sense of a complex, unfolding cinematic narrative: the intercutting of past and present; the contrasting images of her reading their old love letters and him driving the stolen car. I can imagine in the film version how these two very different actions (one private, interior; the other public, exterior) could be intercut as a non-verbal dramatisation of the breakdown of the relationship.

Springsteen's lyrical creativity is inspirational and contains so many lessons for dramatic storytelling.

'Labelled with Love' by Squeeze

As with 'Stolen Car', you can find the lyrics to this song online.

Another ballad, this time with an even stronger narrative thread, another poignantly 'lost' character at its heart, and a particularly strong sense of a developing, progressive narrative. This song almost works as a feature film story proposal in its own right.

And what stands out particularly for me in these wonderful Chris Difford lyrics is the idiosyncrasy and specificity of the visual descriptions. The visceral, visual details of this woman's home, her cat, her appearance, even her smell.

I love the way it tells an unfolding story – and that this story isn't linear. It starts in this woman's sad present – and then cuts back in time to show how she has changed and become this person (personal change is at the heart of so much effective storytelling). This feels like a very cinematic or televisual storytelling technique.

I love the structure of the song, with the repeated verse; how the repetition brings us back to the theme of the song – the romanticising of the past from a less than perfect present.

The title, 'Labelled with Love', articulates so clearly what the song is about – the story cuts between this woman's present and her past, showing us how her fondly remembered past has curdled into a sour present. So many of the visual details leap out at you in their distinctiveness and in the way they help to bring this character alive.

'The Mower' by Philip Larkin

> The mower stalled, twice; kneeling, I found
> A hedgehog jammed up against the blades,
> Killed. It had been in the long grass.
>
> I had seen it before, and even fed it, once.
> Now I had mauled its unobtrusive world
> Unmendably. Burial was no help:
>
> Next morning I got up and it did not.
> The first day after a death, the new absence
> Is always the same; we should be careful
>
> Of each other, we should be kind
> While there is still time.

This Philip Larkin poem is less dense with imagery than the two songs, but there is such a strong sense of character, mortality and personal crisis at the heart of it – and again all dramatised and brought to life through a very specific and powerful set of visual images. I can imagine using this moment – killing a hedgehog while mowing a lawn – as the dramatic catalyst of a very particular, personal crisis. So, this feels more like a powerful, personal taking-off point for a story than a fully realised narrative, but it is nonetheless creatively inspiring for that. The dead hedgehog is a great example of a narrative visual metaphor.

Like so much of the best writing (and this is vital in screenwriting in particular), all three of these examples are predominantly visual. They take you as listener or reader into distinctive, textured, poignant and visual story situations. I can imagine all of these working as either short films or as the bases of longer-form dramatic stories. They are full of powerful, telling, emotive images.

> Here is a (non-exhaustive) list of media and areas of life that can suggest and inspire story for the screen:
>
> * Songs.
> * Instrumental music.
> * Poems (particularly ballads!).
> * Novels.
> * Short stories.
> * Non-fiction books.
> * Newspaper or magazine articles.
> * Newspaper or magazine photos.
> * Adverts (whether in print, TV, cinema, on billboards, the internet…).
> * Feature films.
> * TV shows.
> * Stage plays, operas and musicals.
>
> (I'm not suggesting you shamelessly rip off story and character ideas from other shows and films – but so often there may be a particular moment, idea or image in a show that opens up a huge, related creative vista for you as a writer – whether this is to do with story, character, period, theme or form.)
>
> * History, mythology (e.g. *Kaos*, an eight-part series for Netflix, created by Charlie Covell, inspired by Greek mythology).
> * Documentaries – particularly feature-length documentaries. There are so many valuable lessons and inspiration for fiction storytellers in the best long-form documentary narratives. *Searching for Sugar Man*

(2012) and *The Rescue* (2021) both offer so many lessons about how to tell stories on screen compellingly.

* Podcasts – the recent explosion in podcasts is an example of our hunger for stories. If you proactively research and listen to podcasts that appeal to your sensibilities, you will find a plethora of story ideas (e.g. from interviews).
* Real people observed.
* Public figures observed – the big public figures, the people in the news, can be a great jumping-off point for character and story. Examples include *Vice* (2018) and *Priscilla* (2023).
* Houses or other buildings (whether residential, commercial or institutional). So many buildings contain their own epic, personal stories – whether it's a single hotel room and its many occupants over the years (*Room 104* – Mark and Jay Duplass), an ordinary terraced house (*A House Through Time*) or Buckingham Palace (*The Crown* – Peter Morgan). And, more specifically, historical blue plaques on buildings.
* TV or radio news.
* Everyday objects – works of art (most obviously pictures but also sculptures, installations, etc.); cars, motorbikes, trains (travel and modes of travel are wonderfully rich story starting points – so many great cinematic stories involve journeys); objects of emotional importance to people (clothes, hats, jewellery, toys, shoes, lockets, photographs); the list is potentially endless.
* Talks, lectures or events (e.g. TED Talks as a basis for screen drama).
* Travel or locations – everywhere you go, stories will suggest themselves to you if you are actively looking for and open to them. Going somewhere new is a great way to find a different sort of story and a different perspective on story. Even if you find no stories in this other place, the act of leaving and then returning to your home environment will bring a different perspective to it, and refresh the perspective of your normal, humdrum, daily life.

- ★ Graphic novels – TV series *The End of the F***king World* (Charlie Covell) and *Bodies* (2023), and feature film *Days of the Bagnold Summer* (Lisa Owens) are all adaptations of graphic novels.
- ★ Games – e.g. *The Last of Us* (a computer game that spawned a highly successful HBO TV drama series).
- ★ Dance choreography.
- ★ Acting and performance – there are so many points of comparison between acting and writing. An example: Alison Steadman's chameleon quality – how physically different she is in *Abigail's Party* and in *Nuts in May*. It's all about the character, not about the actor. Similarly in screenwriting, it's all about the story, not about the writer.

Documentaries: the lessons for screenwriters

So many of the best documentaries work because of the ambition and scale of the stories and characters they are examining. In these examples I would argue that the premise, the story starting point, is compelling, even before the brilliant way in which that story is then realised on screen.

The Rescue (2021, directed by Elizabeth Chai Vasarhelyi and Jimmy Chin). Watching this film was an intense experience, I was on the metaphorical edge of my seat throughout its 140 minutes running time. This is the story of the rescue of the twelve eleven-to-fourteen-year-old members of a Thai children's football team and their coach after sixteen days trapped in an underground cave. This is an inherently dramatic story. We know immediately what is at stake: the lives of these young boys.

What is extraordinary about this documentary is the richness and complexity of the story, enriched even further by the skill with which the story is told. The film focuses mainly on the (largely) British team of amateur, hobbyist, to some extent socially dysfunctional cavers who are central to the success of the rescue operation. Theirs is the predominant point of view that carries the story, but there are so many subplots around them and the other 'characters' — so many utterly personal challenges and obstacles, so many knotty individual dilemmas, and so many brilliant uses of the best dramatic narrative devices: for instance, the emotional use of objects in the image of the boys' bikes, waiting at the mouth of the caves to be reclaimed by their owners, watched over by a tearful mother. This is an incredibly powerful and counter-intuitively personal, humanising image (counter-intuitive because it is dramatised through an object rather than through a person).

At every turn, another obstacle is raised in the attempts to free the boys. What underlies the film is an absolutely elemental human instinct: a mother's love for her child. This is the unspoken emotion that compels the audience's attention and — vitally — their emotions (even though the mothers and their sons barely register as characters in the story).

One of the interesting things I learnt from the Q&A following the film's screening was just how many versions of this story are being developed or made — whether as feature films (*Thirteen Lives*), documentaries or books. And this didn't surprise me at all. Because from the film and from the Q&A I got the impression that another twenty-seven equally gripping feature films could be made from this material, all of which would be equally valid, emotive and gripping. (Producer John Battsek talked about some of the subplots they reluctantly had to leave on the cutting-room floor.)

The Rescue made me think about some of the familiar screen narrative devices it uses, familiar to the extent that they have become narrative clichés:

* The idea of the 'ticking clock', the 'race against time' — such a familiar but powerful element of so many effective pieces of storytelling.

* The 'unlikely hero' — there are several in this film: the ordinary person placed, through no choice of their own, in an extraordinary situation. The idea of heroism is so often all the more compelling when the hero is unlikely.

- Stakes – that question of 'what is at stake' here is so fundamental. Not just the life or death of a group of powerless children, but also the reputations and livelihoods of those attempting to rescue them.

- The sense of a driving narrative purpose pitted against a series of seemingly insurmountable obstacles in the rescuers' attempts to get the children out of the underground caves. There is a tremendously strong sense of forward narrative propulsion.

- Specific character considerations and flaws – the detail of the lives of each of the central characters feels so distinctive and specific.

- A series of subplots all connected to the main plot.

Documentary Storytelling

Deep Water (2006, Jerry Rothwell) / *The Mercy* (2017, Scott Z. Burns)

Deep Water is a documentary feature; *The Mercy* is a factual drama feature exploring the same story. In my opinion, *Deep Water*, the documentary, is more successful, largely because it is so much more clearly rooted in research, in the weird, idiosyncratic and mind-boggling reality of this story. *The Mercy* in comparison feels compromised and overfamiliar in its relatively unimaginative use of generic narrative devices and lack of depth. *Deep Water* is an extraordinary story of an epic journey undertaken by the wrong person at the wrong time – and the tragic consequences.

Icarus (2017, directed by Bryan Fogel)

A brilliantly ambitious documentary that takes a massive narrative turn in a way that is unexpected and incredibly effective. A brilliant combination of a very personal story that asks huge, global, ethical questions.

Man on Wire (2008, directed by James Marsh)

The extraordinary story of Philippe Petit, who walked on a tightrope between the Twin Towers (illegally, unofficially) in New York City in 1974. A wonderfully personal, idiosyncratic story given great poignancy by later events. (And another documentary that spawned a less good narrative feature.)

Leaving Neverland (2019, directed by Dan Reed)

A brilliant televisual examination of the predatory sexual crimes of a massive global superstar, Michael Jackson. Both an object lesson in how to tell an investigative story, and a fascinating portrait of a talented, charismatic but very damaged man.

I think there are some big, important storytelling lessons to be learnt from documentaries like these. So many of these documentary stories are created in a technically different way to screenplays – instead of being 'written' conventionally, these stories are often excavated and discovered in the editing process, in the cutting and assembly of many hours of shot footage.

The main thing to take away from these universally excellent documentaries is the choice of story material. These all feel like inherently fascinating, strongly dramatic story areas. These stories, all of which were to some extent big news stories at the time, have something of the epic about them. They feel like important stories that examine the human condition in all its extremes, people at their best and worst; people at heightened moments in their lives. These are stories grabbed from the headlines whilst at the same time feeling utterly specific and particular in the characters, story worlds and detail they explore.

What is Your Story About?

Often, a writer's choice of story material, the idea that sticks with them and demands to be written, is an instinctive rather than an intellectual choice. It's about finding a story that grabs you and won't let you go, that excites and energises you as a writer.

This big question – 'What is this story about?' – may not at first be easy to answer. But it's a question that, as a writer developing a project, you should keep coming back to and re-examining, because this is really important. There may never be an easy answer to this question. Certain stories mean different things to different people – an audience can find meanings in stories that had never occurred to the writer, and this is no bad thing. Often it's a mark of a story that has real emotional range, depth and universal appeal. *Little Miss Sunshine*, for instance, is a script that explores a number of different themes and ideas. So many people who have seen the film have a strong emotional response to it, but it would be hard absolutely and definitively to encapsulate in a couple of sentences what the film is about – beyond its essential narrative engine of a family's journey to a children's talent competition. The film will mean different things to different people and can be interpreted in a number of different ways.

So this question of what your story is about, thematically, is something that you should keep coming back to, exploring and trying to define, as you develop and write your script. If you can get to the heart of what your story is about, why you're writing it, you should then be able to find ways to articulate and dramatise ideas that will have real meaning for your audience.

> ### The Fundamentals of Story
>
> When coming up with story ideas; and when you are developing a particular idea, it's worth thinking about the fundamental values of your story. Here are some of the issues and qualities that drive and generate dramatic narrative:
>
> * Health/Illness and Injury.
> * Wealth/Poverty.

- ★ Youth/Old Age.
- ★ Love/Hate.
- ★ Freedom/Captivity.
- ★ Democracy/Authoritarianism.
- ★ Integrity/Corruption.
- ★ Purity/Decadence.
- ★ Isolation/Togetherness.
- ★ Fame or Infamy/Anonymity.
- ★ Luck/Misfortune (e.g. winning the lottery/losing your winning ticket).

Drama Storytelling Archetypes and Templates

It's also worth looking at the *types* of stories that proliferate: dramatic story archetypes and templates.

Think about which of the following categories your story may fit into (or is it in another category altogether?). Make a study of these sorts of stories. Think about how your story can play with – and subvert – the conventions of this type of story:

- ★ **The Journey** (e.g. road movies) – metaphorical character journeys as well as actual, physical journeys: *The Road* (2009), *Little Miss Sunshine*, *Alice in the Cities* (1974).

- ★ **The Investigation** – stories about journalists, the law, crime. So many dramas are about an investigation: *CSI*, *Columbo*, *Poirot*.

- ★ **The Relationship** – love stories: *Rye Lane* (2023), *Annie Hall* (1977), *When Harry Met Sally* (1989).

- ★ **Coming of Age/Rites of Passage** – stories of growing up and personal challenge: *Stand By Me* (1986), *Ladybird* (2017), *Juno* (2007), *Boyhood* (2014), *Whiplash* (2014).

* **The Confinement** – stories of captivity and escape. This could be about prison, hostage-taking, kidnap, etc.: *Time* (2021), *The Green Mile* (1999), *The Shawshank Redemption* (1994), *Room* (2015).

* **The Haunting** – ghost stories: *Get Out* (2017), *The Exorcist* (1973), *The Enfield Haunting* (2015).

* **The Revenge** – tales of retribution and seeking justice, vigilante stories: *Taken* (2008), *Cold Pursuit* (2019), *Blue Ruin* (2013).

* **The Heist/The Siege**: *Dog Day Afternoon* (1975), *Ocean's Eleven* (2001).

* **The Duel** – a battle between two characters or organisations: *Heat* (1995), *Duel* (1971), *The Fall* (2006).

* **The War** – dramatising a war or battle whether on a smaller, character-driven level, or on a more epic scale: *The Long Good Friday* (1980), *Saving Private Ryan* (1998), *Band of Brothers* (2001), *Dunkirk* (2017).

* **Crime Drama** – there are many different ways to tell and construct crime stories (whodunnit, whydunnit, procedural) and from many different points of view (police POV, perpetrator POV, victim POV).

* **Medical Drama** – stories set in a hospital, GP practice, veterinary practice; or stories about individuals afflicted by illness or injury: *ER* (1994), *Casualty* (1986), *Maternal* (2023), *Scrubs* (2001).

* **Community Drama** – stories about groups of people who come together to fight for a common cause: *Pride* (2014), *Brassed Off* (1996), *Sherwood* (2022).

* **Business/Family Business Drama** – stories of families and their businesses, and quasi-family organisations: *The Brothers* (a BBC TV drama series from the 1970s that ran for seven series), *The Godfather* (1972), *Six Feet Under* (2001), *Boiling Point* (2021), *London's Burning* (1988).

* **The Family** – *Here We Go* (2020), *The Cockfields* (2019), *Howards' Way* (1985), *Mum* (2016).

…and so many overlaps and combinations of all of the above.

Story Ideas: Conclusion

The overall message of this section is that we must remember and recognise that stories are everywhere, all around us all the time in our daily lives. We need to think and live as writers, being actively and constantly on the hunt for stories that excite and energise us, that motivate us to write. And the least productive place to do this is where most writers do it – sat in front of that blank, forbidding Microsoft Word page on their computer.

We need to challenge ourselves to generate story ideas from the most seemingly unlikely of sources. Using the Newspaper Exercise (page 14) during screenwriting courses has taught me that the more limitations and parameters you bring to a creative task, the more creatively enabling it becomes.

Not only do we need to (ruthlessly but judiciously!) cannibalise the events of our own lives, we need to tap into all those other sources and media that suggest and provoke story.

Look outwards, not inwards. Get out into the world. Look at what is happening outside of your room, your home.

Think about what excites, scares, terrifies, infuriates you. What enthuses you, what makes your heart skip a beat? What are your secret passions? It's the things that stir your emotions that you should be writing about. What or who do you love (or hate)?

★ ★ ★

On courses I have sometimes referenced the idea that a drama series about, say, a family-run café is too low-stakes, too lacking in potential drama to feel like a promising story set-up. This example has been blown out of the water by US show *The Bear* – which is about exactly this, and manages to be both viscerally compelling and highly dramatic within the narrow parameters and character values of its very specific story world.

The takeaway from this is that whatever the scale of your story, you need to find the emotional core of the idea – the dynamic between characters and story world that is going to pose powerful story questions for the audience and make us care about what is going to happen to the characters.

Dig into stories that evoke an emotional response in you, issues that 'bother' you, stories that challenge the status quo. Drama should be intellectually engaging but, more fundamentally, visceral, emotive and provocative.

Don't try to anticipate what you think TV commissioners and film producers may be looking for. First, please yourself. If the stories you're developing don't excite you, they won't excite others. And look for the specific (micro) character story that will humanise and dramatise the bigger (macro) idea.

Don't think that because an idea came to you easily, you should be suspicious of it. *Or,* conversely, if you have struggled working on an idea for years, that that somehow confers status or value on it. The opposite is more often true – the best ideas can come quickly and easily.

Some of the best drama is an articulation of a writer's rage (it seems to me that this is true of so much of the work of writers like Jimmy McGovern, Sally Wainwright and Jed Mercurio).

But as a writer you have to put yourself in the right place (mentally and physically) to be open to these ideas.

Identify the essence of what is exciting and unique about your idea, and keep this at the heart of your pitch – and further development of the project.

All writing is political. What are the politics of your story? What political assumptions are you making? Should these political assumptions be challenged?

Use the real world (rather than other TV shows) to inspire story. For instance, the brilliant *Succession* is clearly inspired by the stories of real media mogul families like the Murdochs and the Maxwells. The realities behind the fictional stories in *Succession* give these stories resonance and relatability, as in ITV factual drama *A Confession*, based on a real police case, written and produced by Jeff Pope. Factual drama has become a reliable staple of UK TV and this was an outstanding example of the genre.

Theatre shows too have brilliantly tapped into real news stories – from *A Very Expensive Poison*, written by Lucy Prebble (who co-created the TV series *I Hate Suzie* with Billie Piper) – a writer equally adept writing for screen or stage and one of the outstanding UK dramatists of her generation – or *The Lehman Trilogy*, written by Stefano Massini and adapted by Ben Power – another stage play, a three-hander with limited set that nonetheless explores in epic storytelling terms the history of global financial services firm Lehman Brothers, and in so doing, offers a compelling critique of late capitalism and its fallout.

Small Island is another epic and outstanding stage dramatisation by Helen Edmundson, adapted from the novel by Andrea Levy. Although completely fictional, the story successfully taps into and is inspired by real events of the twentieth century, in particular the arrival of the Windrush generation of West Indian immigrants into the UK, and the issues they were (and still are) confronted with.

The question of zeitgeist, or 'Why now?', is a big issue in identifying the value of your ideas. There is a strange and recurring industry phenomenon whereby similar ideas are initiated and developed by several different producers or writers simultaneously – even though there has been no communication between them. This is one of those weird industry realities that it's not worth getting too hung up about.

One other thought, then, about the notion of 'taking' story ideas from real stories: no story is unique. Don't beat yourself up about this, or get too worried about the uniqueness of your idea, because your voice, your take on a story, *will* be unique.

III
Storytelling for the Screen

The Basis of Your Story

The logline

Loglines are an important element in shaping, defining and selling your ideas. I would define the logline as a description of the central story idea of your script in one or (at most) two sentences. The logline should be something you are constantly honing and developing until you settle on the one or two sentences that clearly define your story and illustrate its dramatic potential. You need to be sure real, substantive drama is at the heart of your idea and in the logline.

Work tirelessly to make sure your logline is short, compelling and distinctive.

> **Some Example Loglines**
>
> These are all from (unproduced) scripts I have read, and I think they are very strong. Each communicates their story clearly and engagingly; they all have a certain emotional pull; and each of them seems to inhabit a story world that feels distinctive and defined. For each of them, something of the tone is implicit in the logline. I would be interested to watch all of these shows:
>
> * 'A young, disabled Scouser manipulates a pilgrimage to Lourdes in order to lose his virginity.'

- 'When Donna's husband John dies, he doesn't quite make it to heaven as he has one last task to finish. He visits Donna and convinces her to search for their first daughter Jayne, who they put up for adoption more than fifty years ago.'

- 'A group of dads meet at a child bereavement charity group and start a football team to raise money for the charity. Within the football team, the dads raise each other up, confronting depression, self-harm and life after their children's death.'

- 'An ensemble of four women, all obsessed with true crime, try to deconstruct and solve three murders committed by 1960s Glasgow serial killer "Bible John", who was never caught.'

- 'A group of young stand-up comedians look to support and encourage one another as they work to improve their comedy routines and make their breakthrough.'

- 'In the wake of 9/11, the mega-wealthy Bin Laden family must do whatever they can to survive in a city still grieving the heinous crimes of their estranged brother.'

The story premise

The clarity, focus and impact of the story premise is so important. Can you clearly and easily articulate the essence of your story in one (or at most two) short, uncomplicated sentences?

Here are some examples of films that have a clear, strongly dramatic story premise (and my attempts to articulate that story premise):

- *Never Rarely Sometimes Always* (2020, written and directed by Eliza Hittman). A feature film in which a seventeen-year-old girl has to leave her home state of Pennsylvania and travel to New York City for an abortion – an intense, personal story but also a compelling examination of the contentious and damaging issues around abortion in the US. (An issue that has become even more powerfully contentious since the film was released.)

* *The Assistant* (2019, written and directed by Kitty Green). A feature film told from the point of view of a personal assistant in a US film company as she observes and clears up after the increasingly disturbing activities of her Weinstein-like film-producer boss. (It's interesting to compare this fictional, tangentially connected version of the Weinstein story to the more factually based *She Said* – both films have their virtues and tap effectively into the issues around the #MeToo campaign.)

* *Money Heist* – a 2017 crime drama series (created and written by Álex Pina) told from the point of view of the mastermind and criminals behind an attempt to steal huge amounts of money from the Royal Mint of Spain. Part heist drama, part siege drama.

The drama and dilemma at the heart of each of these stories is crystal clear.

The dramatic proposition

Establishing the dramatic proposition of your story is key to effective, focused storytelling. A show that does this brilliantly is *Only Murders in the Building* (Disney+), created by John Hoffman and Steve Martin, in which the 'dramatic proposition' is articulated via character voice-over within the pilot episode of the show itself.

>   CHARLES
> A great true crime mystery unpeels
> itself like an onion.
>
>   OLIVER
> First the crime, then the characters and
> then their secrets.
>
>   MABEL
> The secrets are the fun part – who's
> telling the truth, who is lying, what
> are they hiding.

>   CHARLES
>   Because let's be honest, sometimes it's
>   easier to figure out someone else's
>   secret than it is to deal with your own.

This dramatic proposition is not quite the same as the story premise, which, in this instance, I'd describe as: 'A series about three loners who all live alone in the same Manhattan apartment block and come together when they discover their shared obsession with a true crime podcast, to investigate the murder that has taken place in their apartment building.'

But this voice-over sequence encapsulates precisely what the series is about: this idea of three unlikely characters in a very particular setting taking it upon themselves to investigate a murder – and in so doing running away from their own personal issues and secrets.

So there is a subtle distinction between 'story premise' and 'dramatic proposition'. It's the difference between 'What is the story?' and 'What makes this dramatic, what gives this its story engine?'

You might think that such an 'on the nose' articulation by the characters of the dramatic proposition of the series would come across as clunkily expositional. But somehow the opposite is true. This feels like the beautifully satisfying last narrative jigsaw piece of the episode-one story. Once this piece is finally dropped into place, we have the whole jigsaw complete. The episode is coming to that perfect ending in which we clearly understand the idea behind the story, and we are intrigued by the three main characters and their secrets – the contrast between who they appear to be and who they really are. And at the end of this voice-over we receive the final visual clue in the murder story that runs through the series, that will hook us into episode two. Series storytelling of real skill and elegance.

A series that understands itself so well instantly enables you to relax into the pleasures of the story – you feel you are in capable, assured hands.

This clear grasp of the narrative proposition of the show – and the human contradiction or dilemma at its heart – is at the heart of effective dramatic writing.

I remember some years ago, Channel 4 head of drama development, Surian Fletcher-Jones, talking about how important it was for writers on Channel 4 drama shows to clearly establish the dramatic proposition of a show within the first twelve minutes, before the first advert break. This can be incredibly challenging – but I think it's a really helpful challenge for writers to aim for. Ideally the dramatic action of this first section should achieve this, set up the big story questions you want the audience to be asking; or more directly, as with the voice-over example from *Only Murders in the Building*.

Appreciating the clarity of the dramatic proposition in *OMITB* made me think about some other TV shows, films and scripts that I have watched, read and enjoyed – and why I responded to them.

And I think one of the things they all have in common – and the thing we all need to be striving for – is a crystal-clear dramatic proposition at their heart. This doesn't have to be complicated. Often the best ideas are quite simple. But there needs to be a fundamental core of drama, conflict and dilemma to your story idea.

What is the jeopardy and conflict in your story? What is at stake for the central character? These are key questions that you need to be able to answer easily.

This clarity of dramatic proposition is often reflected in the marketing of a film or TV show – in the impact and immediacy of a trailer or poster.

Note There are overlaps between the above three elements (logline, story premise, dramatic proposition). They are different ways of articulating something similar. The important principle is not to get hung up over definitions – but to keep focusing on the dramatic essence and singular idea at the heart of your story.

Some Examples of Dramatic Propositions

While the below all work as story premises/loglines, I have *italicised* the dramatic proposition, the dramatic drive that propels the story.

Mass (2021, written by Fran Kranz)

A feature film in which two middle-aged couples are brought together to meet in an anonymous church hall. Couple A's son has murdered Couple B's son; the four talk – *trying to find some resolution and meaning from the violent tragedy that has overtaken their lives.*

The Tinder Swindler (2022, director Felicity Morris)

A documentary feature in which *two young women join forces to try to bring to justice the man they met on Tinder who seduced them*, won their confidence, then defrauded them out of tens of thousands of dollars.

The Incredible Kitty Fisher (written by Melanie Spencer)

A brilliant unproduced script, inspired by the true story of eighteenth-century courtesan Kitty Fisher. Kitty and her friend Lucy are disenfranchised and living in poverty in London. They realise that their only currency is sex – and so *Lucy helps Kitty go on a journey of self-empowerment*, taking on the toxic male establishment at their own game. (A great example of a period story that has real contemporary resonance.)

Flick (written by Emilie Robson)

One of the many outstanding scripts from the 2021 Channel 4 screenwriting course (as yet unproduced). Set in and around Newcastle. Twenty-year-old Flick has died in a car accident. After the funeral, her two lifelong female friends spend one last indulgent night on the town with Flick's urn of ashes, mourning and celebrating her life. Cut to the next morning, they wake in a house they don't recognise – having lost the ashes (due to be scattered by her family later in the day) – and wanted for murder themselves after a confrontation at the funeral with Flick's obnoxious ex-boyfriend. (This all happens in episode one.) *The two girls must race against time to find the urn, establish what happened on the previous evening, and prove their innocence.*

The Responder (written by Tony Schumacher)

From BBC iPlayer: 'Under pressure, fraying at the edges. In relentless night-time Liverpool, copper Chris is paired with a rookie. Will they save or destroy each other?' The lead character has an impossible dilemma to juggle: *in order to help the victims, he needs to cover up, even facilitate, a larger crime* – and thereby risk his job, his marriage, even his freedom.

Yellowjackets (created and written by Ashley Lyle and Bart Nickerson)

In the first episode (and throughout the first series) the story cuts between:

1996: a US high-school girls' football team's private plane crashes on the way to a game. Stranded in a mountainous forest for weeks, the girls have to do unspeakable things to survive…

…and 2021: Now middle-aged, the women live separate lives, trying to hide the dark secrets of those lost two weeks. *But events in the present force them back together to confront the horrors of the past.*

Life and Death in the Warehouse (2022)

Written by the excellent Helen Black, this feels like a story that needed to be told. It's both powerfully dramatic but also driven by an impassioned political and social agenda. A very specific story – about the workforce of an Amazon-like 'fulfilment centre' warehouse that asks huge questions about capitalism, profiteering and the human costs involved. *The film dramatises the unequal battle of the workers to survive and thrive in a hostile working environment.*

Cheaters (2022, written by Oliver Lyttelton)

After a one-night stand in a hotel in Iceland, Josh and Fola are horrified to discover they (and the partners they cheated on) live opposite each other in a South London street. Written in a series of eighteen ten-minute episodes, the series is predicated on a simple but very smart idea, forcing four characters together in a seemingly insoluble situation: *the four main characters, thrown together unexpectedly, must renegotiate their lives, relationships – and secrets.*

All of the above are, for me, shining examples of shows that have a crystal-clear and compelling dramatic proposition. All seem to me to be relatively easy to pitch because the writers understand the stories that they want to tell – and all are defined by knotty, dense, human dilemmas.

★ ★ ★

The following extract of character speech is from *Growth*, an unproduced project I worked on with writer Nick Flugge. A grown-up son talks about bringing his ageing mother into hospital for an appointment:

```
Yeah, you know because some would say
I was doing a good thing bringing my
mum in today, even if I had to go now.
There's no rule saying you're beholden
to your parents once they get old...
```

This very clear articulation of what this show is about feels 'in character' and absolutely relevant to the moment of the scene – so it works; but more than that, it resonates in the way it so clearly expresses the theme of Nick's show – a character-driven comedy drama about the reciprocal responsibility of an adult child for care of their ageing parent.

Note Having the characters articulate the dramatic proposition in dialogue in the show is helpful in illustrating what I mean by the 'dramatic proposition', but I should emphasise that this shouldn't be seen as an absolute requirement. Most of the above examples contain a clear and powerful dramatic proposition without ever having the characters articulate this within the show's dialogue.

Genre

Closely connected to the idea of drama storytelling archetypes and templates listed in the box on pages 35–7 is that of genre. In both film and TV, there are so many recognisable, acknowledged genres – types of story that writers come back to again and again. It's always worth considering the genre context of the story you're telling, because everything you write will fit into some sort of genre or combination of genres.

> ### Case Study 1: Romantic Comedy
>
> Audiences are sophisticated. We all know or at least instinctively understand more than we realise about how story works. We subconsciously recognise tropes when we see them – those moments that we've seen time and time again in story after story.
>
> The best writing is predicated on the understanding that audiences are smart. The story has to stay ahead of the audience, keep surprising them. Audiences understand genre and the conventions of each genre. In romcom, we understand that the guy will get his gal; we understand that romcoms end happily. The happy ending is implicit in both 'rom' and 'com'.
>
> For screenwriters, 'genre' is all about the history of storytelling, of the development of a certain type of story through the history of film, TV

and fiction. It's your job as a writer to recognise the conventions of genre while at the same time bringing something new and unexpected to them – something that reflects the time, your identity and agenda as a writer, and the particular story you're telling.

You need to understand how your story fits into the overall canon of that particular genre. You need to understand, acknowledge – and then challenge – the tropes and conventions of that genre (will the guy in fact get his gal? See the BBC comedy series *Starstruck* – written by Rose Matafeo and Alice Snedden – as a great example of a show that both works within and challenges the romantic comedy genre).

There's a wonderful romantic comedy pastiche film, *They Came Together* (yes, the double-entendre is intentional) from 2014, written by David Wain and Michael Showalter, starring Amy Poehler and Paul Rudd, in which the entire eighty-three-minute running time is an (extremely funny) patchwork of all the well-worn tropes we've come to recognise from the long-lived genre of romantic comedy. It's essentially a single-joke feature film that nevertheless works because the film-makers have a shared shorthand with their audience. There's much comic pleasure in the way the film pastiches – and revels in – familiar romcom tropes. *They Came Together*, in its subversion of these familiar moments, is wonderfully creative in its own right.

Every genre has its familiar narrative and stylistic tropes. Indeed, most genres have spawned their own subgenres of films that lampoon these generic tropes – like *They Came Together*, or the *Austin Powers* movies (Mike Myers' comic take on spy thrillers). From a screenwriting point of view, these films are doubly enjoyable for their humour on the one hand, and on the other hand their critiques of and nods towards overfamiliar screenwriting tropes. (The Basil Exposition character in the *Austin Powers* films, for instance, is a joy.)

A recognition of and affection for the particular narrative tropes of a genre will give you starting points for your own genre story. What situations are you going to use and how are you going to subvert them? Taking familiar scenes or tropes and playing with all their different possibilities enables you to create new story ideas.

Other films and TV shows that approach the romantic comedy genre in familiar but also fresh, engaging and distinctive ways include *Rye Lane* written by Nathan Bryon and Tom Melia; TV series *The Lovers* written by David Ireland (the clearest romcom characteristic of this show is how superficially mismatched the romantic couple are – always a great story or relationship starting point). And then there are classics, like *When Harry Met Sally* (Nora Ephron), another example of a wonderfully mismatched pairing; *Marriage Story* (Noah Baumbach), about a break-up but still, I would argue, a film that belongs in the romcom genre. *Annie Hall*, *Love Story*, *Palm Springs* (a romcom/time-travel genre mash-up), *Notting Hill*, *(500) Days of Summer*, *The Apartment*…

So if you're writing a romantic comedy, whether for TV or film, it can be really helpful to watch a whole series of films and shows in this genre (both new examples and very old ones) and to think about the story conventions of the genre – the 'meet cute'; the obstacles in the way of the relationship; the character conflicts; and the happy ending (or not?).

Case Study 2: *She Said* (2022)

She Said is a dramatisation by Rebecca Lenkiewicz of the *New York Times* journalists Jodi Kantor and Megan Twohey's investigation into Harvey Weinstein's serial abuses.

There are all the scenes you'd expect from this story genre – tense, hierarchical newspaper-office meeting-room scenes in which the progress of the investigation is discussed; phone exchanges between journalists and the victims of Weinstein's abuse; journalists doorstepping victims who are reluctant to speak out; and interview scenes in which the journalists come face to face with women who have been abused and are finally able to tell their story, to face down their personal demons.

And then there are the more private, domestic, character moments as we learn more about the two female journalists, and the strain their investigative work is putting on their home lives.

Indeed the film in some ways feels like a patchwork of many scenes that are familiar from this genre of the journalistic investigation story (*The Post*, *Spotlight*, *All the President's Men*, *Zodiac*).

And yet, for me, the film works. This story is so emotionally charged. The man under investigation is such a monster, and it's the utterly specific, researched details of how he manipulated and bullied his way to his abuses that really bring home the particular emotional horror of this story, that make it feel truthful and emotionally scarring – for example, the discovery that he repeatedly, in trying to cajole his victims into compliance, would swear that there was nothing untoward in what he was initiating, forcing himself on the women with the line 'on the lives of my children'.

Case Study 3: *Hustle* (2022)

I find something very reassuring about the film *Hustle* (screenplay by Taylor Materne and Will Fetters). It is a deeply conventional film in the genre of sports movie: a classic rags-to-riches tale of a wizened talent scout and coach (Adam Sandler), down on his luck, who invests all his fading hope into a rough-diamond basketball talent from Spain, trying to help him find his place in the glittering NBA. As you might guess from this plot summary, the film has everything you'd expect from the genre – a pre-title sequence setting up this old scout, at the end of his career and in a fruitless search for new talent; then the new kid seen – by chance – doing a street hustle after Sandler has failed to unearth the talent he's seeking in more conventional settings; intense training montages; the opposition he receives from his bosses at the Philadelphia 76ers. (The film is largely set in Philadelphia and even references *Rocky*!) The new kid on the block has a setback when a rival rookie riles him on court, finding his psychological weak spot; the farewell trip to the airport that instead results in 'one last chance'; the coda preceded by a 'Five Months Later' caption…

In other words, so much that is familiar, that we've seen before in general and in this particular genre in particular. So why is this 'reassuring'? Because, for all the familiarity, the conventionality, this also works. It's a really well-crafted, enjoyably immersive and emotive piece of cinematic storytelling.

While it is conventional – it conforms clearly and rigidly to the conventions of the genre – the detail and colour in the texture of the characters and the setting, make the film distinctive and engaging.

This is a deceptively well-crafted piece of cinematic storytelling – far more difficult to pull off, in my opinion, than so many of the ambivalent, hard-to-grasp, narrative-light art house films that will be far more favourably reviewed. In its unapologetic but assured use of familiar narrative conventions, the film feels old-fashioned in good ways – an example that, if you work within genre and conform to the all-important principles of good storytelling for the screen, there is no reason why you shouldn't be able to craft a really successful, engaging and enjoyable story.

In summary, then, so much of strong, surprising film and TV drama writing is about both embracing and subverting the usual over-obviously expositional tropes.

> **Genre Exercise**
>
> If you're feeling blocked or uninspired, I suggest you go to 'genre'. Pick a genre and invent a story you are interested to tell within that genre – whether it's a comedy horror, a musical, a romcom, a road movie, whatever.
>
> Get a daily newspaper and find five stories that could be adapted to the particular genre you've opted for.
>
> Study that genre. If, for example, you want to write a road movie, then watch as many road movies (film and TV) as you can (e.g. *Thelma & Louise*, *The Road*, *Upright*, *Burn Burn Burn*, *Queen & Slim*, *Locke*, *Little Miss Sunshine*) and study the conventions and narrative devices of that genre. List and write up the conventions of the genre, enjoy making a study of it – then work on not just using but twisting and subverting those conventions to serve the particular story you want to tell.
>
> Find the story that feels like it suggests a fresh take on the genre and that excites you. That way you already have certain narrative and structural staging posts in place – the conventions and expectations of the particular genre, to play with and to guide your story. Your starting point will feel less like that scary blank page. And your reader or audience will also have the reassurance of coming to it with their own expectations and preconceptions of the genre, whether you meet those or challenge them. A win-win.

Tone

Like voice (see pages 6–10), tone is a tricky element to pin down and define, but much discussed and unquestionably important. On many TV dramas, the production will have a tone meeting in which every scene in an episode is discussed between director and team (set designer, costume designer, location manager, etc.) to make sure they are in agreement on the tonal understanding of the story they're telling.

In particular, consistency, or at the very least deliberation of tone, is vital. When reading a script for consideration, it's vital that the reader understand the tone of the script from the start. This is about mood, atmosphere and the story values you're establishing – what is meaningful in your story world.

Tone has overlaps with genre. If your story is defined by its combination of comedy and horror, that goes some way to defining tone. Although, having said that, *Shaun of the Dead* and *Get Out* could both be described as 'comedy horror' – but the two films feel unique, absolutely their own things and very different in feel, tone and theme from each other.

Ultimately, whatever the genre, each successfully realised film has its own distinct tone (mood, feel, atmosphere).

Tonal shifts within your story should be clear and deliberate – for example in *The Wizard of Oz*, the change from black-and-white to colour signifies a radical switch in the tone of the storytelling as we shift from Kansas to Oz.

Form

Content is obviously vital – but so is form. How does what you want to say, the subject matter of your story, influence the form and structure of your story? There are so many different ways to tell your story – and it's incumbent on you as a writer to find the best, most effective form for it.

By 'form' I mean anything from a single-shot monologue told in real time to an epic story told backwards in multiple scenes over the course of a hundred years. If you are excited by a particular story but feel that in too many ways it's familiar, think about how the form of your story, the way you dramatise it, can transform and lift it out of the ordinary and the predictable.

So, if you have what seems like quite a conventional love story, would telling this story backwards add something to it? (See Harold Pinter's play/film, *Betrayal*.) Could you tell this love story as two linked monologues in which your lovers never actually meet? Can you take this familiar story and transpose it into some unexpected, contrasting setting that will elevate it?

Case Study: Monologue

In the year of lockdown, for obvious practical reasons, the monologue was everywhere. But even within this one dramatic narrative form, there are a thousand and one ways of telling stories.

As a form, monologues are of particular interest to me. My first TV producer job was a regional ITV drama series called *First Signs of Madness* – four thirty-minute monologues about London-based characters. It included Chris Chibnall's first TV script: a look back on the life of a London Underground driver as he drove the length of the Central Line for the very last time – a wonderful example of a story that combined both a physical and metaphorical journey. I have also made a series of audio monologues, *Tribute*, in which characters muse over life, and a particular death (www.tributepodcasts.co.uk).

One of the more recent examples of this form that stood out for me was Suzie Miller's exceptional stage monologue, *Prima Facie* – given a tour de force interpretation by the brilliant Jodie Comer; and which worked equally powerfully on stage and in the filmed NT Live version.

If you're interested in writing in any new or different form, such as monologue, you need to study that form. Is your monologue a public speech (wedding, funeral, political speech)? A private moment of internal reflection? Is your character locked up? On a journey? If they're indoors, what room are they in and how does this affect what they say and how they say it (e.g. the difference between being in the bathroom and the kitchen)? Is it one single scene, or numerous scenes? A linear story, or one that cuts back and forth in time? All of the above storytelling questions apply as strongly to monologues as they do to any other dramatic story form.

Sometimes, in less interesting monologues, it seems like writers feel the normal storytelling principles don't apply, that they can have the character simply telling you their story in a way that feels too straightforward and uninflected.

> With all forms of drama, so much of the texture and richness of the storytelling comes from the audience trying to perceive what the dynamic is:
>
> * Between the character and the material – whether they're telling us the full story, what they're withholding and why they're withholding it, how the character shies away from the truth and why.
>
> * Between character and environment – how they respond to the environment they are in.
>
> * Between character and how they interpret what is happening to them, and what happens – how they act in response.
>
> If this is a form that interests you, there are so many wonderful examples to study, monologues that are as dramatically powerful as any other form – shows like *Marion and Geoff* (2000, written by Hugo Blick and Rob Brydon), and the pioneering *Talking Heads* series by Alan Bennett.

Principles of Dramatic Storytelling

Introduction

Storytelling is as fundamental to humanity as going to sleep at night and getting up in the morning. Rather than (initially) worrying overly about how to shape our stories, we should first be concerned with the emotional impact of our stories, what it is in our story that in some way expresses our essential humanity, speaks to our existence and its finiteness.

Story attempts to give some meaning to human existence: to articulate the vast range of extraordinary possibilities that life offers, while at the same time reflecting how limited and fragile it is – and while the end is the only thing we can predict with any certainty, we know not how or when it will happen. All of these mysteries of life and death underpin our need to tell stories – these ideas are at the heart of all meaningful art.

We don't have to be constantly striving to articulate this in our stories. We just need to recognise and acknowledge that it underlies the human need to tell them, and remember that many of the best stories touch us because in some way they celebrate or examine our shared human experience – they try to make some sense of what is not ever going to be fully knowable.

Story, like life, can never make total sense. A story that attempts to have all the answers is doing something that life can never do and so may not ring true.

★ ★ ★

This section covers some of the key principles of effective dramatic storytelling for the screen.

I refer to them as 'principles' rather than 'rules'. There are no 'rules' in screenwriting or, at least, all 'rules' are there to be challenged and subverted. To me, a 'principle' feels like something that is to be recognised rather than, like a rule, followed slavishly.

Every script I read and every show I watch furthers my knowledge and understanding of what makes for effective storytelling.

For every film or show you can think of that stands out because of its adherence to these principles, you will also be able to think of shows that successfully subvert and challenge them. But I think it's vital to your craft as a writer that you recognise and understand the principles before deciding whether and how you're going to subvert them.

Research: know what you write

'Write what you know' is common storytelling advice. But my experience of working with so many writers leads me to rethink this to – 'know what you write'. One of the joys of writing, one of the important weapons in your arsenal, is research: the ability to study a world – a profession, a religion, an organisation, an industry, a country, any sort of story setting – and become so expert (however briefly and temporarily) that you afford the reader or audience a privileged insight into that story world. If you're going to write a story set, as a completely random example, in and around a hotel in Moscow, then you need to immerse yourself in the specifics of the way this world works: establish the specific values, tensions and hierarchies of your characters within this world.

The best stories make full use of their settings so that they feel unique and utterly distinctive. They allow the audience a fresh and unexpected glimpse into a world that they didn't know about and that is both fascinating and allows the writer to ask particular questions of the characters who move within this world (the all-important conjunction of character and setting). This is one of the joys of story for an audience.

One of the skills a writer needs is the journalistic skill of research – and shaping research material into dramatic story. It's easy to get too wedded to the process: to get bogged down in the volume of the interesting information you have acquired and try to shoehorn it into your story, show off your newly acquired knowledge credentials. You need to wear your research lightly, shape the research to your own story purposes rather than let your story sag under the weight of the research. Research should be one of your tools, your story virtues – not a chance to show off how much you know or have found out.

Counter-intuitively, so often the way into a new story idea that will feel original and distinctive is through directly using a story or a set of facts that has already happened, that has a basis in actual lived experience.

Just as stories need a shape and structure, so the creative act needs processes, techniques, limitations and prompts to unlock and enable you. Giving yourself a limitless, infinite range of possibilities often just leads us to shutdown, to non-creative inertia. We need parameters, a structure within which to create, and research will help you to find that.

The essential dramatic events of your story should happen on, not off screen

Once you get into writing, your default principle for every scene should be that your characters are *living in the moment of that scene*. From scene to scene, adhering to this principle should be the priority and focus of the drama – rather than having characters commentating on their own lives and actions, discussing what has happened in other scenes, what may happen in future scenes or what has happened off screen.

To put it even more simply, the story you're telling should happen on screen.

This sounds obvious. But in so many of the less successful scripts I read – and even many of the TV shows and films I see – too much of the significant dramatic action is happening off screen.

Part of the process of telling any story on screen is deciding what you show and what you don't show. Sometimes it's interesting to see the aftermath of or build-up to a significant event, without seeing the event itself (*Reservoir Dogs* is a great example of this – a wonderfully tense and dynamic piece of storytelling that subverts this storytelling principle). But I would say this should be the exception rather than the rule.

> As an illustration of this principle, a film that in some ways reminds me in its form (and a little in its content) of *Reservoir Dogs* is a much more recent British film – *The Outfit* (2022). One of the key, defining aspects of the film is its storytelling decision to confine the story to a small set of rooms – the shop and working area of a Chicago tailor's shop in 1956. The story it tells is a relatively familiar genre gangster film – but from the perspective of the tailor caught up in this gang warfare. The film gets bogged down in long dialogue exchanges between the characters about what has happened or might happen outside of the shop. While some very dramatic events also happen within the shop, throughout the film there is a sense that the success of the storytelling is stymied by the decision to confine the action to these two rooms – resulting in reams of straightforwardly expositional dialogue about what

> is happening elsewhere, off screen. It's a film that made me want to yell at the screen – stop telling us what we should know and just show us! It felt like a film that was made because the interiority of the storytelling must have made it relatively inexpensive to shoot – but the storytelling feels fatally compromised.

Something that I see too frequently is characters neutrally discussing and describing something that has happened off screen, away from the gaze of the audience. This sort of scene is often the worst example of undramatised exposition – scenes whose sole purpose is to give the audience information, that use characters as expositional mouthpieces rather than as vibrant three-dimensional people caught up in the moment of the action. For a scene to work as a dramatic unit, it's not enough to convey information. Because, fundamentally, drama or story has to be about *people*, and scenes should be about the people in the moment of the scene, not just about the information these people are conveying – it's people we relate to and engage with.

A corollary of this is if a scene repeats information we've already heard. This too should be questioned; you see action played out, then someone reports what happened to someone who wasn't there. Unless this adds another layer to the story – e.g. the character in question is lying, reinterpreting or repurposing what we have seen, giving a false account of what happened – then you should rigorously avoid this sort of repetition of exposition.

Good writing is so often about the power of the moment in a scene, so, in general, dramatise a situation rather than have your characters discuss it after the event. Or, more simply: 'show, don't tell' – which has understandably become something of a script editor's cliché.

> But it's not always this straightforward. Take, for instance, the excellent Netflix series *Criminal* (2019, written by George Kay). This is a very strong, contained drama series format that is predicated on dialogue and on people talking about dramatic events that have happened elsewhere beforehand – but this doesn't preclude drama in the dynamic between the characters on screen in the present. The setting of the series – the police interview room – is where things come to a head. It's of vital importance to interviewer and interviewee, and is about revealing things for the police character over and above what they know coming into the interview. Crucially, the stakes are clear for the characters on both sides of the table. So showing not telling needn't necessarily mean avoiding static dialogue and discussions of what has already happened off screen. This is one format that both challenges and underlines this principle brilliantly.

Withhold exposition until the moment of maximum dramatic impact

While my default principle is that the crux of the drama of your story needs to play out on screen, you also need to consider the other side of this coin.

'Exposition' can be broadly described as 'story information' – and the big questions for you as storyteller are how and when (and whether) you choose to reveal particular story information.

'Backstory' is exposition from the past that is pertinent to the story you're telling on screen in the present – what has happened to your characters before your story starts. With every successful characterisation will come backstory: what has happened to or between the characters before your story has started will significantly inform your story in the present.

Too often, exposition and backstory can feel like a burden that is being carried by your story when in fact it should be a powerful part of your storytelling armoury, something that adds richness and complexity to your story in the present. How you handle and exploit both of these elements of story is absolutely key to effective storytelling for the screen.

The important principle I think you need to bear in mind is this: your storytelling instinct should be to withhold key backstory exposition for as long as possible; to think long and hard about where and when is the best place to reveal it.

Characters' secrets, their lies, their baggage and any other information you need to reveal about who they are… none of this character information should feel 'neutral'. It should all add another layer of intrigue and depth to your character and their story. Each time you reveal another layer of backstory or exposition it should fundamentally change the status, the stakes, of your story.

Inexperienced screenwriters often think they need to tell us as much as they can as soon as they can, to get past the 'problem' of letting the audience know who your characters are and what their story issues are. But the opposite is more usually true – you should see the issue of revealing key exposition about your character and their story not as a problem to be got out of the way, but as a virtue. Resist the temptation to tell us too much too soon.

Exposition, when and how you use it, is one of the most important and thorniest issues in telling your stories on screen. Although they may not express it as such, one of the biggest turn-offs for an audience is undisguised or undramatised exposition, when the story is parked up, so that characters can helpfully fill the audience in on plot details they may have missed.

So often, a dull, literal scene can be transformed into an intriguing, gripping scene by simply removing certain information from it.

The hook: posing questions is at the heart of effective storytelling

Connected to this principle of withholding exposition is another: good storytelling is predicated on hooks. What audiences respond to, what keeps us turning the page, or our eyes glued to the screen, is the way that story poses questions for its audience.

Each scene should pose a new story question and, as above, you should withhold key story *answers* for as long as possible.

The resolution of story is – finally – answering these questions, providing a pay-off for everything you have set up. And there is nothing more disappointing than a story that doesn't pay off its set-ups. But too often, writers waste the opportunities their stories have given them by answering too many of these questions too early in their story, paying off their set-ups too soon.

> This was a key principle that was brought home to me when working as a script editor on the successful BBC crime drama series *Waking the Dead*. Working on one script, the writer, with the help of the forensic science adviser, had come up with a wonderful piece of detailed evidence and deduction that provided an intriguing and unexpected clue to the solving of the crime of the week. But the writer in question had initially both introduced and resolved this issue within one quite long – and excellent – dialogue scene. Between us, we worked out that this was such a great piece of story that we should break it down into several different stages of revelation over several different scenes, spread across the two-hour story. In this way, one good scene became a much more powerful, weighty and compelling story strand with a more impactful, significant pay-off and reveal. The writer knew where he was going, but withheld the key story information until the optimum moment in the story – far later than he had initially thought. And the time and struggle it had taken the investigating team to reach the right conclusion gave this reveal more story weight and impact – allowing the audience to more fully emotionally invest in the final answer to this question of evidence and revelation.

Questions are what keep us hooked by story – not answers. It's the hook, the underlying narrative questions, that will keep an audience… hooked!

Generate suspense

Suspense is fundamental to film and TV storytelling. When we're caught up in the suspenseful nature of stories on screen, it's a sure sign of storytelling success. That tricky mix of expectation, hope and fear is generated by our desire for things to come right for your characters, for them to achieve the best – or avoid the worst.

At the start of the fourth series of *Trying* (Apple TV+, created and written by Andy Wolton), the main characters are preparing for a funeral. Someone has died – but the identity of the dead person is withheld from us for the first ten minutes or so of the episode. We see the 'order of service' but a wallet and keys hide the photo. This is a real 'teaser' – the identity of the dead person has been so artfully and artificially hidden from the audience. But despite the self-consciousness of the device, this works. I was drawn into the story. Audiences love to be held in suspense like this, it's an absolute story staple – and it comes back to the writer's control of their material.

Other memorable moments of suspense: Chuck Noland (Tom Hanks) on his self-made life raft is almost run down by a vast ship in *Cast Away* – but will he be able to get the ship crew's attention before it passes him by? In *The Godfather*, Michael Corleone desperately moves his father out of his hospital room before the assassins arrive to kill him – will he manage to hide his father before the killers arrive?

These are moments that have stayed with me because of the sheer adrenalin rush the storytelling induced in me. It's about the storytellers getting you to invest emotionally in these characters in these situations; getting you to imagine best and worst scenarios and what either could mean for the character. And it's about postponement of the outcome, keeping you hooked and on the edge of your seat for as long as they can.

Make a virtue of context

All stories are coloured by their context – the knowledge and preconceptions the audience brings to them – and bringing a sense of context to scenes is another key aspect of the dramatic storyteller's work. For instance, if you give your audience a piece of knowledge not accessible to the characters in the moment of the scene, putting us in this position of privilege can often lend real power to an otherwise ordinary scene or moment in a story.

Peter Jackson's Beatles documentary, *Get Back*, has so much power because of its context – the knowledge the audience brings to it of what happened to these people both before and after the events of this film. It's this sense of context as we witness Paul McCartney in real time creating some of the best-known songs of the twentieth century that makes the film feel magical and profound. And the same is true of biopics like *Rocketman* or *Bohemian Rhapsody*.

Subtext and counterpoint are essential elements in dramatic storytelling

The idea of subtext – the counterpoint between what is happening on the surface of the scene and what the scene is actually about – is fundamental to good dramatic writing.

If dialogue is flat and not coming alive, it's very rarely about the dialogue itself – it's more often that the purpose of the scene is too clearly stated and acted out in the superficial action and dialogue of the scene. There will of course be moments in your story when the truth of the scene *does* need to be articulated clearly and straightforwardly, but these scenes should be the exception rather than the rule, and you need to be very clear about why and when a scene without subtext is justified.

In other words, scenes need layers – the majority of scenes need to be performing several functions at the same time, to work on more than one level. (More on this in the sections on Character, from page 126, and Dialogue, from page 175.) There needs to be a tension between what is happening on the surface of your scene and what is *actually* happening, underneath the surface.

Often, secrets and lies are the key to this counterpoint and to intriguing, involving storytelling in general. Good storytelling is often about what *isn't* said, the things characters hide from themselves and each other.

Humour and humanity are the bedrock of story

I think what audiences yearn for above all else is a sense of relatable humanity in your story. If they recognise this well of humanity – often expressed through character 'intelligence' (more about this on pages 133–5), connection between characters, or a sense of joy or wonder – then I think they are willing to forgive a lot, to suspend disbelief and immerse themselves in the story you are telling.

A big part of this element of humanity in story comes from a sense of humour. Even (or particularly) when life is at its darkest, it's a sense of humour and of the absurd that is what makes characters feel recognisably and relatably human. It's this somewhat absurd but fundamental and frail humanity that, for instance, elevates the writing of Martin McDonagh (*Three Billboards Outside Ebbing, Missouri*; *In Bruges*).

Successful storytelling – whether drama or comedy – depends on the audience recognising a truth in the actions of your characters. And a story without a sense of humour is as lacking as a person without a sense of humour. Within storytelling principles as a whole, humour trumps every other consideration for me, because humour – any moment in story and character observation that makes us smile, let alone laugh – is rare and to be cherished. Successful comic writing is a rare gift and not, generally, valued as it should be, compared to dramatic writing.

I believe that your first approach to story should be instinctive: trust in your own storytelling instincts. The emotion you feel as you write a scene will be the emotion you evoke in the reader or audience. Your stories should attempt to dramatise your truths in your way.

So make sure your story has a clear connection to your own experience or observation of the human condition. Make sure you have recognised and dramatised the idiosyncratic humanity of your characters.

Good writing is about accessing an emotional response to an event

What do we (the audience) look for in a TV or film story? This is not a question that can be easily and quickly answered. But I would say one of the things we are fundamentally looking for is that the story elicits an emotional response. An intellectual response is good – but we don't go to the movies to be 'interested', we go to be moved, to have our emotions stirred. Indeed, in my experience, when asking someone for their opinion of a show, the response, 'It was interesting,' often means the opposite. A solely intellectual response is often an inadequate, incomplete and unfulfilling response to art of any sort. We have a fundamental need to be moved, not just interested.

'Sentimental' has become a dirty word. The dictionary definition is 'of or prompted by feelings of tenderness, sadness, or nostalgia' – which sounds to me like a feeling that a (certain kind of) good, successfully realised screen story elicits from us. An alternative definition, 'having or arousing feelings of tenderness, sadness, or nostalgia, typically in an exaggerated and self-indulgent way', seems more like what our perception of the word 'sentimental' has become: a pejorative word, a synonym for 'mawkish'. There is a certain type of character-driven film that wears its heart on its sleeve and will appeal to audiences but not critics – films, for instance, like *A Man Called Otto* (David Magee) and *About Time* (Richard Curtis). I think both of these films work superbly, are examples of outstanding character and story screenwriting – but they are the sort of films critics will often dismiss as 'sentimental'.

But I would argue that 'sentiment' is what many of the best films and TV fiction evoke in us: an appeal to our emotions. And this is absolutely something that as writers we should not shy away from. An emotional response to the death of a loved one, for example, is not (normally) seen as 'sentimental'. It is an undeniable human reality.

In my experience, too many scripts forget or underestimate this all-important function of story. Story exists to help us understand emotional responses to life events, whether that emotional response is positive (smiles, laughter, tears of joy) or negative (anger, jealousy, violence, hostility, tears of sadness and frustration).

The undeniable fact is that every life contains moments of huge joy and sadness – and one of the principal reasons fictional stories exist is to help us reflect on and come to terms with this. The best films make us relate to and process the huge emotional upheavals in our own lives.

> Give me a messily sentimental story any day over a well-organised story that doesn't connect with me emotionally. *I Am Sam*, written by Kristine Johnson and Jessie Nelson, for instance, is an example of a film that, if I was that way inclined, I could pick all sorts of narrative holes in. And some of the reviewers went in hard on it: 'its sentimentality is so relentless and its narrative so predictable' from the *New York Times*. But the film hits the ground running, it instantly sweeps you up in its emotional wake and carries you along for the ride. It's silly, it's fun and it has moments of great beauty. At its heart there is an ultimately insoluble emotional issue; and this is what drives the film and the audience's involvement with its characters.
>
> It's also about things that are fundamental to the human condition – in particular, the parent–child relationship.
>
> As I was watching it with my daughter, she said, 'It's a bit of a tricky situation isn't it?' Every single story requires this 'tricky situation', this dilemma, at its heart.

If the situation isn't tricky, if it's easily soluble, you have no story.

This is not to say that every fictional story has to address a hugely emotive issue or event. But at the same time even the smallest, subtlest, least superficially emotional stories need to be underpinned by something that feels like a relatable observation of the human condition.

Acknowledge and subvert tropes and clichés

Audiences are incredibly sophisticated, in that we have all watched literally thousands of hours of screen narrative (whether fiction or non-fiction, TV, film, gaming, whatever), and are therefore generally unforgiving of the familiar, hackneyed and derivative.

It's very hard to surprise audiences, to tell stories in a completely new and unexpected way. We instinctively understand tropes and clichés – ways of telling story on screen that feel obvious.

So many scripts, for instance, open with the morning wake-up, the shower, characters meeting in the kitchen for breakfast, leaving the house. As a writer, you need to ask yourself serious questions about why you are choosing to include such sequences. You need to think about why these particular scenes are important for your characters and story, what it reveals about them, how it advances the story; and how you are going to write such sequences in a way that feels fresh and surprising.

> The opening sequence of *Four Weddings and a Funeral* (1994, written by Richard Curtis) taps into this trope – but does it in a way that feels fresh, funny and, in a manner that is scatologically inarticulate, dramatises and reveals the characters, and immediately introduces narrative tension. There is nothing that is startlingly original about it – but it is sure-footed, confident, engaging storytelling. It takes a very familiar screen narrative trope and subverts it with confidence, humour and flair.
>
> Similarly, the highly dramatic opening teaser before cutting back to an earlier point in the story, whether that's a year or an hour previously, is another familiar narrative trope. But there's a reason why it's been so overused: when done well it can be so effective. As for instance in the HBO miniseries *The White Lotus*, written by Mike White, where an unidentified death in the teaser leaves us with a huge character question that powerfully informs the following six hours of the story (and was used in exactly the same way in both series one and two).

Some other examples of familiar film and TV tropes:

* Characters vomiting in response to upsetting news.

* The scene in which our hero maverick police investigator is hauled over the coals by their superior for their unorthodox methods. ('Morse, Lewis… a word in my office. Now!')

* The moment when a man spots the missing or dead girl they love(d) from behind in a public place, taps them on the shoulder, they turn round… and it's someone else (who looks a little puzzled and pitying). Our hero apologises confused, 'I'm sorry, I thought you were…'

* The hero emerging unscathed from a huge explosion or burst of automatic gunfire.

* The surveillance team in the car across the road from the target – weirdly never seen by the target.

* Sex scenes that don't have any connection to story.

* Middle-class couples conversing over large glasses of wine in their designer kitchens.

BUT before this starts to feel a like a cynical whinge-fest, I want to emphasise that I'm not saying there is anything absolutely wrong with any of these scenes and devices.

Tropes and clichés become that because they have been proven to work, because they are helpful narrative devices and because, at their best, they can work as the basis of brilliant dramatic scenes.

But I do think you should have a healthy questioning attitude when these sorts of scenes suggest themselves to you – how can you subvert how it usually plays? And in particular, how can you do something unexpected with these scenes in a way that feels utterly specific to and illustrative of your very particular and distinctive characters and story world?

Because I think the two biggest reasons for resorting to these sorts of clichéd scenes are either:

1. A lack of clarity about the characters – not knowing clearly enough how they as individuals would behave or respond in these situations.

Or:

2. A lack of research – not knowing the idiosyncratic possibilities of what might realistically happen in a particular situation – and thereby falling back on what you have seen previously on film and TV, rather than going to observations of real life.

The big thing to avoid is your script playing like a diluted version of other, better, already existing TV shows and films. Instead, it needs to be absolutely its own thing; even if you include many of these familiar sorts of scenes, you need to write them in such a way that they feel surprising, idiosyncratic, real and relatable. Find your own unique spin on the way you use them in your story.

Think carefully about what to include and what to leave out

With every story, you as a writer have a multitude of decisions to make about what you decide to show on screen. These decisions are at the heart of good storytelling. Tell the audience too much and you remove the possibility of tension, intrigue and mystery from your story; show too little and you risk baffling the audience and perversely leaving out the real, substantive drama of your story.

This sounds obvious but it's a principle that needs stating: good screenwriting is about including the interesting bits of your story and leaving out the boring bits.

If, for instance, there is a sequence in your story in which a character is travelling by car from location A to location B (as there is in so much TV and film drama), you need to decide which moments in this journey you need to show. Do you need to show this character leaving her house, walking down her garden path, unlocking the car, getting in, starting the engine, pulling away from the kerb? Do you need to see her driving at various points in her journey, arriving, etc., or can you just jump her from the interior of her house to the interior of the house to which she is travelling? (I use this example because this sequence is such a familiar one.)

There are many rational justifications for including boring scenes in screen drama, for instance as a necessary set-up or introduction – so that the contrast between the ordinary and extraordinary in your story world is clear. But beware of these 'necessary' humdrum set-up scenes. If a scene is dull, it's dull – however much you think you can justify its context within your overall story.

In every context of dramatic writing, words to question are 'discuss', 'chat', 'agree', 'talk about', 'muse' and 'consider'. These are all either passive or internalised verbs. The art of screenwriting is to externalise the internal. There is sometimes a place for scenes of discussion and reflection, but beware the script where these scenes dominate: scenes of discussion have the potential to be resolutely undramatic.

Every single scene needs to change the status quo of your story

Story needs to be taut, pacy and economical. Every single scene needs to count. If it doesn't, you should be able to cut the scene. This is one of the questions you should be asking of every scene – does the scene change the status quo of your story? Do we come out of the scene with the story in a different state to the one in which we went into the scene?

Make use of the infinite potential variety in the nature and character of scenes

There are so many different sorts of scenes: public, private, dynamic, passive, static, wordless, dialogue-driven… It's important to recognise and consider the vast number of choices you have at your disposal when constructing the way a scene works, and the many different elements you can use.

Some specific examples:

- ★ Big, public, set-piece action scenes.
- ★ Private, reflective, wordless, single-character scenes.
- ★ Two-handed scenes of reflective, conversational dialogue.
- ★ More dynamic, multi-character dialogue scenes of confrontation and conflict.
- ★ Characters interacting with a phone, computer or other props.
- ★ Scenes in open, public spaces.
- ★ Scenes in enclosed, private spaces.
- ★ Scenes of characters confined – people in cells, locked rooms, enclosed spaces.
- ★ Static scenes with characters sitting still.
- ★ Dynamic scenes of movement.
- ★ Scenes without people.
- ★ Scenes in cars, trains, planes – people in transit.
- ★ Fantastical scenes – dreams, visions, scenes of the imagination.
- ★ Single characters in vast, unoccupied, open spaces.
- ★ Multiple characters in busy, crowded spaces.
- ★ Scenes at night or day.
- ★ Scenes in extreme heat or cold.

I could go on...

Don't always think scenes need to be active and dynamic – there is often a place for the contrastingly reflective, quiet scene, cut against more dynamic scenes. Look for counterpoints between the action and the location just as you do between the text and subtext (see pages 65–6). Be transgressive in your choice of the elements of a scene.

There is always a place for two-handed dialogue scenes. They are perhaps the most-used scene set-up — but you need to be wary of too many scenes in which the characters talk to each other in a way that feels neutral, informational and passive. These moments should be the exception rather than the rule, because this static two-way exchange is the hardest to make surprising and dynamic. Introducing a third character into the mix will give you so many more choices, in some ways will ask more of you as a writer — but usually will greatly add to the texture and possibilities of the scene.

Conversely, having scenes containing only one character will often force you into bold, interesting, creative (non-dialogue-driven) decisions that will add to the colour and texture of the character in question and their story.

After all, we spend much of our lives by ourselves. Think about what your character does when by themselves — what they do specifically that is interesting, secret, or reveals something about who they are as an individual, that is not revealed in public!

What you should try to avoid is that scene of the solitary person unconvincingly talking to themselves with useful story information, or speculation. This feels obviously expositional. And don't ask your audience to read what your character is reading off a computer screen. This strikes me as an unimaginative use of the medium and can also feel too obviously expositional.

If such a ploy strikes you as the only way to convey a vital piece of information, you need to do all you can to disguise and dramatise its expositional purpose. So, for instance, if your character is reading crucial story information from a computer screen, have them wrestle with the technology, or their eyesight. Introduce some sort of recognisably messy human element to the way you convey this story moment to give it another layer of value and meaning for the audience — so that this moment of information reveal is also (for instance) an enjoyably wry, comic observation of universal struggles with new tech, or of a particular facet of character.

Similarly, try to play scenes in person rather than on the phone (or on Zoom/Skype, etc.) — it's (usually) more interesting. In many ways the advent of the mobile phone is a curse to dramatic storytelling. It enables so much to happen in life that previously couldn't, and it hugely limits your story choices. Connected to the principle that your story should, as a default, happen on screen rather than off screen (see pages 59–61), is one that scenes between characters should ideally happen in person. There is often a place for phone or FaceTime calls – but in pure storytelling terms, they lack the immediacy and intensity of face-to-face scenes, and so should be the exception rather than the rule. (One brilliant exception was the BBC lockdown comedy series, *Staged*, written by Simon Evans and predicated entirely on a series of Zoom calls.)

Tell the story through the cut

So much of your story can be told or suggested in the way you cut from scene to scene. This method of storytelling is economical, subtle and negates the need for clumsy expositional dialogue – it's interestingly suggestive rather than straightforwardly explanatory.

Indeed, using the cut from scene to scene is often a way of disguising expositional reveals.

Some examples:

* Cutting out of one scene on a question which (looks like it) is answered by the way you start the next scene.

* Making unspoken narrative connections through the cuts. In other words, you come out of a scene with a question about a character, and into a scene featuring that character in which the question is addressed, reflected back – even if it's not directly answered.

In this way the best screenwriting dramatises and energises the story through the way one scene connects to the next; how a question at the end of one scene is addressed by what we see or hear at the start of the following scene.

An unanswered question that closes a scene drives us into the next scene on an upward inflection. Conversely, an answer at the end of a scene too often feels final, conclusive – and then the cut to the next scene can feel like you're having to kick-start the story all over again, rather than being an energised transition. One of your jobs as a screenwriter is to judge these cuts from one scene to another, working at finding ways to elevate the energy and dynamism of your story in how you cut between scenes. If in doubt, end on this upward inflection of a question mark – not the downward inflection of a full stop.

A good screenplay is like a good song, with one bar (scene) moving elegantly and beautifully to the next. There is a style and rhythm to the way you move from one beat within a scene to the next, and between one scene and the next.

This is an integral part of the basic grammar of storytelling for the screen, and one of the aspects that makes it such an exciting and compelling narrative medium.

Think also about the moment at which you come into and exit from each scene. Accepted wisdom dictates that you come into a scene as late as possible and get out as early as possible. Arguably, this should be a default principle – but like all principles of dramatic writing, it's there to be challenged and questioned. (For more on this, see page 75.)

Pay attention to the rhythm of how your story plays

Rhythm is closely connected to genre – the rhythm of the cuts, the scene length, will typically be more rapid in, for instance, an action thriller than a relationship or period drama. But a script that contains only long, static two-handed, interior, private dialogue scenes will feel monotonous. You need to be constantly surprising your audience with the way you break up and vary the rhythm of your storytelling. You should mix night scenes with day scenes; public scenes with private scenes; work scenes with domestic scenes; intimate, quiet dialogue scenes with noisy action scenes; long dialogue scenes with short, wordless scenes; and so on.

If you watch older TV shows (even the excellent ones) and compare them with current shows, you will notice how the rhythm of storytelling has changed over the years. Rhythm nowadays is much more rapid, scenes (and shot length) shorter.

At the same time though, in recent years there have been some examples of writers choosing to subvert this trend and challenging audiences by including some extremely long scenes almost as story set-pieces, as stand-out story moments.

> I'm thinking of some of the excellent interview scenes in more recent series of *Line of Duty* (Jed Mercurio), and the climactic meeting between police officer and serial killer at the end of series three of *The Fall* (Allan Cubitt). These scenes worked brilliantly precisely because they were the exception. As writers, both Allan Cubitt and Jed Mercurio have proved themselves master storytellers in their use of visual narrative, in the way their stories are given power and intensity by the way they cut between scenes. They had both earned the right and found a story justification for these exceptionally long – and completely gripping – ten-plus-minute static dialogue scenes.

Hit the ground running

Particularly in this day and age of short attention spans and screenwriting competitions that in the first instance weed out scripts by only reading the first ten pages, it's vital that those first ten pages are packed with intrigue, dynamism and substantive story.

Some of the narrative structure textbooks advocate the first act being set up – establishing the world of your story, the status quo of your main character and central relationship – before shattering this status quo with the story catalyst at the end of act one. But I think audiences these days demand more than set-up in your first fifteen minutes – they also require narrative tension, some form of conflict and, crucially, that you establish the dramatic proposition that is at the heart of your story.

An experienced reader will make judgements from the first words in your script, the first page, the first three pages. The first few pages of your script are the most important. You need a script that opens with a vital, dynamic, dramatic story scene, that hits the ground running, immediately welcomes the audience and infuses us with confidence. What is also vital in these first few pages is narrative clarity – there is nothing more demoralising to a reader than struggling to understand what is happening or who we are meant to be focusing on right at the start of the script.

Key Storytelling Elements

Stakes

What is at stake for the characters in your story? This question has become a script editor's cliché. But like so many clichés, it has become a cliché because it is such an important question. In fact I'm not sure there is any more important question you can ask of your story than 'What is at stake?' It's a question that is fundamental to compelling story.

The principal characters in your story, in trying to achieve their aim, need to be taking a risk. They need to have something to lose. If, by failing to reach their goal, their status hasn't changed, then you don't have a story. Story needs to be about taking risks, characters putting their head above the metaphorical parapet. Narrative tension will be generated by the audience's anxiety about the bad things that will happen to your protagonist if things go wrong, if they fail to achieve their goals.

The nature of what the stakes are will vary greatly from story to story, depending on the story world, the genre, who your protagonist is, and so on. But the audience needs to understand what is at stake for this central character, what they stand to lose, what they are risking. Ultimately, in the context of your particular story, what is the worst thing that could happen to them in attempting but failing to achieve what they are trying to achieve? Similarly, 'What is the best thing that could happen?' is also vitally important.

Stakes vary from story to story. *Detectorists* (Mackenzie Crook) is, objectively, very low stakes in terms of the characters' aims and ambitions. But if what is at stake matters to the characters, then it matters to us. This too is a hugely important principle. The success of *Detectorists* proves that almost any story world or context has dramatic potential if you can find the right tone, the right story detail and, most crucially, establish and dramatise the characters' emotional relationship to the story world in which they exist.

On the other side of the coin, films like, say, *The Silence of the Lambs* (the attempt to find and capture a serial killer), *Love Story* (love thwarted by terminal illness) and *Goodfellas* (a police informant looking back at his dangerous, highly violent life as a member of the mob) are all much more obviously and inherently dramatic – what is at stake in each of these stories is clear.

Narrative clarity and connections

Audiences need to be able get their bearings in a story as soon as possible.

When submitting your spec script to a reader who has no sense of the context, the importance of this can't be overstated. So often, a reader will mentally check out of a script very early if they can't get a handle on what and who the story is about, and what the tone is.

What are your characters trying to achieve and what and who is getting in the way of them achieving this? And who is your lead character? I would suggest that, unless you have a very good story reason for doing otherwise (and you often will), you open on your lead character – to my mind, an important structural principle, one that will give your story a sense of purpose and clarity from the first moment of the first scene.

The first few pages of a script are disproportionately important. If the first few pages are hard to follow or understand, if we're not sure who the lead character is until page ten, then we will disengage from your story.

The best stories have a clarity and simplicity. It's about moving through your story with purpose, and connections that build in escalating narrative intensity from scene to scene.

Scenes and moments should connect, parallel strands should be cleverly interconnected, and you should be clear:

* What the main plot is.
* What the subplots are.
* That the subplots are intrinsically linked to the main plot.
* Where the subplots inform and illuminate the main plot.
* Where the main plot can't exist without the subplots.

It's also essential that the main plot can be expressed clearly and is inherently dramatic – with a dilemma at the heart of the story premise. (For more on this, see pages 41–2.)

Story gaps

Good storytelling is also about the *gaps* you leave in your story – posing questions for the audience about what has happened in the time between scenes, or about what has happened before your story starts.

Sometimes subtle suggestion or complete omission can be more powerful than showing. Leaving gaps in the story for the audience to fill in for themselves is a powerful storytelling tool. The best stories work on the basis that reading or watching them feels like an active, dynamic experience. The best writers trust their audience to fill in gaps for themselves with their own imaginative interpretations, instead of spelling everything out painstakingly.

If the audience feels you are 'spoonfeeding' them, the viewing experience will be flat and unrewarding. Incomplete storytelling generates mystery, intrigue and interesting questions for the audience to ask of your story.

With any screen story, there will be plot holes. It will be impossible to justify everything you have set up. Don't get too hung up on trying to fill these in – the overall effect of this will be to make the story feel plodding and overexplanatory. If you tell your story with enough flair, pace and imagination, the audience will indulge and forgive the potential holes!

Good storytelling is an act of confidence – telling the story in such a way that you win over the confidence of the reader or audience, enabling them to relax into and emotionally engage with your story such that they will be happy to forgive and ignore anything that isn't fully explained or 100 per cent rational.

Less is more. Don't be afraid of making your audience work hard. This is much preferable to the opposite: 'on the nose' storytelling.

> An example from *Happy Valley* [**SPOILER ALERT**], series one, episode three:
>
> The sequence in which Tommy Lee Royce runs over and kills police officer Kirsten portrays an act of extreme violence in a way that is chillingly powerful. But so much of the violence is implied. We don't see the moment of violence. We are with Tommy Lee Royce as he runs over the body; we feel the bumps as he drives over her. The scene is shocking because we are asked to imagine what is happening rather than being clearly shown. We are stunned by the action this character has taken, without it being graphically shown on screen.

Point of view

Point of view (POV), or perspective, is another crucial element of screen storytelling.

Some stories are told clearly from one character's point of view. Our view of the other characters, of the story world in which this character exists, and of the story problems that this character needs to solve, are all seen through this central character's point of view.

This close identifying with a single character, experiencing the story as *they* experience it as a character, is a great way to pull your audience emotionally into your story.

> Sally Wainwright's *Gentleman Jack* is a good example of this. The central character Anne Lister is in almost every single scene; and her occasional direct address to camera is a reminder that she is in charge of the way the story is filtered through to us, even if she is not as in control of events around her as she'd like to be – which is itself one of the successful narrative tensions of the show.

This idea of viewing the whole story from a single character's POV poses questions for you as a writer – and imposes restrictions. Because if we view the whole story through the prism of a single character's POV, then it also means we are not allowing ourselves to show the audience any scenes from outside of this character's experience – no scenes that don't involve this central character. So often this single, focused POV can be frustratingly restrictive – which is why it's not something you see in that many stories.

> Another example is the excellent US indie film *Fruitvale Station*, written by Ryan Coogler. [SPOILER ALERT] This is a fictionalisation of a tragic true story, about the killing of Oscar Grant by police in San Francisco in 2009.
>
> The story is told almost exclusively from Oscar's POV. We see him through the day that leads up to his tragic and unnecessary death. Every single scene is framed so that the story is primarily told through his prism on the world. This works wonderfully well, as we empathise deeply with his relationship with his girlfriend and young daughter, the fact that he has lost his job in a supermarket, and his dabbling with the drug trade to supplement his income. But alongside this single-character POV are fleeting moments in which we see Oscar through other eyes – primarily

through the eyes of his mother, as we flashback to see her visiting him in jail. And, importantly, as Oscar gets into a fight in the prison visiting room and is overpowered by prison guards, we leave the scene with his mother, rather than staying with Oscar.

After Oscar is shot, the story POV clearly (and necessarily) shifts – first to his girlfriend, the mother of his child, and then for the last few heartbreaking minutes of the movie, to Oscar's mother as she corrals friends and relatives waiting in the hospital to hear news of Oscar's condition. This shift in perspective is a clear storytelling decision and, having so strongly set up the character of Oscar's mother earlier in the film, is a narratively satisfying and emotionally gripping pay-off to Oscar's story.

Other Examples of Interesting and Successful Use of POV in Screen Story

Cast Away (2000, William Broyles Jr.)

The film is striking for its one-hour-plus sequence of the Tom Hanks character (Chuck Noland) alone on his desert island, in which the film explores dramatic questions about isolation and survival. The film is book-ended by shorter – but equally powerful – sections of Chuck before and after his six years alone, and beautifully dramatises not only how he has changed but how the world has moved on without him. It is a wonderful example of an organic, richly dramatic, three-act structure, where Chuck's perspective on the world is so powerfully different in the three acts of the film. The film is told predominantly from Chuck's POV, and this adds greatly to the intensity of the story.

Room (2015, Emma Donoghue)

[SPOILER ALERT] Another film in which the character POV is striking, and another film with a simple but brilliantly effective story premise.

The story is in some ways a familiar one, plucked from or inspired by the headlines – about a woman who has been kidnapped and kept in secret captivity for many years ('inspired' – if that's the right word – by the real Josef Fritzl case in Austria). But one of the many brilliant things that elevates this film is that the main character POV is that of the captive woman's child, conceived by rape in captivity, and who, for the first half of the film, has known only the world of 'Room' – the tiny space in which he lives with his mother. The transitional sequence at the film's turning point in which the boy escapes is a wonderful, cinematic narrative sequence. The first time I saw the film I was literally squirming in my seat – so caught up in the emotional power and tension of the story, so desperate for him to make good his escape, that I literally couldn't sit still. (Evidence of screenwriting at its very best!)

While the entirely different second half of the film doesn't have the consistent POV focus of the first half, it still packs a powerful narrative and emotional punch, and still uses the boy as the main focus of the story. But we also see the POV of the characters around him as they try to help him find his place back in conventional society. Indeed, this shift in story POV – from the simplicity of the son–mother relationship in captivity, to the relative complications of the broader POV, and so many different people's response to both child and mother – is at the heart of what is brilliant about the storytelling. A brilliant example of how the form of the storytelling and the decisions writer Emma Donoghue made about how to change the point of view over the course of the film, brings a powerful and razor-sharp focus to the content and nature of the story.

Little Miss Sunshine (2006, Michael Arndt)

Part of this film's brilliance is that it's a true ensemble story that nonetheless feels like it has a wonderful sense of unity and momentum. At certain points in the story, we are clearly experiencing moments from each of the main characters' points of view – Olive in her desire to win the 'Little Miss Sunshine' contest; her grandpa in his effort to enable this; Frank coming back to his sister's family after his attempted suicide, seeking respite; Dwayne in his determination to get to flight school; Rich trying to strike the deal that will elevate his 'Nine-Step Guide to Success' philosophy and seal financial security; and Cheryl in her attempts to hold the family together. At certain times in the film, we are absolutely emotionally in tune with each of these characters in their individual agendas. So while it's far less easy with *Little Miss Sunshine* to sum up clearly whose POV we're following at any one point in the story, as the POV shifts subtly between characters within scenes and from scene to scene, there is still such a strong sense of audience engagement with the point of view of each character. And the fact that it's harder to clearly define whose POV we're with at any one moment doesn't make it any less successful as a story for the screen. A wonderful example of multiple-POV, ensemble storytelling.

Consideration of point of view is one of your most important and powerful tools as a storyteller for the screen – and not only in the overall story but within individual scenes. It's a huge part of enabling the audience to identify with your characters and engage with your story.

Story for the screen is all about immersion in character – and considering from whose point of view you are telling your story is a key element in this.

Set-ups and pay-offs

The best storytelling is circular. In some of the best dramatic writing, there is a sense that the story has come full circle and arrived – in a different version and in unexpected ways – back where it all started.

> In the one-woman play *Prima Facie*, by Suzie Miller, there is a reference at the start to the character's first day at university, being asked to compare herself to those sitting to her left and right. This is then echoed at the end of the play by a similar question in a different context, and the way the story ironically self-reflects adds greatly to its power.
>
> And in the lovely *Rye Lane* (written by Nathan Bryon and Tom Melia), we come back full circle to the idea raised near the start of the film: is Dom someone who waves at people on boats or not?! A sweet and meaningful pay-off.

These sorts of 'callbacks' so often add resonance and emotional weight to a story.

The best storytelling is characterised by a sense that every single moment in the story is significant and purposeful and – in particular – that every single set-up will have a pay-off; that every single moment has meaning, that nothing is wasted or unconnected. This sort of storytelling is deeply satisfying, one of the elements that makes you feel like you're in the hands of a capable storyteller who is in control of their material.

This circularity of story and paying off of all your set-ups is such a vital part of good practice in creating your story. Ideally, every single moment in your story needs to have (often unexpected) meaning – and connection.

Signposts

But, always be careful to distinguish between the narrative satisfaction of set-ups that are paid off, and those moments that less helpfully 'signpost' what's about to happen and thereby drain the story of surprise, tension and energy. Unhelpful signposting is exemplified by characters accurately anticipating what is about to happen in their story.

While pay-offs should feel recognisable as such, and satisfying, they also need to feel in some way surprising.

> For instance, in Jimmy McGovern's outstanding three-episode miniseries, *Time* (BBC, 2021), there is a seemingly unimportant incident when Eric McNally's car brake light gets broken. In the best storytelling no incident is wasted, no event is without consequences, and everything is connected in surprising ways. With a storyteller as skilled as McGovern, we instantly sense that the broken brake light is going to become much more significant than it at first appears – and we aren't disappointed.

In the best scripts, while there is a remorseless narrative logic, the story is still surprising and unpredictable.

Metaphors, imagery and motifs

There is a moment in *Fruitvale Station* when protagonist Oscar witnesses the running over of a dog. This has no real narrative link to anything else in the story – but it's a beautiful, brutal, poetic moment – that acts as a metaphor for the story as a whole. It's the sort of poetic, cinematic, emotionally resonant moment that turns a good film into an outstanding film; a moment that articulates everything the film is about in a way that is indirect but profound.

The best story works on more than one level. There is the story – with the themes, the incidents that go into making up this story – but the best story also works on a more visceral, poetic, metaphorical level, with little moments, images, or tableaux that express or suggest what the story is about. Often these are moments that as a writer come from your heart rather than your head. (And actually many of these moments are to do with the 'objects' mentioned on page 97.)

Often, a single image of your character in a particular setting, or undertaking a particular action, or with a particular object – articulates the essence of the whole story. This is the sort of image that could work as a poster.

Movement

So many of the best films and TV drama stories are predicated on movement, energy and dynamism. Story needs to *move* in every sense of the word:

1. Elicit an emotional response in the audience.

2. Move forward from moment to moment, scene to scene, with pace and energy. In every story, there needs to be a strong sense of a shifting emotional landscape; of narrative issues changing and moving within the dynamics of the relationships between the characters; of the story moving forward through time and space. Your story needs to have this sense of propulsive energy and drive from scene to scene.

3. Physically move. There is no scene more difficult to make interesting (although it is the most common scene you will find in most screenplays) than one in which two characters sit on seats in a room exchanging information. In general, scenes are so much more interesting, dynamic and layered when the characters are in motion. So many of the best stories dramatise journeys with progressions that are both physical and metaphorical.

Story needs to be about friction and energy – not about contentment and peace (until the end – and often not even then). The best storytelling exudes energy – even if it's a frustrated, constricted energy. Static scenes should be the exception not the rule.

> *The Disappearance of Alice Creed* (J Blakeson) is an example of a film that – although largely limited in its long middle section to an enclosed, interior three-hander – displays great energy, movement, and continuing narrative shifts. The film's opening five-minute action sequence, leading up to and dramatising the incident that is the catalyst for the whole story, is an example of a story using movement and dynamism brilliantly.

In an interview, I heard Lucy Prebble talking about finding the process of writing relatively easy when in motion – travelling on a plane, train, bus, etc.

Around the same time I heard Bill Nighy talking about an acting self-discovery – that the worst thing he could do as an actor was to have his arms hang still by his sides. Once he realised any movement of his arms was better than no movement, it was liberating (this is my interpretation of his words).

It comes back to the idea that so much of the most effective screenwriting is visual and active. If you have two characters undergo a significant or emotional change over the course of the scene, it's hard to convey this with both sitting down throughout. It feels counter-intuitive to stage moments of emotional turmoil and change, of revelation or inspiration, when two characters are sitting.

There are, as ever, exceptions to this principle. If, for instance, the characters are obliged or forced to stay seated when they're bursting to get up or move in some way – at a big public gathering, in church, school assembly, on military parade ground, whatever – then there's the potential for a fascinating tension within the scene. The characters not being able to do what they physically need to do creates a feeling that their natural self-expression has to be restrained, channelled in some other way. In this way restrictions can be used to dramatise a situation – this sort of inner conflict is key to effective dramatisation.

> *Little Miss Sunshine* (Michael Arndt) subverts the movement principle brilliantly with its early, long dinner-table scene: a ten-minute, largely static scene that brilliantly introduces the key characters and their story agendas for the whole film.

Story world

Your story world is the basis of everything in your drama. It's the context within which your characters exist, the context that is going to challenge and ask questions of them. Whether your story world is rooted in a real-world setting – an institution like a hospital, a police station, a business or some other organisation – or if it's entirely imaginary, your own unique creation, it's essential that you know this world inside out, that you understand both the possibilities and the parameters of the story world you have created. What does it look like? How does it function? What are the rules of this world? And how does it release and enable these characters' stories?

Things to Consider Carefully

Random events and deus ex machina

Random accidents and events undermine the story values of your film, because they feel to the audience like a betrayal of their emotional engagement.

The clearest example I can think of to illustrate this point is the random car crash that suddenly and unexpectedly kills your main character(s). This is undoubtedly and sadly true to life – but in a work of fiction, often this feels frustrating and unsatisfactory, like a breaking of the narrative rules and parameters within which your story operates.

This sort of event – that comes out of nowhere and completely takes over and redirects your story – so often feels like a story cheat: a pay-off without a set-up. When it feels like this, it undermines all the work you have done to get the audience to invest in and engage with your characters and their story; it cheats your audience and cuts your story off at the knees. At their worst, these moments cause your audience to disengage when, until now, they have gone along with your story, emotionally investing in the characters and the choices they make. Big, shocking story events need to feel narratively and tonally integrated and not like jarring, over-convenient story devices.

That's not to say that this sort of big, unexpected story event can never work – TV drama and film are full of these sorts of moments. It is a tricky balancing act. Occasionally, these sorts of random events can be exactly what you need as a story catalyst – they can be the keys to unlocking character, disrupting and intensifying story in an exciting, unexpected way. (Indeed Kay Mellor created a whole long-running series format out of another potentially random, unmotivated story event – the idea of winning the lottery, in *The Syndicate*.) But as writers you need to judge when these sorts of events are a narrative virtue and when they undermine your story and the story values you have established.

> [SPOILER ALERT] An example of a car crash that *does* work, that doesn't feel like a 'random event', is in the first five minutes of episode one of HBO series *Six Feet Under*. In Alan Ball's wonderful script, it feels like the catalyst for the whole series, the event that propels the story forward. And the event itself is wonderfully well-written in its illustration of character and of the ironic, dark humour of the series as a whole (the crash happens just after the victim has been lying on the phone to his wife about starting smoking again; and as a result of him taking his eyes off the road to light up). Not only is this incident not random, it's like a narrative and tonal signature of the series. It instantly sets up both the story of the series and the heightened, darkly comic tone.

So your judgement as a writer has to be about when these events feel like they are a pay-off that has been set up – an event that feels rooted in character and tone – and when they feel like they come completely out of the blue, like a '*deus ex machina*': solving a tricky plot issue conveniently but without narrative or tonal integrity.

If you're going to include this sort of 'real life', random event – whether it's catastrophe or triumph – then the event needs to feel like it's absolutely integral to the way your story unfolds and that it earns its place in your story. Even if it's a surprising and unexpected moment, it should feel like a natural story development that adheres to the story values you have established.

Similarly the *deus ex machina* is about a random event that resolves your story, that doesn't feel integral to what you have set up, narratively or tonally. It feels imposed and too neatly ties up the loose ends of your story, without your characters having earned that resolution by their actions. Audiences will feel let down by this sort of ending. The resolution of your story should feel earned – both surprising and inevitable.

Politics and preaching to the converted

A lot of the best writing is political – writing that has a strong, impassioned political agenda. One of the tricky aspects of political writing is to make sure your story doesn't feel overly didactic or preachy, that it still feels surprising. Preaching to the converted doesn't make for challenging or intriguing stories.

If you are telling a story about politics – for instance about financial mismanagement, abuse of refugees, or corrupt right-wing politicians – you need to think about how you approach these stories. Write so that the message isn't immediately crystal clear; so that you're not instantly boxing yourself into a corner and giving yourself nowhere to go with your story.

It's too easy to make your villains instantly dislikeable, your heroes upstanding and morally superior. Try not to allow the audience to instantly dismiss and judge the villains – and avoid having your hero being on the right side of the political argument from the start. Stories and characters need to be more ambivalent and complicated than this.

If we can discern your political stance as a writer from very early on, the story becomes too much about the message, not enough about the development of the characters and their story. Ultimately stories can reassure and convey your political agenda – but before this, they need to challenge, subvert and provoke.

Character-driven versus plot-driven

Should you aim to make your scripts 'character-driven' rather than 'plot-driven'? Sometimes in TV drama that feels plot-driven rather than character-driven, as an audience we aren't made to care when dramatic things happen, because we don't feel enough empathy or connection with the characters.

At the same time though, I would argue that some of the work of the most successful UK TV dramatists is more plot- than character-driven – in particular Harry and Jack Williams, and Jed Mercurio. But it's instructive with shows like *The Missing* and *The Tourist* that if the plot is sufficiently twisty and action-packed – constantly surprising – then it can make up, to some extent, for the lack of believable, rich, human, empathetic and recognisable characters.

Personally I would always advocate for character-driven stories and am not a particular fan of shows like *The Tourist, Liar, Angela Black*, etc. – shows that, it seems to me, focus on twists, turns and surprises, often at the expense of believable, empathetic characterisation. But there is no denying the success of these shows.

As new writers, I think you will make things hard for yourself if you focus on plot over character. Ideally you need both – but the characters should drive the plot rather than the other way round.

In some TV drama (particularly bad crime drama), there is a tendency to think that making the plot complicated (often to the point of incomprehensibility – for instance making the clues leading to the eventual reveal of the identity of the murderer really over-intricate) will in some way compensate for flat characters. It won't.

Characters should not exist only to support and carry a plot. The characters need to *be* the plot. What we watch drama and read fiction for is to experience people and their behaviour. Sometimes TV crime drama can feel like a crossword puzzle – a mass of clues and red herrings that eventually coalesce into a solution. To a small extent this can feel slightly satisfying when all the clues are unravelled and resolved – but this sort of drama will always feel thin, insubstantial and less emotionally fulfilling than the best character-driven drama.

Two Further Thoughts

Be specific

Good screenwriting is utterly specific. It should be set in Derby (say), not an anonymous Midlands town. And it's about specific individuals – not about a group, or a vague, general mood.

Making a narrative or character virtue of specific, distinctive visual and physical detail is a vitally important part of screenwriting. It's about finding the universal and relatable in the specific. Telling, relatable detail in setting, clothes, hair, facial hair, personal tics, dialogue tics, period or regional observations, etc., is much more persuasive and effective than general, vague, non-visual action.

And remember that a film or TV show can only show us one thing at a time. Plurals and generalities aren't filmable. Make sure your action is singular as well as specific. Directions like, 'A succession of people enter the building' are hard to visualise for the reader and to film for the director.

Get your story onto the page

When you are creating a new story, one of the things that will excite you is that you can immediately envisage certain scenes in this story. I would suggest that you make a list of these scenes, even write them rather than delay gratification – don't think you need to methodically write your script in story order. Often, it's a really helpful tactic in easing the difficult process of writing to write whichever scenes leap out at you from whatever part of your story – and not to rigorously stick to story order.

One of the things that I find most effective when working with writers on scenes that aren't quite working, that aren't quite coming alive clearly off the page, is to ask them to articulate both the purpose or function and action of the scene under discussion. So often what the writer articulates in conversation is both more exciting and clearer than what is on the page.

One of the hardest aspects of screenwriting is actually getting your story onto the page effectively and clearly. What may feel clear in your head can sometimes lack clarity on the page. This is one of the hardest things to nail down – it requires a level of objectivity that it's very hard for writers to attain when they are deeply embedded in their own story; and it's where a script editor can come in very useful.

Aspects of Exposition

By 'exposition', I mean story information. How you handle exposition is one of the thorniest aspects of screenwriting. Revelation of necessary exposition needs to be seamlessly woven into the story – it should never feel like the action of the story is on hold while the writer fills us in with important information.

Choices and questions about exposition and how you choose to dramatise it are at the heart of successful dramatic storytelling. Audiences will sniff out clumsy expositional devices – we've all seen so much of it – and whether we view it technically or just instinctively, our hearts all sink a little at the familiar news conference, news report voice-over, two characters trading information about their past the first time they meet, etc.

Disguise or dramatise exposition

You can disguise exposition with a joke, an argument, a denial. Have your cake and eat it – scenes can exist *primarily* for what is compelling in the moment of immediacy between the characters, but *also* give us exposition.

The long dinner scene at the beginning of *Little Miss Sunshine* (also referenced on page 89) is a great example of this – exposition through the prism of brilliantly created, clearly defined character dynamics. The specificity of the relationship dynamics – the tension between Frank and Rich, the grandfather's misplaced pride in Olive's dance routine, the fact that Frank is a newly arrived outsider into the family – enables the characters to trade information that is helpful to the audience in a way that feels motivated, believable, and framed in the completely credible idiosyncrasy of brilliantly observed characterisation. And the scene concludes with the phone call that sets up the journey cross-county that is the heart of the film's story. While generally you should avoid the trope of using phone calls to give your audience exposition, in this scene, writer Michael Arndt pulls it off because of the brilliant, hugely well-defined character dynamics (and humour) in the moment of the scene.

This is a long, largely static dialogue scene, packed with exposition for the audience, but all brilliantly disguised and dramatised through the prism of beautifully written character relationships.

Reveal exposition through action rather than dialogue

Try to reveal story exposition through character action – i.e. what characters do rather than what they say, or what they do when it is in direct contradiction to what they have said.

The opening non-dialogue sequence to *The Disappearance of Alice Creed* does this superbly. It tells us so much about the story, and about the relationship between the two characters in it, through their actions and behaviour. One character helping the other to tie his tie is a strangely revealing moment of both relative status and intimacy. The way the two men go about a shopping trip, which sets up intriguing and unsettling questions about the intended use of what they're buying (rope, a saw, a bed)… all of this brilliantly and intriguingly precedes and prefigures the chilling abduction that concludes the sequence.

It's so often the moments of visual poetry, non-naturalism and imagery that elevate a script, and are memorable and emotive. Cinematic images often tell the story with greater emotional clarity and power than dialogue. (This is true not just of scripts but also of pitches, outlines and treatments.)

There is a moment in the opening episode of Abi Morgan's *Eric*, when the father finds his missing son's drawings of a monster that the boy has imaginatively created. Somehow this monster – in the various drawings that the father first rifles through and then recreates in his own cartoonish drawings and sketches – powerfully informs the tone of the story. The monster the boy has 'created' feels like a metaphor for the dark forces in the urban world around him that have led to his abduction. But the moment also dramatises both the boy's secret talent and passion for drawing; and his father's previous lack of sensitivity to his son's inner world.

Exposition and evoking an emotional response through the use of objects

All our lives are characterised by the possessions with which we surround ourselves – use these objects and possessions to tell your characters' stories (a wedding ring, a gift shared, a hidden bottle of gin, banknotes under the mattress, photographs – although this particular device is too often used!). Make the way you dramatise your characters' stories through their possessions distinctive and surprising. What are the objects, keepsakes, pieces of furniture or personal possessions that have meaning in your own life? What are these objects that have emotional meaning for your characters?

This is a key part of successful screen storytelling. The way you use props can be hugely effective in making the audience engage with your characters – and in advancing the story.

> Wilson the volleyball from the movie *Cast Away* (2000, William Broyles Jr.) is one of the best-known and most successful instances of this. This inanimate piece of plastic becomes a key character in the movie. It is a device to enable Chuck Noland to have someone (here, some*thing*) to talk to – but it's more than a device, because this use feels psychologically true. We can all empathise with a man feeling so isolated that he has to resort to 'humanising' and talking to a volleyball. When he loses the volleyball at sea, calling, 'Wilson! Wilson!' as it floats off into the distance, is a properly tear-jerking moment – that's good writing!

Who knows what, when?

One of the most important questions in how you use and dramatise exposition concerns the relationship between characters and information, by which I mean: how much do your characters know about each other and about the substance of the story in which they're existing? What does each character know and what don't they know? And what happens when one character thinks they know something about another – but is wrong? What each character knows or think they know about every other character is at the heart of your story and how you dramatise it.

But it's also about the audience's relationship to the story. At any given point in your story, how much information are you giving the audience? And, in particular, how much information are you giving your audience in comparison to the information you're giving your characters?

Do we know more or less than the characters in the scene? Are we having to work out what is going on, to catch up with where the characters are up to? Or do we find things out at the same time as the characters find them out? And, to complicate these questions even further, does one character know as much as the audience knows, and other characters in the scene, less? (These questions could get more and more complex – but I hope you get the point I'm making here!) All of these seemingly minute changes and decisions have the power to radically alter the nature of the scene.

A simple example, to illustrate: a scene from a thriller or crime drama in which our hero is entering a dark, derelict building looking for a shooter or baddy whom she has reason to suspect is hiding inside this building. Do you the writer show the audience that this armed baddy is inside the building, waiting for our hero? Or do we only reveal this shooter to the audience at the same moment as our hero sees them? Or do we show that our hero knows where the shooter is (a set of footprints through the dust...)?

These are three different ways to play this scene, and of course there are very many more – but all are altered by the information we give (or don't give) the audience and the characters going into this scene. There are a multiplicity of choices in the creation of every single scene, all influenced by the context of these moments in your story: the tone, style and narrative conventions.

Consideration about what the characters know about each other and what the audience knows about the characters is key to how your story plays out on screen. For example, there is the notion of the 'unreliable narrator' – is what you're telling the audience about your characters 'the truth, the whole truth and nothing but the truth'? In the best stories, this is very rarely the case.

To illustrate, here's another familiar type of scene:

```
Night. Man A sits in his car down the street from
a house. He sees Man B and Woman C coming out
of the house together. Man B and Woman C kiss
passionately and then get in another car and drive
off. We cut back to Man A, looking at them.
```

There are all sorts of ways of framing and playing this scene that will evoke very different responses in an audience. Because this is a familiar scenario, I imagine our first thought is that Man A in the car and Woman C who leaves the house are a couple; and that this man is spying on the woman's affair with Man B.

Without altering the action of the scene, there are so many different ways to keep changing the nature of this scene.

Even in the seemingly neutral way in which I have framed this scene, you would probably infer that we are experiencing this scene from Man A's point of view (because I'm opening the scene on Man A). But how about if we play it from Woman C's POV? Or how about if the kissing couple are in their seventies and Man A in his twenties? Or if Man A smiles and then laughs when he observes the kissing couple? There are so many choices you as a writer have to make. Avoid the obvious, the predictable, while getting to the truth of your characters and the crux of the drama of the scene. Scenes should almost never feel 'neutral'; they should feel inflected and loaded with meaning.

Often, you should reject the first idea you have about how to play a scene, and explore ten other possibilities before coming to a decision. Everything is about character and context – about what makes sense of the character and their actions – making the scene meaningful, but also surprising.

Familiar expositional devices and tropes

Here are some examples with which we are all familiar, where the way a writer conveys exposition feels too obvious or visible:

* A group of press clamouring around a key character with cameras and microphones, asking questions.

* A background (or foreground) TV news report conveying story information.

* Similarly, an audio news report in the background.

* On-screen captions with reams of hard-to-follow exposition (see the opening to episode one of *His Dark Materials* (2019) for an example of what I mean here).

* A character remembering or thinking about other characters by looking at photos of them (especially photographs on a domestic mantelpiece).

* Police squad-room conferences that open with 'Now listen up!' In fact, police-station multi-character conferences more generally as 'exposition dump' scenes.

* Police officer arrives at taped-off crime scene, PC lifts the tape. Police Officer: 'So what have we got?' Exposition follows.

* Obvious and under-motivated leading questions and expositional feeds such as 'What are you thinking?', 'Just a crazy idea but…', 'Penny for them…?'

* An actual ticking clock to tell us the time.

* Letters read in voice-over as they are written – particularly in period films (desk, quill pen, etc.).

* Characters reading aloud from a screen (phone, laptop, etc.).

* Characters talking to themselves in a way that isn't real but is helpful to the audience's understanding of plot.

* 'Walking and talking' scenes in police station corridors where the junior officer reels off expositionary information for the senior officer.

* TV news conferences in which tearful relatives of the victim or missing person appeal for anyone who knows anything to come forward.

* The interview room scene where a police officer interviews a suspect. (There is a brilliant example of where this trope is subverted in series one of *Criminal Justice* by Peter Moffat: the interrogating police officer's decision to remove the table brings a fresh and surprising perspective to this familiar type of scene. The George Kay Netflix series, *Criminal* (2019) also has many excellent examples of how to bring these often familiar and potentially 'tropey' police interview scenes to life – through depth and detail of character, through brilliant story hooks and twists.)

Note   As above, on page 69–70, I'm not saying there is anything inherently wrong about these familiar storytelling scenes – just that, in being aware that they may feel familiar, you might find ways to make them feel unique and integral to the distinctive way you tell your own story.

Stylised Storytelling Devices

These are all devices specific to screenwriting, often helpful in revealing and dramatising exposition. At the same time, you must be careful that these devices feel like they are integral to the character and tone of your story, and that they don't come across as over-convenient, over-visible expositional devices.

Voice-over

Voice-over and flashback – as screenplay storytelling devices – are sometimes viewed with suspicion and uncertainty by screenwriters (and producers and script editors). There seems to be a perception among less-experienced screenwriters in particular that this sort of device is not to be trusted and to be used as sparingly as possible, and a perception that TV producers and script editors in particular will turn their noses up at the use of voice-over. I don't think this is true – but if there is any negativity towards voice-over and flashback, it's because they are too often seen as synonymous with poor writing.

Voice-over shouldn't be used as an unimaginative expositional prop. As a principle (and like all 'principles', this one is there to be challenged!), there should be a counterpoint between what we are seeing on screen and what is being said in the voice-over. If the voice-over is just describing what we can see for ourselves on screen, it's redundant. If it's giving us another perspective, adding another layer of meaning and intrigue to the scene, it's potentially valuable. If what the character is telling us is in opposition to what we see them doing, then it can work brilliantly.

Voice-over also brings us back to the question of POV and perspective (for more on this, turn to pages 81–5). If, for instance, your story is punctuated throughout by the protagonist's voice-over, one of the key questions you need to address is – from what perspective is this character's voice-over coming? And how is their voice-over perspective different to the perspective the character has in the present moment of the story? One of the most obvious examples of this is the Kevin Spacey character voice-over in Alan Ball's *American Beauty* – in which the voice-over perspective is from beyond the grave. Another memorable use of voice-over is in Nicholas Pileggi's *Goodfellas*, where the story POV is provided by mob newcomer, Henry Hill, played by Ray Liotta. [SPOILER ALERT] As the story develops, we come to learn that this voice-over is provided by Hill from the perspective of his new life and identity in a witness protection scheme; and the story he is telling is in his guise as police informant.

And in Richard Gadd's dark, chilling *Baby Reindeer* (2024), the voice-over feels like an absolutely vital, integral part of the character and tone of the storytelling, as the central character reflects in present-day voice-over on the mistakes he made in the past of the story he's telling. This was a seven-part TV series that made a virtue of its origins as a one-man stage play.

Voice-over is such a familiar element of screenplays generally – but it's really important that the way you use it adds another layer of dramatic impact and intrigue to your storytelling.

Flashback

Similarly, with flashback the thing to avoid is using it as a straightforward expositional tool, as an easy (and uninventive) way for your character to fill in their backstory. As with voice-over, if you're to use flashback, it needs to be surprising and to provide a fresh, unexpected perspective on the story in the present.

The thing to be aware of with flashbacks is that by definition they take the audience out of the immediacy of the moment in the story. As a general principle of dramatic storytelling I would say this is not a good thing, so you need to question the intent and effect of flashbacks, with this in mind. But as with voice-over, there are so many examples of where flashback is an integral, exciting element of a screenplay. One of my favourite recent examples is the flashback from the courtroom to the marital argument that preceded the 'fall' in *Anatomy of a Fall*, written by Arthur Harari and Justine Triet (2023) – arguably the key, standout sequence of the film.

Direct address to camera

As with flashback and voice-over, you must judge your use of a device like direct address to camera by what it adds to your story and how integral it feels to the way you are telling it. Phoebe Waller-Bridge in her TV dramatisation of her stage monologue *Fleabag* uses this device brilliantly, in that it feels so integral to the tone of the show, to her character, and it intensifies her bond with the audience as we share confidences not accessible to her fellow characters. There is something very seductive about feeling narratively privileged in this way as an audience member.

Direct address to camera has been used in countless shows – *This is Going to Hurt* by Adam Kay and *Gentleman Jack* by Sally Wainwright are two other recent and, in my opinion, very successful examples.

If considering using this device, you need to feel strongly that it is a completely justified part of the character and tone of the storytelling. As with flashback and voice-over, direct address to camera risks taking the audience out of the immediacy of their engagement with a scene or story moment. Like those other devices, direct address to camera needs to bring an added layer or dimension, additional intrigue to the story, for it not to feel like an overly self-conscious, unnecessary, expositional device.

Mockumentary

Since Ricky Gervais and Stephen Merchant's seminal *The Office*, 'mockumentary' has become a hugely overused narrative stylistic device in situation comedy. Too often, this comes across as derivative, unimaginative and not integral to the idea. Too often, rather than adding to the richness of the storytelling, the device feels tired and uninspired and takes you out of the world of the characters in a way that feels self-referential and stylistically empty.

As with all these sorts of stylised narrative devices, the device or form needs to enhance and elevate the content – it needs to really add to the texture and effectiveness of the storytelling.

This device can be used in drama even if it is more familiar as a comedic device – see Jeff Nichols' *The Bikeriders* (2024) as an example of a drama feature in which the device is used as a really effective narrative framing device.

Montage

Of all the many stylistic devices used in screenwriting, it seems to me that montage is the most ill-used. It is so common for me to read a screenplay that uses montage only as a straightforward, rather predictable way to condense and rush us through the less-interesting and tricky-to-dramatise passages within the time frame of a story.

There are of course exceptions – for instance, that wonderful sequence at the start of the Pixar movie *Up*, written by Pete Docter, Bob Peterson and Tom McCarthy.

As with every familiar screenwriting narrative device, your use of montage needs to be surprising, fresh and, above all, narratively justified. Too often montage feels like the least difficult way to convey a lot of story information economically rather than as a real storytelling virtue in its own right. Uninteresting use of montage sequences begs huge storytelling questions about the way your story is told and structured.

Your montage sequence should be the best way to tell this particular part of the story, not just a way to rush us through a slightly dull or problematic part of it.

But again, I don't want to be completely negative about the use of montage in story because, like all narrative tropes, it has become a trope because it is so often a real narrative asset and can work well as a way of advancing the story with a skilfully light touch. It can be a brilliant way to distil a lot of story into a short, visually driven narrative sequence.

It's up to all of us to study how montage has been used as a narrative technique in the years and years of screen stories – to learn how it works at its best and its worst, and use it in unexpected, imaginative ways that add intrigue and richness to your story.

As a writer, you also need to be utterly specific in the images you use within any montage. You need to select the images and actions that are going to convey the story – not delegate these decisions to the director by writing a montage in vague, general terms.

You need to view a montage as a mini-movie in its own right – a section that elevates the film as a whole, that brings a distinctive and surprising new perspective, maybe throws a whole new light on a particular character or relationship; or tells part of the story in a different and very particular way.

Captions

Captions, used at their best, can really enhance screen storytelling. We've all experienced the thrill and satisfaction, in particular, of reading those captions at the end of movies based on true stories that tell us more about how the story panned out after the story of the film has ended. It's even the case sometimes that this is the most enjoyable part of the film. (Not a good sign for the film as a whole!)

But as a general principle I would advise you to seek alternative, more cinematic ways of conveying information than using on-screen captions. And if you are going to use captions, make them feel like an integral part of the way you tell the story; make sure you are confident that they bring something extra to your film.

Ultimately my feeling about captions is that they are sometimes used when the writer can't think of a way to convey necessary information more elegantly and cinematically. Too often they are used unimaginatively and as a last-resort, expositional device.

Treatment of Time

How you treat the passage of time in your screenplay is an important storytelling consideration. What is the relationship between past and present in your story? After all, that is one of the guiding aspects of the way we live our lives. Are we the same person at sixty-one that we were at seventeen? Both physically and temperamentally we are entirely different people; and anyone who has stayed exactly the same is an anomaly, and socially dysfunctional. Cutting between different time frames is a highly effective way to energise storytelling, to pose intriguing story questions.

Do you tell your story in a linear, chronological way? Or disrupt the chronology? In most cases, I would argue that moving forward from scene to scene, in such a way that the connections create an escalating narrative intensity, is done best by telling your story chronologically. This should be your default. Question whether you are striving for impact through seemingly artificial, unnecessary and sometimes confusing disruptions of the story's chronology.

Having said this, playing with story order, with time sequence, can sometimes transform a predictable story into something that is more fascinating – but be clear that if you are messing with the story's chronology, it is enhancing the power of your story.

You need to think about:

* How much time, if any, has passed between each scene – whether action is continuous or not.

* What has happened in any time elapsed between scenes.

* Whether two different, intercut story strands are happening simultaneously or not.

More broadly, you need to consider how you are going to dramatise effectively events that take place over a long period of time. For instance, I worked on an ITV two-hour film, *Anybody's Nightmare* (2001, written by John Flanagan and Andrew McCulloch), a factual drama in which the central character spent four years in prison. We wanted to cover this part of the story relatively speedily – but how do you compress four years of life into twenty minutes of on-screen drama? One of the answers is the narrative device of montage (see pages 105–6). The other device in this instance was the use of repetition. Showing repeated events – in this case subtle variations of Christmas non-celebrations – evoked both the tedium of prison life and the passage of time.

How do you convey the story moving from one day to the next in ways that feel sure-footed, clear but interesting or surprising?

There are certain stories (although not many) that will be enhanced by telling them in reverse – starting at the end and going backwards to the start.

One such example that comes to mind, was a proposed (as yet unproduced) feature-film adaptation of a stage play that, because of the necessarily enclosed, interior and small-scale nature of the story, seemed to too obviously betray its stage-play origins while also feeling in screenplay form a little too linear and predictable in the way the story played out. The story in question was about a woman in her fifties who admits herself into a care home, against her family's wishes, when diagnosed with early-onset dementia. The suggestion that we reverse this story, change it so that we told it backwards, seemed to me to give the story a power and poignancy – we start with the character with chronic dementia, and gradually work our way back to who she was, her 'true self', before she was struck by this terrible illness.

Other dramatic stories that work brilliantly because they are told in reverse include Harold Pinter's play *Betrayal*, and *Memento* (2000), written by Christopher and Jonathan Nolan.

Condensing time

As a general principle (there are exceptions!), I think the more you condense time, the more focused and intense your story will feel. Don't insert unmotivated three-week gaps between scenes that introduce unwanted questions and detract from the intensity and focus of your story.

> The series *24*, in which each episode took place over an actual hour of the characters' lives – a story told in 'real time' – was a stronger series premise than BBC show *Five Days* (Gwyneth Hughes, 2007), in which a criminal investigation took place over five non-consecutive days.

The ticking clock

This is such an important and fundamental factor in creating narrative tension. Life is a ticking clock – and so should drama be.

Pressure of time is one of the story elements that escalates intensity. It's something we all have to deal with. As we get older, as time starts to run out, how does this affect our decisions and our actions? This is the macro but there is also the micro – the two hours of an exam, the twenty years of a prison sentence, the meeting for which you're late, etc.

Think about what it is that can bring urgency to your story. What time pressures are your characters under? Is your protagonist's ballgown going to turn back into rags when the clock strikes midnight?!

You should try to load each scene with dynamic intensity – fired by a thwarted desire, complicated by urgency, a lack of time or other situational stress.

Look for elements that introduce urgency into your story.

Structure

> We shall not cease from exploration
> And the end of all our exploring
> Will be to arrive where we started
> And know the place for the first time.
>
> T. S. Eliot, 'Little Gidding' in *Four Quartets*

Introduction: what is 'structure' and how can it be useful to us?

A conversation I had with a writer a few years ago…

```
                    ME
       So what are you interested in writing
       about? What stories do you have in mind?
```

> **WRITER**
> I'd like to tell a story backwards.
>
> **ME**
> Interesting. What's the story?
>
> **WRITER**
> Oh, I don't know that yet, I just want to tell a story backwards.

While I was initially intrigued, I was rather dismayed that the writer in question was putting this structural consideration at the front of their planning, rather than marrying content with form. You need to know what story you want to tell before thinking about the best way to tell it.

★ ★ ★

A quick internet trawl will tell you that dramatic stories for the screen are structured thus:

* Forty beats in a feature film.
* John Truby's twenty-two steps.
* The fifteen steps of *Save the Cat*.
* The nine-act structure of feature films.
* The eight-sequence structure model.
* Seven basic plots.
* The six main arcs in storytelling.
* Five acts.
* Four acts in a UK commercial TV-hour episode.
* The traditional three-act story.
* Two acts in a UK commercial half-hour episode.

★ ★ ★

How easy it is to disappear down the rabbit-hole of 'structure'. All of the structural theories above can be helpful, but none are compulsory. And none should be the starting point for the creation of your story for the screen.

It's important to recognise that 'structure' is not your story material, your content. Structure is what you do with your story material, how you order and organise it. It is about looking at the story material you have and thinking about how to order it so that the story you tell is the most dramatic, exciting version of itself. Sometimes that means a straightforwardly linear, chronological approach, but sometimes it means you play with the time sequence in radical and unexpected ways.

There is a lot of noise around the idea of story structure — in particular, many attempts to reduce story structure to formula, to the idea that every story can be distilled down to the same essential shape. Whether this is true or not, I'm not sure it's a very helpful idea for writers trying to create stories. The last thing you need to be doing at an early stage of story development is trying to fit your story into a preordained shape or structure.

A writer's voice is not defined by the structures of the stories they tell. Their voice is defined by what they write about and the attitude, agenda and style they bring to the stories they tell. It's about what you have to say, about your unique perspective on the world.

In other words, structure, while undeniably important in helping you maximise the dramatic impact of your story, should not be the primary consideration in your writing.

Writing this now almost feels like screenwriting sacrilege, it's so counter to the impression you will get from some of the more reductive theorising about how you create stories for the screen.

There are no short cuts. Each story, each project, presents its own unique challenges. It's never easy. You have to approach each story issue on its own merits.

Structural considerations can be incredibly helpful when trying to maximise the dramatic effectiveness of the story you have created. Structural landmarks are sometimes a useful point of reference when stories stubbornly fail to come alive – but I think the attempt to use a set formula within which your story must exist makes for predictable, shallow, superficial storytelling. It's putting the cart before the horse.

Your stories should be attempting to dramatise your truths in your own way – not conforming to hours and years of conventional series television or genre feature films.

Television and film drama must be entertaining – but it is most entertaining when it aims to be fresh, distinctive, challenging, provocative, playful and creative – both in its content and in its form and structure. Rigid, imposed structures are an attempt to standardise content, to take the risk out of creation. But screenwriting is not a set, finite or measurable form. It is ultimately subjective and, at its best, organic. And while structural considerations are an element of how you tell every story, pre-imposed structural requirements are anathema to the creativity of bringing a story alive.

Supposed structural weaknesses often have a deeper, less geometrical cause – the lack of a true dramatic dilemma; characters who lack a sense of purpose or inner conflict; a story world that feels flat, colourless, inauthentic, derivative, under-researched.

Structural narrative effectiveness is about making connections, paying off set-ups, about the story coming full circle. You must focus on every moment in your story having meaning – even if this meaning is not immediately obvious to the audience in the moment of that scene. The best storytelling is economical, purposeful, streamlined and circular.

If you become a slave to a whole series of plot points and structural diktats, your story will feel more mechanical than spontaneous.

The most complicated theories of structure I think we should be wrestling with are those traditional story considerations of the three-act structure – beginning, middle and end; thesis, antithesis, synthesis; set-up, conflict, resolution.

Other, more complicated ideas – whether it's five acts or seven acts, twenty-one beats, the midpoint, etc., too often seem to me like artificial constructs imposed onto stories retrospectively to explain them, rather than integral elements of that story's creation.

Confronted with so many different theories and necessary points to hit and acknowledge in your story, these theories feel to me like they are more creatively crippling than inspiring.

Some of these structural ideas can be helpful at a later stage of development, when analysing your story and trying to maximise its dramatic impact or work out why it doesn't have the dramatic intensity that you'd hoped for.

But I would advise you not to get too hung up over structural strictures too early in the process of story development. You need to allow for your story to be able to surprise you, for your characters to take you in directions you hadn't anticipated. Imposing rigid structural rules on your story can sometimes lead to a script that is plot-driven rather than character-driven (for more on this, see page 93).

My suspicion of structural 'rules' and formulae is strengthened by my own experience as a script editor and producer. I have been working with writers for decades, and one conversation I never seem to have with writers is about structural formulae – e.g. where one act ends and another begins, where the 'midpoint' of your story is, how many acts your story breaks into... These all feel to me like over-analytical, theoretical attempts to simplify the process of creating story, that have no real application to the reality of how it works with writers in the industry, in the real conversations between producers, script editors and writers.

Similarly, the overuse of technical screenwriting jargon is often viewed with suspicion – the language of the amateur rather than professional writer.

Discussion between producer and writer is about how this particular story is going to work, what will keep it driving forward and make it dynamic and surprising – scene by scene, episode by episode.

The exception to this in my experience is working on a TV drama series that is necessarily split into four parts because of the commercial breaks. So on an ITV drama (with three advert breaks), for instance, we'd talk (as a very loose framework and only one of many different ways to break the story down) about:

* Act one making a big splash, grabbing the audience's attention, establishing the dramatic proposition of the episode and series (if this is the pilot episode).

* Act two being able to afford to take its time and establish a deeper connection between the audience and the central characters as they respond to the action from act one (usually containing more private or personal scenes than the first act).

* Act three being the key story section of the episode, the section in which the story action comes to a head.

* Act four resolving this story of the week whilst also setting up a compelling hook for the next episode.

This is absolutely not to say that structural considerations are not of the utmost importance. So, for instance, often in a BBC one-hour drama episode (at fifty-nine minutes, significantly longer than a 'commercial' TV hour of forty-six-or-so minutes), it's the middle section, the second of the traditional three acts, that is often the trickiest – the section in which the story tension may dip, where the story often needs most attention.

And those preordained structures may be useful for script editors working in the mass production of five-episodes-a-week soaps, or continuing drama, where it's essential to have some sort of broad technical consensus about how stories are created and developed through the drafts. But in general, these structural markers should be useful background guides rather than the considerations that are driving the creation of your story.

We have all watched and read so many stories. Our lives, whether we choose it or not, are dominated by the experiencing of stories in so many different forms. We all have grown up with and developed an instinct for how stories work, how they are 'structured'. Don't try to over-analyse story, to break it into artificial, preordained shapes.

As you create a story, the characters and the choices they make need to surprise you. If you haven't at some point surprised yourself with the unexpected direction in which your characters or story take you, then you won't be surprising the audience – and it's vital that you do.

Ultimately, 'structure' is about scenes and sequences and how you put them together. It's about ordering and organising your story into a shape that maximises its dramatic impact. On a simple level, it's about deciding what to include and what to leave out, and in what order you tell your story.

The units of storytelling for the screen

SHOTS

As you write, you can visualise your story in shots, but it's a convention of screenwriting that you don't *write* a screenplay as a series of specific shots – this is very much considered treading on the toes of the director. The way you describe action can imply how you might shoot a particular moment – but avoid specifically describing shots (even though as we watch film or TV, any content is just a succession of different shots).

BEATS

This is an often-used term for a moment within a scene. Each scene could be described as a succession of story 'beats'. It's hard to define how long a 'beat' is: it's one of those frustrating non-technical screenwriting terms that means different things to different people. I would describe a beat as a unit of drama within a scene (a dramatic movement, an exchange of dialogue); a smaller unit within a scene that advances or changes your story in some way.

SCENES

We're on firmer ground with 'scenes'. Scenes are the storytelling units of screenplays on which writers should focus. Each scene can be considered as a mini-story in its own right, a unit that moves your story forward in a significant way.

A scene is a unit of storytelling action that takes place within a particular location and in a contained time frame. There are infinite possibilities in the nature of scenes. Scenes and the cutting between them is the lifeblood of storytelling for the screen. (See page 72 for more on the nature of scenes; and page 75 for more on cutting between them.)

ACTS

We're back to a less firm footing with 'acts'. Where one act ends and the next begins is so open to different interpretations that it feels more problematic than valuable. If you feel that your story naturally breaks down into three acts, that can help you to see your way through your story – but it's important to be aware that the act structure should absolutely not be visible to your audience (or your reader). No audience member anywhere (at least if they are engaged with your story!) will say to themselves, 'Oh great, that was the end of act one, now we must be at the start of act two.'

SEQUENCES

The idea of sequences can be very helpful. Within your story, there will often be a particular run of scenes that makes up a sequence (the various scenes in a car chase, for instance). And it may be useful to identify sequences so that you can then intercut two separate sequences together. To continue the car chase example, how about intercutting a parent and child walking on a pavement, preparing to cross a road – several scenes – with a car chase – several scenes. The intercutting might imply the question: are these pedestrians going to be hit by the chasing cars?

The beginning and end of your story

Where do you start your story? Most TV drama pilot episodes will consist of several story strands, which in the best episodes will connect and impact on each other in surprising and powerful ways.

The best writers will not start every one of their stories at the 'beginning'. Rather, as an audience, you will be placed unceremoniously into the middle of story strands and have to work to get up to speed with that story. Gradually the skilful writer will drip-feed to the audience glimpses of the backstory — what has happened in the characters' pasts to create the status quo as we discover it on screen. (For more on this, see page 61.)

When you look at a brilliant example like *Happy Valley* series one, it's almost as if Sally Wainwright has started halfway through and left out the entire first half of her story. The backstory that gradually leaks out through the series could make up a series of its own, there is so much drama and heartbreak in this story before the on-screen story. (For more on this, see page 157.)

Just as you don't want to start every script with characters waking in the morning and going through their morning rituals (see page 69), so you don't want to start each story strand at its beginning with the first meeting between characters. The audience want to work harder than that — to be thrown into the middle of situations and relationships and to have to do their own imaginative work to figure out how things got to this point.

Similarly, the way you end your story strands needs to feel relatively jagged and unpredictable. If you have five story strands, you don't want five resolved, happy endings — this will feel predictable and repetitive. These are important structural considerations.

Aspects of structure

There are so many different aspects of 'structure' to consider in your story. Here are a few prompts to get you thinking about different aspects of narrative structure:

TIME STRUCTURES

* A story over a life, a year, a day, an hour, a century, a story that exists within a minute (that is repeated from different perspectives?).
* Stories told in real time, told backwards, etc.
* A two-hour story that happens in real time (a one-take movie?).
* A story of one particular sport team's season (*Friday Night Lights*), school or university term, etc.

The rhythms and temporal structures of life should be reflected and used creatively in the way you tell a story. We live life within clearly defined temporal structural parameters (at its simplest, the twenty-four-hour day: awake in the day, asleep at night).

Think about the time structures of our lives and how these can be used to shape your dramatic, fictional stories. The time span of your story can be one of its key, defining characteristics. Think about how life and the processes of living are broken down and defined: exams, the working day, a prison sentence, the hours of a complicated medical procedure, the duration of a job, an education, even a whole life, etc.

FORM STRUCTURES

* Monologues, duologues.
* Single protagonist, multi-protagonist.
* Journeys.
* Films or episodes without dialogue…

Consider the rhythmic structures of storytelling, the number of scenes: a two-hour film of one scene, or two hundred scenes – two completely different structural approaches to storytelling.

SOCIETAL STRUCTURES

* Communities.
* Organisations.
* Businesses.
* Teams.
* Gangs.
* Families.
* Relationships.
* Rivalries.

Think about the dynamics and hierarchies, the character tensions, within any of these societal structures.

PHYSICAL STRUCTURES

Story worlds:

* Planets.
* Buildings.
* Jungles.
* Cities.
* Villages.
* Caves.
* Spaceships.

Physical structures within which to tell a story:

* A house; individual rooms within that house.

* A public building – office, school, hospital, prison, hotel, pub; and the rooms within those buildings.
* Private buildings or spaces – homes in multifarious forms.
* Private spaces within public spaces (for instance, an intimate exchange on a park bench or in a hotel room).

Creative approaches to story structure

Try to think outside the box. Rather than the broadly accepted theories of screenwriting story structure, think about the variety of narrative structures that you encounter in your own life and how these can act as creative inspiration for the stories you want to tell. Compare your dramatic story and its shape to other structural forms; think of alternative narrative shapes that may help your story. For instance:

FOOTBALL MATCHES

All football games have the same basic structure – two halves of forty-five minutes each, fifteen minutes' pause for half-time, and added time at the end of each half. And yet, within this rigid structure, the narrative variety of football games is infinitely unpredictable.

The idea that the exact same shape can contain so many different narrative shapes, twists and turns is extraordinary.

The narrative template of a football match has this juxtaposition of a rigid, predictable, repeatable structure, and a completely unpredictable and unique sequence of events within that template (the same should be true of the best TV series formats).

But not only does football have this clear, limiting, rigid parameter of timings, it also has a whole set of other rules from which the game cannot stray (overseen by the referee and their assistants); and on top of that, the complex, dynamic relationship between participants and audience; the influence of other external factors such as weather; the difference between 'home' and 'away' matches; the societal impact of the relative geography, wealth and resources of each club or team; and so on. So many different factors that can influence and affect the 'story' of each match.

And each and every sport has its own particular narrative structures, parameters and quirks of organisation. So many of these can act as creative parallels and inspirations for how you structure your screen stories.

OTHER MEDIA

Think about how particular songs are structured (verse – chorus – bridge). Or poems. I think, in their use of language, rhythm and rhyme, these are particularly interesting structural creative units – with many lessons and inspirations for longer-form screen story.

Also look at novels, newspaper articles, and documentaries for particular, potentially transferable structural ideas. For instance, the BBC TV documentary series, *A Life in Ten Pictures* was a brilliant example of using a very particular structure and form – as expressed by the title! – to tell compelling biographical stories.

Structure ≠ story

Story and structure are not the same thing. You need to first create your story before you can decide how best to structure it. But structural considerations are always incredibly important to the success and effectiveness of your story.

> The documentary feature *Searching for Sugar Man* (2012, directed by Malik Bendjelloul) is a great example of story structure at its most effective. The film-makers ordered their material in such a way as to get maximum dramatic and emotional impact – and surprise – from their story.

> I don't wish to spoil the film for you if you haven't seen it, but there is a moment of revelation quite late in the film that is incredibly powerful. It has stayed with me in the years since I first saw the film. It has been artificially withheld from the audience until the optimum moment of reveal. If the story had been told in a linear, chronological way, it wouldn't have been half the film it was. I hesitate at my own use of the word 'artificially' – it is artificial because it is not chronological. But then all storytelling is, in this way, 'artificial'.

It's about how you order and organise your material as well as about the story material itself. Having a great idea for a film or TV show is both about the idea itself and also about how you realise it – how you turn a dramatically or comically promising idea into a fully fledged film or TV show.

Exercises on Structure

Take a story from another medium – a newspaper article, the lyrics of a familiar song, a poem, a short story, an advert – and analyse its structure. How does the structure, the way the sentences are ordered and organised, enhance the content?

Experiment with the structure of the way this story is told and:

1. See if you can play with this structure and find ways to reorder and enhance it.

2. Take this structural approach and experiment with imposing it onto your screen story.

Take these lessons and think about how you can use them in your screenwriting.

Structure: Conclusions

Structure is meaningless without a heart and soul to your story, without invention and imagination, without complicated characters who we can care about. Structure is nothing without primal emotion – fear, love, horror, jeopardy, etc. – and without ideas and events that engage and fascinate an audience.

It's never as simple as saying, 'These are my structural "tent poles": story catalyst in act one, break into act two, midpoint, act two climax, break into act three, final confrontation or story climax, followed by coda.' All of these staging points can be helpful – but they aren't where you should start from.

Note This question of structural 'tent poles' is importantly different to the idea of narrative 'tent poles'. Narrative or story tent poles are key moments in your story – big story set-pieces or turning points. The sort of moments, events and incidents that probably first attracted you to this story. Working out how you move through your story from one tent-pole moment to the next is a vitally important consideration in the creation and construction of your story.

So rather than asking 'Where is my end-of-act-one hook?', 'How does this story break into five parts?' or 'What is the midpoint of this story?', ask 'Who is this person?', 'What do they want?', 'What is the world in which they live?', 'What are the values that define their lives?' These are the interesting, rich, human questions.

At root, good storytelling is about instinct – it's intuitive rather than rational, it's about feelings, emotions and momentum.

The best writing happens when the characters and their world come alive in a writer's hands, when the characters feel so real that they are dictating to the writer what they do, how they will respond in any particular situation.

It's possible to spend all your time worrying about structure – and missing the point of what dramatic stories are all about. Stories at their best are unconventional, surprising, slippery and hard to define. Trying to impose the same, rigid structural shape onto all the stories you want to tell feels artificial and restrictive.

Sometimes the best writing happens when it slips out of the writer's control, when it takes on a life of its own – but this usually only happens when you have prepared the ground for it, when you know the dramatic imperatives of your story: the nature of the relationships between the characters; between them and the world and genre in which they operate; when you have a solid background of research.

Some of the best writing is elusive – it asks a lot of its audience, with no easy lessons, no clear narrative answers, just a succession of strange, fractured, incomplete scenes that loosely combine into a filmic whole that is somehow more coherent than the sum of its parts (e.g. Ruben Östlund's 2017 *The Square*). Far sooner this than a film that tells a story competently, straightforwardly and professionally, but predictably and unimaginatively. This is the difference between the luminous documentary *The Rescue* (see pages 30–2) and less powerful film *Thirteen Lives*.

'Structure' is nothing without compelling raw material.

Write a Drama Series Pilot Episode

If you're looking to get work as a writer in television drama, a series pilot script is what you will almost certainly write (whether that's a one-hour or half-hour script).

One of the big questions with any pilot episode, whether you're writing it as a 'sample' or as something that is going into production, is: how much do you 'front-load' this opening episode in order to illustrate what the series will be about at its very best?

★ Above all, the pilot episode has to demonstrate how the overall format of the series will work. In other words, I would advise against writing a standalone episode that introduces and sets up the series – but is significantly different in its form and construction to subsequent episodes. This opening episode needs to demonstrate the virtues and specifics of how the series as a whole will work.

* The pilot episode needs to set up the dramatic proposition and the overall story premise as quickly as possible. It needs to introduce us to the lead characters and establish their agendas and what is at stake for them, both in this opening episode and in the series as a whole.

* It needs to tell a completed serial story within this episode while also delivering a strong hook to bring the audience back for the next episode.

* It needs to introduce and dramatise a distinctive, persuasive and engaging story world or precinct.

* You need to hit the ground running, get straight into the story. The temptation is that you use this episode as the setting-up episode, introducing the audience to the story world and characters – before an end-of-episode hook that will lead to the real story kicking off in episode two. But I think this should very much be the exception rather than the rule. Audiences are both smart and impatient. They don't want everything explained and set up, they want to be thrown straight into the dramatic action, even if they have to work hard to figure out initially exactly what is going on. The audience would far rather be struggling a little to keep up. After all, this approach generates exactly what you as a storyteller want: that the audience is asking questions of your story, that they're emotionally engaged in the process of getting their head round your story, rather than being ahead of you, sitting there thinking, 'Yes, yes, we know this, you don't need to be spelling this out, just get on with the story!'

IV
Character

'*The subconscious is always talking shit.*' – film-making duo the Safdie brothers, @Josh_Benny on Twitter/X

'*Characters resist their condition.*' – producer and script editor Hilary Norrish

Introduction

Story and character are indivisible – what characters *do* constitutes your story. The emotional arc of your character *is* your story. There is no more important element in story than character.

We have all watched those shows in which, however smart, dramatic and surprising the plot is, we just don't care in the way we'd like to. Whatever happens in your story, it's the characters, the people, with whom we engage. And to engage with and care about them we need to recognise something in them.

We want to have the experience of inhabiting your story through your characters, of experiencing the story vicariously through these characters. We need to be able to empathise with and understand the characters – whether we like or approve of them or not.

Invest time and care in the creation and development of your characters. Rich, textured characterisation is at the heart of successful storytelling in any narrative medium – and this is especially true in screenwriting.

Elements of Characterisation

Empathy

Empathy for characters is all-important. We don't need to agree with or even like characters, but we do need to be able to empathise with them in some way. So give your villains the best lines – enable the audience to see or empathise with an antagonistic point of view. Don't make it easy for your audience. There should be no easy answers in your story. Every character, even those who are objectively unlikeable, should feel to some degree empathetic and fascinating. It's important that all your characters have at least a hint of humanity.

> For much of the three series of *Happy Valley*, antagonist Tommy Lee Royce is something of a monster – but at critical points in the story he is partially redeemed and made interesting through his momentary flashes of humanity. The way Sally Wainwright makes him difficult to completely dismiss as a character makes the story so much more involving and interestingly complicated.

The challenge is to make your characters imperfect but ultimately redeemable. There are of course the truly monstrous, psychopathic exceptions to this principle – the character of Ben in Sarah Phelps' excellent *The Sixth Commandment*, for example (but even he could at least mimic a sense of relatable humanity).

Character choices

A character is defined by the choices they make. Your story should present the lead character with a series of situations that force them to take decisions and make choices.

A real, flawed character will often make bad choices – this is part of the fun of the journey you take your character on.

Generating empathy in the audience is about you, the writer, identifying with impossible choices and questions – 'What would I do if I were that person in that situation?' (Importantly, not as yourself, but as this character.) Sometimes storytelling is no more complicated than that – placing yourself in your character's situation and getting inside their head to imagine and weigh up the choices, the decisions they would make.

This is a minimum requirement when approaching the creation of story. If your audience is doing this and can see a clear solution to a problem that the character hasn't seen, it will immediately cause that viewer to emotionally disengage from your story. Your characters will almost certainly not have exactly the same sense of logic and reason as you – but they need a specific sense of character logic, of their own individual values, to navigate their way through the world of the story in which they find themselves.

These choices, decisions and character actions are at the heart of character-driven stories. One film implies this idea in its title – *Sophie's Choice* (1982, written by Alan J. Pakula). I don't want to spoil the film for you, but the central character has to live with the consequences of the impossible choice she has been given.

What is the ethical difference between bad characters who do good things and good characters who do bad things? It's this sort of dilemma and ambivalence that is at the heart of compelling and relatable characterisation.

Characters need to be the determining element of the plot, they need to instigate and drive the plot. Give your characters a crisis, a dilemma. It's how we react in extreme, tough situations that really reveals who we are as people.

The harder the choices you give your characters, the more gripping your story will be.

The character journey

Once you have established the world and circumstances of your story, you need to create a character at the heart of the story who has a journey that they need to undertake. It can be a physical journey, but it absolutely needs to be an emotional character journey.

Character in story is about how they change – or about how they change the world they inhabit. Your story needs to keep moving forward – and your character's journey, their narrative, needs to keep changing and moving from scene to scene.

Connected to this, no one is settled in their personality. We are all works-in-progress – as we grow up, as our circumstances change. As the world around us changes, we change. Our views change. Our relationships change. Our work changes. Things we hold dear and do at eighteen would shame us at fifty-eight. And vice versa – if our eighteen-year-old selves knew how they're going to end up forty years later, they would probably be dismayed! We are all undergoing change, at different rates and in different ways. The fact is that we change because we *need* to change. This change in personality and attitude is at the heart of story. Story must be dynamic. Each scene is a unit of change. And each story is about how a person changes. These are all potential aspects of the 'character journey'.

What is particularly interesting about this for story is that it's a truth we rarely acknowledge. The idea that we are constantly changing is a scary, unsettling one. But this generates a brilliant narrative tension – between the fact and way we change, and our opposing desire to slow or deny this change within ourselves. It's this inner conflict, our self-denial about the truths of our experiences, that is at the heart of so much effective storytelling.

Distinctive characters

Everyone is eccentric to some degree – we all have our own individual quirks, obsessions, secrets, activities, beliefs. Think of every house or flat you've ever lived in and all the people who lived around you. I don't know about you, but virtually every single one of my neighbours have been strange to some degree – and I imagine they have found me equally strange. And if someone you know has no eccentricity whatsoever, well that's equally strange and noteworthy – what are they hiding? What is going on underneath the seemingly placid, neutral surface?

In other words, characters need to be distinctive. Quirks, eccentricity, particularities are all part of the rich tapestry of characterisation. Whether that's external, observable quirks – what they wear, how they walk, tics and foibles – or internalised, less observable or secret quirks, obsessive habits carried out only in private.

> In *Little Miss Sunshine*, the character of Dwayne is defined by his vow of silence, his refusal to speak. This decision/quirk adds so much richness, humour and humanity to every scene he's in. And pays off brilliantly when he finally speaks.

Internal conflict and contradiction

Dramatic characters need to be conflicted, flawed, damaged. Internal tensions are at the heart of successful characterisation. So often your story will be of the characters undergoing that journey from conflicted to resolved.

Furthermore, damaged, flawed characters are the ones we all relate to – we are all imperfect, flawed, damaged, lacking self-awareness – so this is what we recognise and identify with in fictional characters.

These flaws and contradictions can be external and observable (the wealthy person who dresses like a pauper), or internal (the pilot who has developed a secret fear of flying).

Successful dramatic characterisations should manifest a contradiction – a gap between what the characters say and how they act, on the one hand, and who they truly are, or could be, or aspire to be, on the other hand.

> In the BBC series *Normal People*, adapted by Sally Rooney from her own novel, lead character Marianne has come from a dysfunctional family background and feels that she is unlovable. We can see that this is a self-protection response, that her real fear is making a commitment – and being hurt again. So she continues to punish herself and resist the reality of her genuine feelings for Connell. The external events of her story articulate and dramatise this deep-seated inner flaw. Marianne's internal journey is to learn to love herself.
>
> This is the basis of so many character stories – for example, the excellent Amazon Studios film, *Brittany Runs a Marathon* (2019), written and directed by Paul Downs Colaizzo. As the title tells us, central character Brittany's external 'want' is to get fit and complete a marathon. But her internal 'need' is to defeat her negative feelings about herself, to rebuild her self-esteem – so that she can form a meaningful romantic relationship.

It can be helpful sometimes to approach the creation of character in quite a mechanical way – in thinking about the contrast, the gap, between the reality of a person's nature and how they appear.

So, for instance:

* The person who is outwardly happy – the extrovert life and soul of the party – but inwardly sad.
* The person who is outwardly calm but is in fact seething with internalised, unexpressed rage.
* The person who is outwardly kind but is in fact a nasty piece of work (see the antagonist character Ben in *The Sixth Commandment*).

If you write a character who is, for example, vile and unlikeable from the first moment we meet them and continues to be exactly that over the course of the whole story, this doesn't make for interesting, progressive storytelling; and (arguably) neither does it ring true.

We will recognise all of the above contrasts, combinations, contradictions, and gradations of character – they feel real, relatable and fascinating – whereas the characterisation of a person who is both outwardly and inwardly angry feels colourless and flat.

Character should be something of a mystery, a puzzle for the audience to unravel. After all, isn't that true with nearly everyone we know? Everyone has their strengths and weaknesses, their surprising traits, areas in which they are transparent, other areas in which they are unknowable, areas that are not open for discussion. No one is exactly as they appear to be – are they?

The 'worst' person I have ever met, a person who behaved consistently hatefully, destructively and dishonestly, was superficially plausible, friendly and likeable. I liked him and warmed to him until I found out what he had done. And when finally challenged with the truth of his actions – his true nature – his hatefulness finally emerged. I think this sort of person or character is far more common and recognisable than the phenomenon of the person who is both instantly, superficially awful, and *also* awful and horrible beneath the surface impression (although people who are superficially hostile and unlikeable can also be richly interesting bases for fictional characters!).

Just as the story of a scene that has no subtext, that only exists for one purpose, is dull and flat (see pages 65–6), so a character whose appearance and reality are one and the same – who does what they say they're going to do, who is totally transparent – is not just uninteresting, they're not real and therefore not believable.

Characterisation is about struggle – the outer struggle to achieve, but more crucially, the inner struggle to come to terms with who they are.

As with so many of these principles, there are often exceptions. Sometimes the exception to this principle of counterpoint works – a character clearly and unequivocally stating their intent in a scene. For instance, a character articulating their innermost fears, hang-ups and contradictions can sometimes be ultimately satisfying. If their ability to articulate their condition feels like the resolution of their personal story, this can work. It's about striking that tricky balance between flat exposition and narrative clarity.

The guiding idea should be that our true identity is masked from ourselves. We all think we know ourselves better than anyone else can. So often we are wrong. In this gap, drama thrives. (See pages 147–9.)

We are also all trying to present as someone better than or different to who we really are. Vanity in characters can be a big motivating force! (For more on this subject, see pages 140–6.)

Subtext

This question of internal character contradictions connects to the issue of subtext in story. The counterpoint of text and subtext is fundamental to good storytelling. So – your story default should be that what characters say and what they do is at odds with each other. There should be a tension between what characters are saying to each other and what is really going on in a scene – that gap between what characters say and what they really think or feel; and also, the gap between what they say they're going to do or have done, and what they actually do.

Subtext, secrets and lies are the staple of intriguing characterisation, and are expressive of flawed, conflicted – and relatable – characters.

Character 'intelligence'

There is something engaging and intriguing about characters who exhibit intelligence, and something uninteresting about characters who act stupidly. 'Stupid' behaviour too often feels more like a writer's failure of imagination than genuine, relatable stupidity! It's a failure to really dig into that key question, 'What would I do if I were this character in this situation?' There is a subtle distinction between characters making bad choices based on their flaws and weaknesses, and characters who make stupid decisions for expedient reasons of plot. I enjoy reading and watching characters who are brilliant, smart, incredibly able. If characters do stupid things or act stupidly it saps our interest in them.

Audiences enjoy characters who are impressive, who are ingenious and surprising, who find unexpected, imaginative ways to confront problems, whether they are your protagonist or antagonist. (Although this isn't to say they should get everything right – this will severely limit the possibilities of your story.)

What sort of 'intelligence' does your character have? And what sort do they lack? For instance, there is the archetype of the brilliant academic who has limited practical or emotional intelligence (like so many clichés, this taps into something that has a ring of truth, that we recognise). Or the street-smart character from the 'university of life', who more than makes up for their lack of formal education.

Think about all the different sorts of intelligence – emotional, social, business, academic, mathematical, literary... Which of these does your character possess and which do they lack? And how does that inform and define them as characters?

Think about what your characters excel in, whether that's sports, education, romance, career, popularity... Where there is excellence and high achievement, there is more room for the hidden weaknesses and secrets that will contrast with this external success, e.g. characters who are immensely popular and well-liked (emotionally intelligent) but unsuccessful in their finances and careers (lacking organisational, practical intelligence). It's these sorts of contrasts and contradictions that feel real and bring characters alive.

It's important to make a distinction between smart, talented, impressive characters and 'perfect' characters. 'Perfect' people don't exist. They are a two-dimensional fantasy rather than a three-dimensional reality. If people are wonderful (even close to perfect) they are wonderful in very distinct ways and for very distinct reasons. Often, for instance, people who are motivated to do good deeds are driven by tragedies or injustices in their pasts – by a lack in other parts of their lives.

Heightened but identifiable

Dramatic characters in film and TV, particularly your lead characters, need to be heightened in some way; to be subtly exaggerated versions of reality. Here are some examples:

* Anne Lister in Sally Wainwright's *Gentleman Jack*.

* Randle McMurphy in *One Flew Over the Cuckoo's Nest* (1975, screenplay by Lawrence Haubman and Bo Goldman).

* Howard Ratner (played by Adam Sandler) in *Uncut Gems* (2019, written by Ronald Bronstein and the Safdie brothers).

This doesn't necessarily mean characters need to be larger-than-life or extrovert. This applies equally to smaller, quieter characters:

* The Rodney Williams character (Bill Nighy) in Kazuo Ishiguro's *Living* (2022).

* The titular character in *The Unlikely Pilgrimage of Harold Fry* (2023, adapted from her own novel by Rachel Joyce).

* The two lead characters in Mackenzie Crook's *Detectorists*.

Characters need to have strong definition. They need to be utterly distinct – whether they are loud, attention-seeking extroverts or private, isolated introverts.

Conjunctions of character and story world

Dramatising your characters, bringing out the qualities you wish to show, often depends on the conjunction of character and setting, particularly the *tension* between character and setting, the friction caused by this conjunction.

Tom Hanks's character's attempts to survive and escape his desert island in William Broyles Jr.'s *Cast Away* for instance; or *The Truman Show* (1998, written by Andrew Niccol), in which a real, private man is caught up in a public, fantasy existence.

This tension can be found in any number of prison-set stories – Jimmy McGovern's *Time*; *Orange Is the New Black*, created by Jenji Kohan; *The Shawshank Redemption*, adapted by Frank Darabont from Stephen King's novella. This entire genre dramatises the incarceration, the containment, of prisoner characters – how specific characters each respond to this ultimate life crisis.

You need to find the setting, the environment, the story world that is going to enable you to unleash your characters. Think about how to challenge them through the settings in which you place them:

* Put the gentle, rural loner into a thrusting, stressful metropolis.

* Compel your shy, reticent character to have to make a big, public speech.

* Have your underachieving, low-functioning character inherit a thriving business to which they are unsuited.

This is why police interviews and court cases are such a staple of drama – they are situations that literally ask demanding questions of your characters. Other examples of spaces and situations that put characters under the sort of pressure that creates drama and emotion include:

* A job interview.

* Enforced isolation.

* A physical challenge, e.g. *127 Hours* (2010, written by Simon Beaufoy and Danny Boyle), J. C. Chandor's *All Is Lost* (2013), or J Blakeson's *The Disappearance of Alice Creed* (2009).

Throw stones at your characters

Make things as hard as possible for your character. Challenge them. Good storytelling is about placing obstacles in the way of your protagonist achieving their aims.

Some writers will subconsciously (sometimes consciously!) avoid doing nasty things to their protagonists because they like them and don't want to see bad things happen to them. This shows how much they are invested in their characters but is not helpful to story effectiveness. It is a very understandable human response but is anti-dramatic. The more pressure you heap on your lead character, the more difficult you make things for them, the more pleasing it will be for the audience (and your character) when things come right for them. The deeper the troughs, the higher the peaks.

As a writer, you need to cause your audience to worry about how things will turn out for your character – you have to introduce doubt into your character's story and inner life.

Our fundamental hunger for story is so often driven by stories of success against the odds. The story of someone born into great riches who then goes on to greater riches is not a story that has great appeal. A story of someone who comes from poverty to great wealth (success) is appealing. There is a trajectory to it. (Even if, in the reality of life, the former is, sadly, very much more common than the latter!)

Character and risk

Stories grip us when there is risk involved for the characters. If a character is trying to achieve something and the cost of failure is that their initial, peaceful life can be resumed unchanged, then there is no real story – there's not enough at stake. Only if our protagonist knows that by failing they will lose everything (or at least something significant) in the attempt to achieve something, then there is risk and a story worth telling. Audiences may not be able to articulate this as they watch a story – but they will feel it. If what is at stake in the story isn't meaningful for the character, the question over the successful outcome will not be meaningful to the audience. (More on stakes on pages 78–9.)

Character and tone

What is at stake for a character in, for instance, a romantic comedy and a police or serial killer thriller will be very different. Character and story values are dictated to some extent by the tone and genre of your show. What is at stake for your character isn't always life and death. Sometimes it can be smaller and more mundane than this.

> In the BBC TV series *Boiling Point* (created by Philip Barantini, James Cummings and Stephen Graham), while there are many bigger character issues in play, we are made to care deeply about the kitchen staff fulfilling a restaurant order successfully – the show clearly establishes what is at stake for these characters in the immediacy of this particular workplace setting.

Active versus passive

What does your character *do*? Your central character should be active rather than passive – this should be a default story principle.

There are, of course, exceptions. Some of the most effective stories are when a character progresses from passivity to activity. Sometimes, the longer you as a storyteller maintain this character's passivity, the more narratively satisfying is the moment when that character finally explodes into action.

But as a default, it's the actions of your protagonist – whether well-judged or disastrous – that should drive the story forward.

Character arcs

Character and story are indivisible. The narrative arc of the character is your story. The default is that an event happens to disrupt the character's status quo: a catalyst, forcing your character into crisis or action. Your character responds to the crisis and *changes* – resolves the crisis and reaches the end of your story a different person.

There are, though, variations to this arc:

* The character, forced by an event or circumstances to change and rise to the challenge, who then returns to the status quo we found them in at the start of the story – someone who has risen to a crisis but remains essentially unchanged.

* The character who remains unchanged through a crisis and remains the same throughout – for instance, a character who is somewhat of an empty vessel, whose words and actions are misinterpreted by others: the Peter Sellers character in *Being There* (1979), the Tom Hanks character in *Forrest Gump* (1994).

* The character who changes for the worse, who begins functional and at peace, and ends the story corrupted and compromised.

> In *The Godfather*, Michael Corleone must suddenly and unexpectedly take on the mantle of head of the family, and in order to do so successfully, he must change and develop a darker side to his character – a side that his wife hasn't seen before and which, understandably, alienates her. He has exchanged integrity for status – the classic arc of corruption.

There are so many variations on the nature of your central character's arc of change (or non-change) over a story. What is essential is that you, the writer, understand the journey you want to take your character on; and that you chart this arc across the story of your film, episode or series.

And while, with the benefit of hindsight, we may be able to articulate these examples quite clearly, in the best stories, these underlying story ideas and arcs can often emerge slowly and only gradually come to light for the audience as the characters themselves slowly begin to recognise their own deeper needs.

Real people

One of the best templates or starting points for fictional characters are real people. Probably not the people you know well, but people you know little about or just observe in public – *and* public figures who you may have read about and observed through news reports, etc.

Below are some examples of both. These were characters created on the Creativity for Scriptwriters course that I run, and are useful illustrations of how creatively fruitful it can be to create fictional characters from the starting point of a real person. This way you are more likely to access observed truths and avoid falling back on TV and film clichés and tropes.

> **Characters Inspired by Observing Real People**
>
> These three characters were all inspired by the physical appearance and mannerisms of a real person observed in public who intrigued the writers. These templates, their superficial appearances, inspired the creation of fictional counterparts.
>
> *Isaac – an Orthodox Jewish man in his mid-forties. Dresses in traditional Jewish clothes. On the day in question he was walking around carrying more boxes than he could manage, in a sweaty, anxious state. Isaac works in his father's long-standing, traditional hat shop in Golders Green, and hates it. His father looks down on him and has always chipped away at Isaac's self-esteem. Isaac is not good at the job and has no real interest in it. Isaac is single and very private. He is not happy. But what Isaac is good at is gambling. He is obsessed with gambling and has a real flair for it. It is an addiction but it's one he (thinks he) is in*

> control of – and over the last few years he has made a very decent income from his secret gambling that has supplemented the paltry income he makes in his father's millinery.

I'm very interested in this character – his secrets and inner conflicts are instantly engaging.

> Maud – an unexceptional woman in her mid-fifties. She lives alone. She divorced fifteen years ago and has no desire to enter into a new romantic relationship. She is emotionally self-contained but at the same time dependent on having people who will listen to her – Maud talks a lot and doesn't really care to listen. Her current interest is beekeeping, which she has been into for the last few years. She will talk endlessly about it to anyone who will listen. Mostly this is to her resentful work colleagues – she is an administrator for an addiction charity. She used to be a regular member of an all-female book club but reading has had to take a back seat to beekeeping. She's from the Midlands originally but now lives in the suburbs of Oxford.

Both of these characters grew out of initial observation of and eavesdropping on a real person on London Euston Station concourse. They are a demonstration of how creativity can be opened up and facilitated by looking outwards at people and stories in the real world – as opposed to staring at a computer screen until your brain bleeds.

And here's an example from a more recent course, by Claire Rowlands. Firstly the description of the character, then a monologue that captures her voice:

> I spotted Grace, a girl in her early twenties, browsing in Waitrose on Holloway Road with her glamorous mum and two older sisters. One sister pointed out that Grace had a leaf stuck in her flip-flop. Grace giggled. 'I know, but I'm leaving it there because it's annoying everyone.' Her sisters looked at her with a kind of fatigued disdain. This is a voicenote to her university housemate:

                    GRACE
                   (croaky)
　Babe —

Voicenote ends.

New voicenote.

                    GRACE
                   (cont'd)
　Baabe. Sorry my finger slipped off the
　thing. I'm literally dying.

　So... news flash... I'm actually
　speaking to you from your bed. I knew
　you'd be super-chill about it.

　So Spike was begging me to bring him
　up to Nottingham for a night out so
　we came up yesterday and it was so
　fucking funny. We had the maddest
　night. Like I'm literally dying.
　Actually deceased. You seriously
　need to meet him. He'd love you.
　Anyway he ended up bringing this
　guy back and they were in my room
　doing debaucherous things, so I just
　jiggled the little lock thing on
　your door which we can totally get
　fixed, because I just knew that out of
　everyone you'd be the chillest.

　So I'm just looking at all your
　little photos on the wall! I don't
　think I've ever been in your room
　before. So cute. There's you and
　the fam at the... are they caravans?
　Are they caravans if they don't have

wheels? Cute little chalets made out of plastic. Such a vibe. I'd love to sleep in a caravan. We should actually do that.

Oh and the other thing I've been meaning to say and I'd actually totally forgotten about it was, you know that fifty quid you borrowed when we went to Magic Radish? Totally don't worry about that. I'd actually forgotten anyway so seriously don't worry. Is that your brother with the leg tats? You should bring him up to stay some time. Tell him I said his ink is sick.

Aw, look at you with your little granny. Is that the one that died? R.I.P. Granny.

Oh! And I have some good news — you know that jacket that was your mum's and we all rinsed you for wearing it? Well Spike was trying on some of your clothes last night and he actually totally found a way to make it work. I took pics, so you can wear it if we style it up in more of an ironic way. I think there's a tiny rip under the arm because he's pretty hench but he can sew that up because he is a qualified fashion designer. I was thinking I could wear it out tonight but it's just so massive on me. Why is everything so fucking huge on me? It's really annoying being

> tiny sometimes. I'm an actual Polly Pocket.
>
> Aaanyway let me know when you're back in Nottingham and we can hang... sorry I'm just trying to find the label on your little owl cushion to see where it's from... Home Bargains. Iconic.
>
> Okay, sweets. See you soon. Lots of love.

What excites me about the creation of these characters (aside from the richness of the characterisations) is that they were created by these three different writers from the outside in. The writers found real people who, for whatever reason, they found visually interesting; and then created inner lives inspired by their external appearance and manner.

But, importantly, they are very much these particular writer's creations. The writers made a personal choice in picking these particular people; they then coloured them in with their own ideas. I think this merging of the real with the imagined is such a fruitful way to create character and begin to transform character into story.

Two people who have been in the public eye in recent years and who fascinate me for the lessons they offer for writers of fiction are Lance Armstrong and Jimmy Savile.

Both, at certain times in their lives, were wildly popular. Both were driven, and in their own ways charming and persuasive, and both performed charitable acts of spectacular generosity, raising vast sums for good causes. Both were unquestionably instrumental in changing many people's lives for the better. But at the same time, ultimately both are defined by the awful things they did.

What fascinates me about both is their plausibility. Savile effectively 'groomed' an entire nation. Loath though we might be to admit it, the whole country was in his thrall. At the height of his popularity, he was a national treasure and revered by both ordinary people who watched him on TV and many establishment figures – politicians, the Royal Family and the police, whose favour he worked so cleverly to cultivate.

Only after his death (and to a lesser extent in the less-celebrated later years of his life) has he been viewed in a different light – weird, creepy, sinister, evil, a hideous serial rapist and paedophile.

How Savile 'managed' his image, his PR, how his outward appearance and public acts of charity were so at odds with the reality of his nature and intentions, is a fascinating illustration of contradiction and ambivalence in character.

He is a very extreme example. But this principle of ambivalence – of the gap between public appearance and private reality – between what a character expresses and what they actually do, all of this is key to fascinating, rich and, above all, real and credible characterisation.

Savile and Armstrong are the ultimate examples of people who were or are living contradictions, deeply flawed, both living for many years with dark secrets and both in their ways larger-than-life, 'heightened'. Crude – but real! – templates of what you should strive for in fictional characters: flaws, ambivalence, contradictions, dramatised through the contrasts between public persona and private acts.

One example of a fictional character who I'm reminded of here is the J. K. Simmons character, Terence Fletcher, in Damien Chazelle's *Whiplash* (2014). He is a striking, charismatic character whom we meet in a public, performative role (apart from one key scene late in the film). For the most part, Fletcher is a monstrous, bullying character, but there is also a sense that he does what he does for (arguably) noble reasons – it's this contradiction that keeps him fascinating. He is a character who demands attention, larger-than-life but at the same time, to me, recognisable from life. As in many of the best-told stories, while he is recognisable and relatable, he is also a heightened, concentrated version of reality. This is what the best screenwriting gives us — this recognisable reflection of a reality that is at the same time heightened and intensified.

One of the things that fascinates (and appals) me about Boris Johnson is his completely self-evident lack of empathy, what journalist Peter Oborne has called his 'chilling inhumanity'. Every time he gave a speech to camera during the pandemic, every time he had to make a public announcement acknowledging a tragedy or disaster, both what he said and how he said it fell so short. He never seemed to find words that were any solace at all. He never *seemed* to care — and what's more, he never seemed to care that it looked like he didn't seem to care! He consistently lied but never lied with any care — he didn't care that we knew he was lying. He is ultimately 'entitled' — he acts like he can get away with whatever he does, that there will be no comeback, no consequences (and, horrifyingly, he seems to be right). Even when he was forced to resign, his lack of self-reflection or acknowledgement that he'd done anything wrong was striking.

I don't mean to get 'party political' here, but what strikes me about Johnson (and some other politicians) is that there is a part of him missing. He completely lacks empathy. He is desperate for power for its own sake but has no purpose with it when he has it, except to abuse it. And yet people love him — they vote for him in their millions. Whether cabinet colleagues or voters, people are unquestioningly loyal to him. So there *is* something about him that is winning and persuasive, charming, funny and engaging (although I hate him so much I even find it hard to write these last words), but he evokes strong feelings in people, both negative and positive — and that's something that you find in memorable fictional characters too (Deborah Vance in *Hacks*, Terence Fletcher in *Whiplash*, Anne Lister in *Gentleman Jack*).

> **Character Newspaper Exercise**
>
> Look through today's newspaper. Find three examples of people who exhibit this contradiction, this gap between what they profess publicly and how they live privately. Find people who are clear, extreme examples.
>
> Describe in writing the two extremes of their personality, and think about how to turn each of these into a fictional character, to the extent that the source or inspiration for these characters isn't obvious.

Self-awareness

When characters are able to articulate their condition, there is less room for subtext. We are all to some extent a mystery to ourselves. We are the only people who never get to see ourselves as other people see us. We've all experienced that uncomfortable feeling of hearing our voices recorded or watching ourselves on film and thinking, 'Is that really how I come across?' And – let's be frank – feeling some degree of disappointment at how our appearance is so disappointingly at odds with how we'd like to think we appear.

This gap between self-perception and how we appear to others is at the heart of effective characterisation. It's the key to subtext.

What alcoholic will freely articulate that they are alcoholic? The tragedy of the alcoholic is how they work so hard to convince themselves that they are normal, that they don't have a problem. What insane person discusses their insanity in cool, objective terms? Self-deception is fundamental to effective dramatic characterisation.

The moment an alcoholic is able to openly and objectively discuss their alcoholism is the beginning of the end of their problem – and the beginning of the resolution of your story.

What should be interesting about alcoholism (as one example of countless possible character issues) is the deeper cause, what it is in the character's life that is driving them to this act of self-destructiveness – and what needs to happen for them to come out the other side. Self-destructiveness, self-sabotage are such common traits. It's this internal lack of resolution that is so fundamental to effective characterisation, that is at the heart of involving, emotionally rich storytelling.

Look for the gaps in characters – the gap between who they see themselves as and how they appear to other people, the gap between how they present themselves and who they really are. The intrigue and power of a good story are constructed out of these gaps.

The following is an excerpt from David Hare's review of Gordon Brown's autobiography in the *Observer*, in which Hare quotes a close ally of the former PM:

> *Brown was like an actor who could watch and assess everything in the film except his own performance… the most brilliant person I ever met when analysing any problem not to do with himself. But… the worst judge alive of anything which is to do with him.*

Hare goes on:

> *…he has always exhibited an everyman dimension that is unexpectedly moving. Brown has in abundance what the rest of us have to some degree – a haunting ignorance of our own place in the picture… It is this quality – knowledge of absolutely everything except himself – that connects the distant, frustrating Gordon Brown to the human race.*

I am the only person I will never see. We are all to some extent fictional character constructs of our own making. We make conscious decisions about who we're going to be, or at least how we appear to other people – what we do and what we don't do. But who's to say this is our true self?

My daughter, applying for university accommodation, is asked on a form, 'Are you an introvert or extrovert?' What an impossible question to answer about yourself!

We all make decisions about how we're going to behave, how we would like to 'present' – but who's to say that is the real us? I make a decision not to do certain things – drink alcohol, go to opera, dance, sing karaoke. Why do I make these decisions? Are any of them functional, rational decisions? (Probably not!) What have you chosen not to do? What character have you 'decided' to be? What inadequacies and insecurities do these decisions (attempt to) mask?

So, character self-knowledge is generally unhelpful to story. The moment a character is able to articulate their 'condition' is the moment they begin to solve it, and is the beginning of the end of your story. Self-denial creates friction, conflict and drama. A clear articulation (particularly early in that character's story) of their own issue tends to feel too straightforwardly expositional, dramatically flat and narratively unhelpful. It's all about taking the audience on a journey of discovery with your characters.

> **How Characters 'Present'**
>
> (This is a private exercise, not to be shared!) Find examples of three people you know and how they choose to 'present' – particularly people where the choice seems quite deliberate and to some extent artificial.
>
> List the ways in which this person chooses to present themselves – how they dress, what they talk about, their attitude towards certain people, etc., and use these lessons in the creation of three parallel fictional characters.

Character agenda

Characters come alive through their agenda, their aims, their attitude. In every story and scene, each character needs to be pursuing their own individual agenda, however petty or grand that might be.

Your lead character may be pursuing the love of his life; a minor, one-scene character may just be trying to prevent this character from entering a private room. But a character's agenda within a scene or story is an important part of what defines them. Characters become distinctive through their own particular, individual agendas – what they want and how they are going about trying to achieve it.

Character detail

Alongside this – and what should connect to their agenda, to what is driving a character – are the minutiae of character: the tics, foibles and idiosyncrasies that we all possess. Everyone is unique. Even identical twins are different to each other.

> The character of the solicitor, Stone, in *Criminal Justice* (Peter Moffat) is often referenced in this respect – and the detail of his athlete's foot and open-toed sandals as a telling character detail. There is something about this detail that brilliantly brings the character alive – a dramatic expression of his seemingly bumbling inefficiency, his professional adequacy (but arguably a deliberate strategy to cultivate this misleading appearance). Peter Moffat's story was rewritten in a US version, *The Night Of* (2016, by Richard Price and Steven Zaillian), and this character detail was maintained in the US adaptation.
>
> A comparable character trait is in the US crime procedural series, *Columbo* (created by Richard Levinson and William Link), in which the titular character's most memorable and defining characteristic was his deliberately cultivated incoherent and shambling exterior, and most memorably his grubby mackintosh – this superficial first impression being at odds with his razor-sharp powers of investigative deduction.
>
> So often, the most memorable characters are defined or remembered through the particulars of their physical appearance and what they say about them – as with Columbo's raincoat. Take for instance, in *Breaking Bad* (created by Vince Gilligan), Walter White's external transformation from soft-around-the-edges Middle America family man to hard-as-nails, deliberately styled crook.

Appearance and physicality

So, in this visual medium, the question of your character's appearance is of key importance. The obvious basics are gender, age, ethnicity. But then there is the detail that really brings them alive: accent, costume, make-up, anything about them that is physically noteworthy and expressive of who they are.

What do they like to wear? How do they wear their hair? How do they hold themselves? All these elements are an articulation of how characters choose to present themselves, how they wish to be seen – of how they 'present', even if the effect they are going for is not exactly what they're achieving.

For some people, outward appearance is all-important and is evidently worked hard at. For others it's less important; they have more of a 'thrown on' quality, although sometimes the casual, 'thrown on' appearance is just as artful, deliberate and self-conscious as something more obviously styled.

Defined, specific and characterful physical appearance really helps in the first instance to bring the character alive off the page for the reader. When, for instance, you are introducing several new characters in a scene or short section of your script, it's so helpful if you allow the reader to clearly visualise the physical specifics and idiosyncrasies of your character – these should always be a key, defining element of your characters.

Character status

Think about status and hierarchy, in each scene, and in your story as a whole. What is the relative status of the characters in a scene or story? How does this change over the course of a scene or story? This development and change in the relative hierarchy between characters is a key component in dramatic storytelling.

This question of relative status and power – the hierarchy – is an intriguing ingredient of every family and organisation; a mainspring of conflict and drama. Who has the power in any particular scene? And how does the power dynamic ebb, flow and change over the course of a scene and a story? Story is all about changes and developments within relationships as relative status between characters changes – the rags-to-riches story archetype, for instance. Think about how differences in character status manifest themselves in a scene.

> In *Succession* (by Jesse Armstrong), the relationship dynamic that drives the whole series is that between the patriarch Logan and his children – who are constantly competing to gain their father's favour, to take over his position. It's all about status and relative power within both the family and the corporation. Logan has the status and the authority, and one of the key narrative dynamics of the series is his children vainly struggling and competing with each other to acquire them.

On a more fundamental level, think about whether your character is 'high status' or 'low status' – where they operate on the 'status scale', and whether their story is about a shift in their status.

> In Sarah Phelps' excellent *The Sixth Commandment*, the relationship between antagonist Ben Field and his sidekick Martyn Smith is a clear illustration of the importance of character status. Throughout the story, in this relationship Field has all the power and Smith is completely in thrall to him – this master–pupil dynamic defines their relationship.
>
> Similarly, in the film *Whiplash*, pupil Andrew cedes all of the status to sadistic teacher Terence Fletcher.

High-status characters are often defined by their composure, their stillness and certainty, lower-status characters by their indecision, their twitchiness. Body language is an important communicator of status in character, so find ways to weave this into your writing. So often the action lines are more revealing of character even than dialogue.

Characters and communities

Tell stories about characters in communities that feel fresh, unexpected and distinctive. One such recent story for me was the stage play *House of Ife* by Beru Tessema, about the specific values and relationships within a Somali immigrant family in London.

The very specific community of the blue-collar Chicago sandwich restaurant in Disney+ series *The Bear* (Christopher Storer) or the Nottinghamshire ex-mining community in James Graham's *Sherwood* are other examples.

Relationships

An interesting, rounded characterisation is nothing without the context of relationships. It's the relationships that bring a character to life, the combinations of people that generate sparks. You can illustrate and dramatise character through the contrast in their different relationships – how they relate in different ways to different people. So many police procedurals, for instance, are elevated by the working relationships at the heart of each episode – Morse and Lewis in *Inspector Morse*, Cassie and Sunny in Chris Lang's *Unforgotten*.

Other series are defined by the developing relationship dynamic between protagonist and antagonist – Joel Fields and Joe Weisberg's *The Patient* is a prime example, focusing on the fluctuating relationship between kidnapper and victim, in which so much is at stake.

There is something deeply narratively satisfying about a long-term duel or stand-off between protagonist and antagonist. Both *Happy Valley* and *The Fall* (Allan Cubitt) were essentially about the long-standing conflict between two characters – and both concluded, memorably and powerfully, at the end of their third and final series with a set-piece confrontation between these two central characters coming together.

Loyalty, betrayal, unspoken bonds between characters and the breaking of these bonds are all worth considering in the development of the relationships between your characters.

The entire romantic comedy genre is predicated on the richness and specificities of the romantic relationships – between Harry and Sally (*When Harry Met Sally*); William Thacker and Anna Scott in Richard Curtis's *Notting Hill*; Alvy Singer and Annie Hall in Woody Allen and Marshall Brickman's *Annie Hall*. So many of the more memorable romcoms work because of the superficial unsuitability, the friction, between the two romantic leads.

NON-HUMAN RELATIONSHIPS

As well as human relationships, think about the non-human relationships that also define and dramatise character. For instance, there are so many screen stories that tell powerfully emotive stories by dramatising human relationships with animals – *Marley & Me*, *Born Free*, *Turner & Hooch*…

And then think about relationships with property, with objects: a character's connection to their home, for instance, but also with particular objects – whether that's a prize, or treasure, that they're in pursuit of, or something more mundane like jewellery, photos, letters from dead loved ones. Or relationships with machines – a car, a bicycle, a motorbike, etc. Or in the fantasy genre, objects that have magical powers that are in the possession of an individual. Think about the relationship with and juxtaposition to particular machines, objects, creatures and property that is going to challenge and dramatise your character.

For instance, in the film *One Life* (2023, written by Lucinda Coxon and Nick Drake), a prized scrapbook acts as the tangible and emotional bridge between the story's two different timelines (1938 and 1987).

RELATIONSHIP UNITS

Organisations in which characters come together are rich breeding grounds for story, particularly organisations and communities with a strong hierarchical order – the military, schools and colleges, prisons, hospitals, businesses. The family-business saga, medical drama, crime drama, and legal drama are all genres predicated on a specific community or organisation. And so many of these professional or working environments act as quasi-families for a group of characters. Recent examples include *The Bear* and *Boiling Point*, both set largely in and around the kitchens of restaurants, where there is something of a 'family vibe' (or actual family connections in the case of *The Bear*) in the hierarchy of the staff.

Think about creating stories within worlds like this that naturally and organically force together groups of disparate, contrasting characters.

THE FAMILY UNIT

So many dramatic and comic stories focus on a family unit (*Succession, Arrested Development, Mum*) — and if not an actual family, so often a substitute, quasi-family (*Friends*).

The importance to story of the family unit — both actual and symbolic or suggested — cannot be overstated. The dynamics of family are at the heart of so much film and TV drama, so much fiction. Think about the infinite variety of family situations — as with every person, every family is unique. From the New Testament to *EastEnders*; *The Godfather* to *Little Women*; *Father of the Bride* to *Little Miss Sunshine*; *The Crown* to *About Time*.

All families and their dynamics are unique but also fit a universal template. The family unit or quasi-family unit is a story constant.

If your story is about family, consider what is uniquely at stake in this particular family? What are the unique tensions and rivalries? What makes family so dramatically and narratively rich is that underneath the family dynamics there are always those huge dramatic considerations — of love, loyalty, betrayal, tension, resentments, shared history and shared secrets. A loving upbringing is what we all aspire to. Love within families is enabling. Conversely, a lack of familial love is damaging. There is so much story to be tapped from the narrative richness and dramatic potential of the family unit.

> **The Family Unit**
>
> Write up descriptions of three real-life family set-ups that are rich, interesting, conflicted, unique and true. This can either be taken from your own family, or people you only vaguely know – but they should be taken from your own experience, not from newspapers, news, internet, or something you've read.
>
> Once you have these three family groupings clearly described, keep what is uniquely interesting, but fictionalise them; use them as the basis for a family unit or combination that you wish to explore further and dramatise.

Stereotypes

Earlier, I referenced the high-achieving academic with limited emotional or practical intelligence (pages 133–4). Other examples of character stereotype include:

* The 'jock' – good at sport, sociable, aggressively heterosexual, not very bright.

* The posh, 'establishment' male – who has been through public school, Oxbridge or the army, now works in the city or as captain of industry; chauvinist, arrogant and entitled.

* The invisible housewife, low on confidence at a middle-aged crisis point.

* The waster student, living the good life; too many drugs, too much alcohol, not enough work.

All of these stereotypes are only helpful when you examine them in more detail, challenge the stereotype and subvert what we have come to expect with these characters. If you start turning some of their values on their heads, questioning these character profiles, suddenly they can become interesting, unexpected and fresh. But you can't challenge these stereotypes until you have acknowledged and recognised them.

Character history and backstory

Backstory is a vital component of any successful story. As people, we are freighted with our history, defined to some extent by our pasts – the people and experiences in our life leading up to the present moment. And the same is true for your characters before the moment we first meet them on screen.

For great examples of how to use backstory, see the work of the wonderful Sally Wainwright in both *Happy Valley* and *Last Tango in Halifax*. Both of these outstanding series are powered by what Wainwright knows about her characters – the experiences they have undergone before her on-screen story starts. She masterfully uses these backstory events and character history to power and change the story in the present. In *Happy Valley*, the all-important central relationship between Catherine and Tommy Lee Royce is defined by something terrible that has happened before the first series. We don't need flashbacks to dramatise these events on screen – but they are an ever-present shadow in the lives of the main characters, and have irrevocably changed and tainted the lives of all the main characters, particularly Catherine.

Indeed, like *Better Call Saul*, the *Breaking Bad* prequel series, I could envisage a *Happy Valley* prequel that is as powerful as *Happy Valley* itself. Catherine Cawood and her family's dark history leaks out over the course of the three series in a way that both informs and drives the story in the present. None of this backstory plays like undramatised exposition. The way and place within the story that each piece of backstory comes out, adds another fascinating layer of intrigue and intensity, ratcheting up the drama of the story in the present.

At what point in your character's life you start your particular story is a key storytelling decision. Make sure that the events and secrets in your lead character's past are an integral part of their story in the present.

Audience perception of character

It's important that you give the audience questions to ask about your character. Don't, as a storyteller, be in too much of a rush to tell your audience too much about them.

If as a writer you are instantly telling your audience the real nature of this character (often, for instance, a character who provides the antagonistic energy in a scene), then you leave yourself nowhere to go with them. If you have instantly defined them as unlikeable and unsympathetic, even if a necessary foil for your protagonist, they may well feel more like two-dimensional functions of plot than rich, three-dimensional, real people. Characters whose essential nature is exactly as it seems on first meeting should be the exception.

Characters who are engaged by their own story

The characters in your story need to be seen to care about the outcome of their endeavours. It doesn't matter how inherently dramatic your story is, if your characters don't seem to be emotionally engaged with the task at hand, your audience won't be either. In order for the audience to feel invested in what is at stake in your story, the characters need to be similarly invested.

Memorable Characters

Here is a list of eight fictional characters from film and TV whom I've enjoyed. I will describe what it is that I enjoyed about each character, and then come up with some conclusions or lessons you can take from this (unscientific) survey…

Happy Valley – Catherine Cawood (writer Sally Wainwright)

Catherine is driven, empathetic, spiky, intelligent, difficult – she has blind spots, moments when her intelligence is overtaken by emotion. She is good at her job, perceptive. She is rooted in a very particular region. She is unpretentious. She is fiercely protective of those values and people that are important to her, but in career terms not overly ambitious. She is hugely empathetic, even if objectively we can see that she can be difficult and confrontational at times. I think the things we recognise and respond to in Catherine are her integrity, her humanity – but also her fury, her hunger for vengeance, driven by her sadness over the tragedy in her family backstory. Catherine goes through extreme emotions. The events of the story over three series challenge and threaten her equanimity and the life she has constructed out of her past tragedy.

Whiplash – Terence Fletcher (writer Damien Chazelle)

Fletcher is antagonist rather than protagonist – the character who threatens and challenges the story's hero. He is morally complicated. On the one hand, he is driven to get the best out of his music students, but the way he drives them is excessive. He is high-achieving but ultimately a bully. The interesting question about him as a character is – even though he is clearly a deeply flawed, even sadistic, character – can it be argued that the way he drives his students to be the best musicians they can be is in some way in their best interests? As dramatised in the film, he is almost exclusively a character we only meet in 'public' situations – principally in band rehearsals and concerts. So the few moments in which we meet him in more private moments feel crucially important. Fletcher is charismatic. It's easier to be blinded to his faults because he is so magnetic as a character.

The Virtues – Joseph (writers Shane Meadows and Jack Thorne)

As played by Stephen Graham, Joseph is one of the most memorably damaged characters. Unable to cope with life and consequently alienated from those around him, Joseph goes on a compelling journey of redemption, as he tries to come to terms with the traumas in his past. The story digs into these traumas and his attempts to finally confront them. Objectively, many of Joseph's actions are alienating and excessive. He is a man out of control. But it's this sense of crisis that makes him compelling.

Hacks – Deborah Vance (writers Lucia Aniello, Paul W. Downs and Jen Statsky)

Deborah Vance is one of the screen characters I have most enjoyed in recent years. She is objectively highly unsympathetic – pretty much uniformly hostile and mean to all those around her. But she is also highly engaging and empathetic, because beneath her nastiness, we are given occasional hints and glimpses of her vulnerability, her insecurity over her career and fame coming to an end. The central idea seems to be that the public image she has so painstakingly created and maintained for so long is starting to crumble, and the character's challenge is, without that, who is she and what does she have to cling on to? She's also extremely funny (in a cruel way) as a character.

I Care a Lot – Marla Grayson (writer J Blakeson)

Another hugely unsympathetic character – even more so than Deborah Vance because we really aren't given any glimpses of the vulnerability or humanity beneath the appalling surface. But what I responded to were the challenges she faces as a character – the questions asked of her, the way she is forced into survival mode and how she so deftly confronts these challenges. An objectively loathsome character who somehow is very engaging because of the way she so resourcefully responds to the challenges she faces. A great example of an active, driven, intelligent, ingenious character.

The Fall – Stella Gibson (writer Allan Cubitt)

Stella is a more self-contained character than the above. What is interesting about her is the strength with which she faces up to the challenges of her male-dominated world, the contrasts between her feminine and masculine qualities – and the hints at what it costs her emotionally. As with *Happy Valley*, this series is very much predicated on the face-off between protagonist and antagonist; and as with *Happy Valley*, the third series culminates in the face-to-face denouement between Stella and her nemesis.

Mid-Morning Matters – Alan Partridge (writer Steve Coogan)

Partridge is quite simply one of the great comic creations. His longevity as a character, returning in so many different formats over so many years, is testament to the brilliance of the creation and the writing. Another objectively unlikeable character – bigoted, opinionated, insecure, boastful – so why is he so engaging, enjoyed by audiences for so long? I think because he is so recognisably absurd in his gaucheness, his insensitivity, his skewed values, insecurity and lack of self-awareness. There is something pathetic but nonetheless relatable. He is also a brilliantly observed reflection of a very particular, increasingly obsolete, 1980s culture of sexism and bigotry. The way he parades his insecurities and prejudices is somehow incredibly funny.

Partridge is an extraordinary example of the power of brilliant characterisation. He is such a hit with audiences, apparently so relatable, he has appeared in so many different shows and formats over such a long period of time and continues to be enjoyed. What a huge achievement of writing (and performance) this character is.

> *This Is Going to Hurt* – Adam (writer Adam Kay)
>
> An interesting character in that he is the loosely fictionalised version of the writer himself in this brilliant, autobiographical series. The main reason that this character stands out for me is that he is so flawed. As portrayed, he is essentially a good man, trying to do the right things in very difficult circumstances. But he is at times unkind, insensitive, defensive and uncommunicative. On the surface, he is not overtly sympathetic, but it's this spikiness, his superficial lack of warmth as a character, that makes him fascinating and watchable. He makes mistakes and so feels human, identifiable and unresolved, even if not objectively likeable.

Engaging characters, characters we care about

So what conclusions can we draw from the above? What do we look for in characters? What do the audience find engaging and gripping in on-screen characters?

* People who are ragged, jagged around the edges, people who feel conflicted.

* People who live life to the full, characters who feel a little heightened, who undergo intense emotions.

* People with a fierce desire, with an aim, an ambition – a desire that in some of the best stories is in direct conflict with what they actually need.

* People who are flawed or damaged in some way. I'd go as far as to say, we respond to characters who aren't straightforwardly likeable.

* Characters with an edge, an attitude, even a snarl, who are superficially unpleasant, confrontational, negative – these are entertaining, challenging, interesting characters, because we want to know what is going on underneath this surface negativity. We anticipate with intrigue how this inner conflict is going to be confronted or resolved.

* Characters who in some way lack judgement or self-awareness – again, this feels recognisably human – characters who make mistakes.

* Dysfunctional characters. The word 'dysfunctional' covers a multitude of sins, but characters who are a bit of a mess are fun.

* Characters who are buttoned up, inhibited, or controlled, are also fascinating. We will sense that underneath the calm, measured exterior, there is something they are covering up, something uncontrolled within, that contrasts with the exterior appearance of calm and order – that counterpoint between what's on the surface and what's beneath it.

Secrets, lies and deceptions – a superficial appearance that is hiding something beneath – are fundamental to effective characterisation in story.

Loyalty and betrayal – the challenging of loyalty and bonds – are key character values.

Issues of status and power – and perceptions of status and power – are also key to character and story. This is very much the case, for instance, in Deborah Vance's central relationship in *Hacks* with younger employee and co-lead Ava; and between Terence Fletcher and younger protagonist (and pupil), Andrew, in *Whiplash*.

Physical considerations are a key ingredient of characterisation: physical specifics such as costume, hair and make-up, voice, accent and tics. The human face and body language can often convey more – and more interestingly – than dialogue. Character action (directions) should be as important a tool in dramatising and bringing your character to life as dialogue.

Dramatic characters need to have strong feelings – yearnings, desires, secrets, needs and wants. Drama is about knocking characters off their even keel. Focus on the primal need they have that is driving their story. What is your character searching or striving for? What happens when we either fulfil all our ambitions, or learn that we are never going to?

Character choices are also important – consider the road your character *didn't* take.

I also realise there is a strong personal aspect to the characters I have chosen above. This choice of these characters says something about me and my foibles and flaws! You need to think about the fictional characters who you respond to and what it is specifically about them that connects with your own sensibility.

> ### Creating and Shaping Character
>
> *Molly* – an unproduced feature-film script written by Andrew Lynch
>
> Andrew had created a really engaging, richly drawn central character: Molly, Zambian, fifty years old. She is a live-in carer for an elderly English couple. In her bedroom, she is lying clothed on her bed, face bathed in the light of her laptop screen as she plays an intense online poker game, sipping from a large glass of wine on her bedside table.
>
> This is a character image that has stayed with me. (This sort of imagery that dramatises the character is so often the key to successful characterisation, enabling the reader – and then the audience – to appreciate and understand the character through clear but simple visual representation.)
>
> In discussing this story with the writer, we were both a bit flummoxed as to why all the excellent elements – the colour and texture of the characterisation; the uniqueness and specificity of the story world (a middle-aged, Zambian female carer with alcohol and gambling issues, living in the home of her elderly clients) – weren't quite coming together to make a cohesive, compelling, emotionally satisfying story.
>
> One of the elements of the story is that this Zambian woman and her daughter (in her thirties) are estranged because of some as-yet-unspecified, dark family history. Our protagonist Molly reaches out to her daughter to try to make peace with her – but her daughter refuses to accept her mother's olive branch.
>
> But in this scenario, it's the mother (the protagonist) who is the functional, able character, and her daughter (the secondary character) who is blocked, refusing to move on.

The key to solving this story issue was to reverse this set-up – so that it is the mother who refuses to talk to or have anything to do with her daughter, and the daughter who reaches out to her mother, only to be continually spurned.

In this revised scenario, the protagonist (Molly) has an emotional journey to undertake. Her story starting point is one of emotional dysfunction, a refusal to confront the painful truth of her past, which is poisoning her life in the present and her relationship with her family.

With this simple character swap, the story emerged: Molly's painful, reluctant journey to a confrontation with, and investigation of, the dark events in her past, that would eventually lead her to a new understanding with her daughter in order for them both to begin to heal – and which would also be the beginning of resolving her issues of loneliness (dramatised through solitary wine-drinking and online gambling).

Once we had made this change, all the rich, original elements of the story had a solid, emotionally rich character issue on which they could be hung, and all these other elements suddenly made sense.

We had established the central character's internal conflict that is so essential to compelling story.

Character Checklists

We can never do enough thinking about our characters or how we define them. I have compiled two slightly different lists below. The first is a list of character qualities – a selection of opposites – and the second is a set of questions you can ask yourself about your characters.

As an exercise, consider these lists in relation to a character you have created and are currently working on in outline or script form.

Character qualities and their opposites

None of these qualities are absolute, but I hope all are useful in helping you assess the particular proclivities and qualities of the character you're creating.

* Introvert – Extrovert
* Active – Passive
* Gentle – Aggressive
* Bitter – Philosophical/Accepting
* Open – Secretive
* Rich – Poor
* Materialistic – Thrifty
* Honest – Dishonest
* Cruel – Kind
* Solitary – Gregarious
* Indulgent – Self-Denying
* Knowledgeable – Ignorant
* Scared – Bold
* Urban – Rural
* Articulate – Tongue-Tied
* Snob – Person of the People

- Anxious – Relaxed
- Self-Assured – Full of Doubt
- Religious – Sceptical
- Carnivore – Vegan
- Drinker – Teetotaller
- Fashionable – Dowdy
- Graceful – Clumsy
- Athletic – Out of Shape
- Beautiful – Ugly
- Humorous – Serious
- Funny – No Sense of Humour
- Conservative – Socialist
- Patriot – Internationalist
- Royalist – Republican
- Sporty – Studious
- Old – Young
- Greedy – Charitable
- Fast – Slow (Mentally and Physically)
- Loving – Hateful
- Animal Lover – Animal Hater
- Neat – Messy
- Superficial – Deep
- Sly – Open
- Conventional – Unconventional
- Slim – Obese
- Tall – Short
- Smiley – Grim-faced
- Volatile – Calm

- ★ Oversexed – Asexual
- ★ High-status – Low-status
- ★ Hirsute – Bald
- ★ Penetrating Stare – Avoids Eye Contact
- ★ Energetic – Sloth-like
- ★ Ambitious – Unambitious
- ★ Bully – Victim
- ★ Employer – Employee
- ★ Employed – Unemployed
- ★ Corporate – Freelance
- ★ Brazen – Discreet
- ★ Wind-up Merchant – Sincere
- ★ Superstitious – Rational
- ★ Challenging – Conciliatory
- ★ Anally Retentive – Spontaneous
- ★ Organised – Chaotic
- ★ Sociable – Unfriendly
- ★ Academic – Uneducated
- ★ Predictable – Mercurial
- ★ Ordinary – Eccentric
- ★ Vain – Unselfconscious
- ★ Healthy – Sickly
- ★ Carer – Cared-for
- ★ Tolerant – Intolerant
- ★ Patient – Impatient
- ★ Original – Derivative
- ★ Happy – Sad
- ★ Arrogant – Humble

Character questions

It wouldn't be practical to ask every single one of these questions of your character – you would lose yourself in the excessive detail. So instead, identify the five questions from this list that have most relevance and application for this particular character.

Ask these five questions of your character, write out the answers to them, and see how you can include this new information in your screenplay in a way that elevates the story and adds to the richness and quality of the characterisation.

Alternatively, it may be that adding to your knowledge of the particular details around this character in this way helps you to really flesh them out, without ever having to make the answers to these questions an overt, revealed part of their story.

* Where are they from?
* Where were they born?
* Where do they live?
* What are the details of their home – is it a house, flat, caravan, barge, etc.?
* Is their home cluttered or minimalist?
* What is their job?
* What is their height, size or physicality?
* Who do they live with?
* Who do they love?
* Who do they hate?
* Do they have any pets?

* What is their attitude towards animals?
* Do they vote? Who for?
* What do they eat/drink?
* Where do they shop?
* What newspaper do they read?
* What are their most-visited web pages?
* What is their sexual orientation? What are their sexual proclivities?
* What do they wear? What colours do they wear? What shoes do they wear?
* How do they wear their hair and/or facial hair?
* Who are they close to?
* Who are their friends?
* What are their interests or hobbies?
* What or who are they afraid of?
* What makes them laugh?
* Are they able-bodied or in some way disabled? If disabled, is this a visible or invisible disability?
* What makes them happy or sad?
* What do they like about themselves?
* What do they dislike about themselves?
* What do they watch on TV?
* What mode of transport do they use? Motorbike? Horse? Mobility scooter?

- Do they have a car? What sort?
- What is their religion?
- What is their ethnicity?
- What public figures do they most admire or hate?
- Who would be their four dream dinner party guests?
- What are their secrets? What secret habits do they have? Who do they tell their secrets to?
- What accent do they have?
- What is their significant family history?
- What are they good at? What skills do they have?
- What are they bad at?
- What are their strengths and weaknesses?
- What have they always wanted to be good at (but aren't)?
- How does their self-image differ from the way others see them?
- What are their obsessions?
- What constitutes success and failure for your character?

Note Some of these questions will be relevant to the character you're writing in the story world they inhabit, and some won't. Select the questions that are most helpful and fertile in revealing and building a particular character.

More Character-Creation Exercises

Person – Place – Prop

In a public space, observe and find interesting conjunctions of person, place and prop.

For example, I was on a train journey and observed a young East Asian man with a Dyson vacuum cleaner.

Think about the character quirks and stories this combination of factors could generate. On the same train journey:

* A sixty-year-old white woman with a small white dog.
* A man in a National Car Parks uniform watching a video on his phone.

Character Shopping Lists

Observe the contents of people's shopping baskets at the supermarket checkout. Choose five items in their supermarket trolley or basket, and create a character from these items. What ideas do you have about them and their lives from their purchases?

Ten Valued Possessions that Define Character

What possessions define your character most clearly?

* Their watch?
* Car?
* Shoes?
* Paintings?
* A musical instrument?
* Their pet rat?

Make a list of ten objects that may define and enrich a characterisation.

Ten Life Events that Define Character

What are ten key life events that have helped mould a particular character? For example:

* Watching a sibling drown?
* Spying on their father having illicit sex?
* The bullying they did at school?
* Seeing the love of their life for the first time?
* Being involved in a traumatic accident?

Again, make a list of ten chronological events that define and dramatise your character, that have led them to being the person we meet for the first time on screen in your story – a whole life in ten short chronological sentences as a character backstory and starting point.

The Five Best and Five Worst Moments in Your Character's Life

A variation on the above. Think about and list five of the very best moments in your character's life, and five of the very worst moments. What do these moments tell you? Can you craft a story out of them?

The Best and Worst People in Your Character's Life

Think about your character's three favourite people in the world, and their three least favourite. What is it about these people that means something to your character, that informs your creation of them?

Character Monologues

1. Think about either of these questions: 'What was the worst day of my life?' or 'What was the best day of my life?' Then write a short monologue in the character's voice, looking back and describing either (or both) of these days. This will help with dialogue too – in creating and establishing this character's voice.

2. Take a character and have them describe their average morning in their own voice. Think about where they wake up, the specifics of their routine – alarm, shower, dressing, breakfast, leaving the home (or not)…This is a creative way to help you address a lot of fundamental character questions. What is unique to your character in their morning rituals?

Note With all these creative exercises, give yourself a time limit – e.g. set yourself a fifteen-minute alarm when you write the monologue. A time limit will focus your mind, and you will be surprised by how much you can pack into fifteen minutes of concentrated writing. If you give yourself an hour for this sort of exercise, you will either write far too much (and the quality will suffer) or you will take too many pauses (which will sap your creative motivation).

V
Dialogue

Introduction

Dialogue, at its best, has enormous dramatic power. Here is an example from Mike Alfreds' brilliant stage (and later film) adaptation of Evelyn Waugh's novel, *A Handful of Dust*.

The story is about the break-up of the marriage of landed gentry Tony and Brenda Last. Brenda is having an affair with a feckless, shallow, unsympathetic, younger male character named John. While she is away from her country home, living the high life in London, her young son John Andrew (also known as John) is killed in a horse-riding accident. A friend of her husband's (Jock) goes to see Brenda in London to tell her the awful news. The passage runs thus:

> 'What is it, Jock? Tell me quickly, I'm scared. It's nothing awful, is it?'
> 'I'm afraid it is. There's been a very serious accident.'
> 'John?'
> 'Yes.'
> 'Dead?'
> He nodded.
> She sat down on a hard little Empire chair against the wall, perfectly still with her hands folded in her lap, like a small well-brought-up child introduced into a room full of grown-ups. She said, 'Tell me what happened. Why do you know about it first?'
> 'I've been down at Hetton since the weekend.'

> '*Hetton?*'
>
> '*Don't you remember? John was going hunting today.*' *She frowned, not at once taking in what he was saying. 'John… John Andrew… I… oh… thank God…*' *Then she burst into tears.*

I can still remember the audience's gasp of shock at this moment as it was dramatised in the theatre, at the notion of her relief that it was her son rather than her lover who had died. I think this is one of the most chilling, affecting moments of dialogue, and it's an illustration of how powerful and memorable dialogue can be at its best, in the service of story and character.

Dialogue Considerations

Dialogue and exposition

Note All of these dialogue and exposition points have been addressed (with different emphasis!) in the Storytelling chapter – but it's important to think about how these ideas impact on dialogue specifically.

In itself, there is absolutely nothing wrong with using character dialogue to convey exposition – story information – to the audience. This will always be one of the key functions of dialogue, just as in real life one of the key reasons we speak is to pass on information.

But long dialogue scenes in a script are a red flag. This is not to say there is never a place for them, but they should be the exception rather than the rule. If you have a long dialogue scene, it should feel earnt – a major story set-piece moment. It should not only be this long because you have a lot of exposition to convey and having two characters exchange this information to each other is the best to way to do it. (It rarely is!)

* If you have a dialogue-heavy scene that's predominantly the characters' exposition, it's difficult to make it work dramatically without some subtext – a counterpoint between what is being said and what is actually going on below the surface. Exposition needs to be dramatised and disguised. Audiences are sophisticated and will smell a rat if characters

neutrally trade information supposedly for their (the audience's) benefit. (For more on this, see pages 95–7.)

* Be careful with devices like having your character speak aloud to themselves. This can sometimes be justified and made to feel like an accurate reflection of character and circumstance – but be careful not to use this as an artificial and unconvincing way of having your character communicate information or their emotional state.

* Find the interesting dynamic between the characters in the moment of the scene that is going to dramatise and disguise this exposition.

* The words 'conversation', 'discussion' and 'chat' describe the sort of situations that should be the exception rather than the rule. Dialogue scenes need to feel more like, for instance, confrontations, disputes, interrogations, arguments, challenges. All of these words imply a dynamic that brings friction and energy to the exchange of dialogue.

* There are other dialogue devices that can fall into the same trap of over-obvious, under-dramatised exposition: public speeches; news reporters telling a story; TV or radio news in the background; a letter or report being read in voice-over. There is a time and place for all these, but when they are used primarily for exposition, to feed the audience with information, they start to feel flat, overfamiliar, functional and uninteresting.

Reality versus economy

Should screen dialogue be 'realistic' – an accurate reflection of how we actually speak?

I would say that it has instead to be a slightly heightened, more deliberate and economical version of real dialogue. The reality of most conversations is that they are messy, repetitive, overlapping, and so often the two participants talk in parallel, each pursuing their own agenda, not really listening to each other.

It's great if screen dialogue has elements of these observed, relatable realities – but at the same time screen dialogue needs to feel like a more distilled, succinct version of most people's real conversations.

Articulate versus inarticulate

Having said that, I am a firm believer that some of the best screen dialogue is inarticulate. When you have two characters who, for whatever reason, are unable to say what they really want to say or what they are thinking, then the dialogue will have subtext – and this is what you should always be looking to achieve.

Below is a scene from *Succession* that made a huge impression on me. It was very powerful because there was a strong subtext to it, while at the same time it is a great example of 'inarticulate', superficially banal dialogue.

In this scene, Kendall is dealing with the emotional fallout of a death he was involved in – and the subtextual question in this scene is whether he is going to bring up this death with the family of the deceased…

```
INT. DODDY'S FAMILY KITCHEN – DAY

                    PAUL
      I'm doing teas.

                    KENDALL
      Er. No not for me thank you. Thanks.

                    PAUL
      Water?

                    KENDALL
      Er, actually. Yes please.

Paul flicks the kettle on to boil.

                    PAUL
      You staying at your mother's?
```

                    KENDALL
          Um. Yep. Yes I am. Yes.

Paul pours him a water, hands it over and leaves.
Kendall left holding a glass of water he didn't
want. [He takes a sip. Cloudy water — a little bit
of a smear on the glass.

Kendall stands, rubs at the smear. The sounds of
talking — maybe sobbing — from the room next door.

A photo on the wall — a young man (early twenties)
giving two thumbs up. Kendall can't look.

Kendall looks around intently at the walls.
Looking for things in the room. Cracks, chips.
Kendall fixates on little details. Something
tangible to keep him together. Steadies his
breathing. Another small sip. Looks at the tiles,
the wallpaper.

More conversation from next door. Kendall closes
his eyes, just for a couple of seconds, anything
to make the time pass.

He opens them again. He clocks Paul in the
kitchen — did he just see me with my eyes shut?
Did that look weird? Kendall nods and smiles.
Looks down at the ground.]

Until finally, mercifully —

The door opens, and Logan comes out.

                    LOGAN
          Okay? Let's go.

                    KENDALL
                    (low)
              Dad — ?

> Kendall draws close to Logan. Paul watching. What is this?
>
> > (cont'd, low)
> > Should I maybe, speak with them — ?
>
> Logan just shakes his head: No.
>
> He follows blindly after his dad. And exits.

What this scene dramatises is Kendall wrestling with his dark secret. As he speaks to the uncle, Paul, the audience are asking the question, 'Is Kendall going to confess his secret?' This subtextual question gives the scene such power and tension, and yet on the face of it, the written dialogue couldn't be more banal and unexceptional – a brilliant example of really well-written dialogue, and a brilliantly conceived scene.

Good dialogue so often isn't showy, doesn't draw attention to itself.

This sort of inarticulate dialogue so often feels more real, more recognisable – and more dramatically intriguing – than the dialogue of characters who are able to articulate their emotions and thoughts. Think also about the power of quiet characters, who speak very little.

Subtext in dialogue

Like scenes, dialogue needs to have layers. There needs to be a counterpoint, a friction between what is being said and what is actually going on in the scene – as perfectly demonstrated by the scene above from *Succession*.

Scenes that are obvious in what their story function is should be the exception. The meaning or intent of the scene shouldn't be the text of the scene, it shouldn't be spelt out in the dialogue. It should be the subtext.

Think about oppositions within dialogue – this is where drama, friction, conflict, and tension come from. Beware of 'on the nose' dialogue – characters expressing themselves too readily.

Dialogue isn't about how real people talk, but we can learn a lot about dialogue from listening to how they talk. Much of the time people don't say what they mean, and this can be funny or dramatic but usually interesting. When people talk, there's usually something else going on in their brain, a line of thought that is different to what they're saying. Think about how this works, how you can use it – especially when tackling scenes that feel initially 'on the nose'.

Dialogue and genre

Certain genres will have particular dialogue conventions and expectations. In the TV police procedural, for instance, there is often a tendency towards under-dramatised exposition – those scenes, for example, in which the senior officer describes the information of the case to his team in the squad room, or scenes in which police officers talk about the case to the press. These scenes become viable because they are accurate reflections of the reality of police procedure – but this doesn't remove the need to make these dialogue-heavy scenes about more than just the information they are giving us, to give them a dramatic dynamic that will take the curse off the exposition.

It's important that you identify conventions of dialogue for the genre within which you're working, and find ways, having recognised them, to challenge and subvert these conventions.

Dialogue and story

The way you write dialogue can define the way you pace and structure your story. For instance, make sure you enter and exit a scene dynamically. As a general rule (there will be exceptions!), an uninteresting way to come into a scene is at the actual beginning of that scene – instead cut into the middle of the scene, have the audience have to work to catch up. So, rather than having the start of a scene where characters are methodically (and realistically) introducing themselves to each other, taking a drinks order at the bar, buying something in a shop – in other words all those sorts of mundane dialogue exchanges that do nothing for your story, for revelation of character, for dynamic, dramatic moments of tension and intrigue – come into the middle of an argument, after the drinks have been bought. When you cut into the scene at a moment of energy in the dialogue, the cut from one scene to the next energises and drives the story forward. Avoid dialogue that has no real story purpose in the service of some sort of mundane 'realism'.

Dialogue and the intention of the scene

So often, when dialogue isn't working, it's because the writer isn't certain about the narrative intention of the scene – of what they want the scene to achieve, how it changes the story, moves the story forward. If you understand the intended dynamic between the characters in a scene, it will be so much easier to find the dialogue to achieve this.

Dialogue is speaking and listening

Think about how your characters listen as well as how they speak. Dialogue is a two-way street. To be a good writer you also need to be a good reader and listener. And you need to think about the dynamics of a dialogue scene – the non-verbal behaviour of the listener is as important as the dialogue. Think about how each character within a scene will react to what is being said. It's this rhythm of dialogue and response that will drive the content and arc of the scene.

Dialogue means little without engaged, responsive listening. A character listening should be listening in a particular, 'active' way – listening shouldn't feel passive. Or is one of the points of your scene that the interlocutor isn't listening? Or that they're wilfully misinterpreting what they're being told? Is the scene about your characters blithely pursuing their own agendas, and are you dramatising this lack of connection?

Dialogue and research

Sometimes the best way to address flat, lifeless, predictable dialogue is through research. Research can reveal the sort of authentic detail and colloquial phraseology that feels real rather than received. Dialogue can feel unconvincing when it feels like a version of previously heard TV dialogue. If you do the research, talk to the people in the know, you will come up with the sort of idiosyncratic colour and detail that will bring the dialogue alive off the page – whether that's about dialogue from a particular period, region, job, hobby or activity. Jargon can often feel like a revealing, persuasive element of dialogue.

Distinctive dialogue

The best dialogue is distinctive to character. We all speak differently – accents, verbal tics, rhythms, use of particular words, etc. Quirks of character are often expressed through dialogue. Everyone is to a greater or lesser extent articulate or inarticulate, florid or plain-speaking, verbose or clipped. Think about how your character uses language, how the way that they speak dramatises them as a person – how what they say either reveals or conceals their true nature. All your characters need to speak with their own individual voice.

Characters are dramatised, defined and illustrated not just by what they say, but how they say it. Making speech feel distinctive to character is a key aspect of dialogue. This doesn't mean that you should be aiming to clearly define your character through what they say. As explored elsewhere, sometimes it's just as narratively helpful that what they say and how they say it conceals their true nature.

One of the best examples of a writer whose characters all seem to speak with their own distinctive (and in this case comic) voice is John Morton, writer of *Twenty Twelve* and *W1A*. The verbal tics and often meaningless phrases that his characters use feel so true and well-observed. Morton's dialogue is such a strength of his writing in the way it brings characters to life. The way Morton writes dialogue is an essential aspect of his own voice as a writer –

but the way in which they each speak also brilliantly dramatises each of his characters.

So, work on giving every character a distinctive speech pattern and way of expressing themselves. Think about all the character traits and how they translate into dialogue. But don't make those traits straightforward or too obvious a window into that character. Try to resist the idea that dialogue should instantly reveal character. Characters should be revealed by what they do over the course of a story, the actions they take when presented with choices, *not* instantly by what they say or profess. In many ways, just like life, drama is about what characters *do*, not what they *say*.

The rhythm of dialogue – for instance, the contrast between staccato, blunt speech and continuous speech that runs sentences together – will immediately make two characters feel very different from each other.

A theatre play that emphasised this for me was *Tactical Questioning* (2011) by Richard Norton-Taylor at the Tricycle (now Kiln) Theatre in North London. The play was a verbatim dramatisation of the judicial inquiry into the death in British army custody of Iraqi hotel receptionist Baha Mousa.

Tactical Questioning was striking in that all the play consisted of was a QC questioning six members or ex-members of the British army, and armed forces minister Adam Ingram. None of the dialogue was 'written', it was all edited from the transcript of the inquiry.

It really brought home to me the potential dramatic power of distinctive dialogue, and how the mechanics of dialogue work. There were such contrasts in the varying but distinctive and idiosyncratic speech patterns, rhythms, accents, and use of language between the characters – every character sounded utterly distinctive.

One spoke much too fast in his nervousness, and the chairman kept having to tell him to slow down. One was in a state of repressed fury and spoke monosyllabically. He was abrupt, uncommunicative. The main officer had a totally different way of speaking to the squaddies – far more labyrinthine, and constantly using meaningless words like 'actually', 'in fact' and 'nonetheless'.

The MP Adam Ingram was hugely repetitive and endlessly evasive. His dialogue caused laughter – the transparency of his lying, his desperate evasions, were comical.

What this play reminded me of was that everyone has their own verbal tics, their own rhythm of speech, a different music to the way they speak. Some people constantly go up at the end of sentences, others go down, others speak in monotones. All of this is hugely revealing of character.

Dialogue is also coloured and influenced by situation – for instance, there can be 'tells' and indicative tics if a character is lying. Status is often indicated in dialogue by both deliberation and rhythm of delivery – more assured, higher-status characters tend to talk in a more deliberate, clear, unhurried way than lower-status characters, who are often more hesitant, mumbly and verbally uncertain.

When you're writing dialogue, think like an actor – think about how your characters' voices sound. Try dialogue out, see how it trips off your tongue.

Dialogue as 'voice'

Distinctive dialogue is one of the key indicators, one of the most easily identifiable traits of a particular writer's 'voice'. For instance, writers as different in sensibility as Aaron Sorkin and Jimmy McGovern are most easily recognised by the way their characters speak. Sorkin's work is often characterised by the super-smart, verbose way in which his characters talk; McGovern's through the more economical, often Liverpudlian, working-class, less articulate, tortured dialogue of his characters.

I think this identifying of a writer's voice primarily through dialogue can be slightly misleading. In my view, the important aspects of writers like these two examples are more deeply rooted in theme, story and character – but these differences come out most visibly and obviously through the dialogue.

Dialogue and dialect

Journeying up the M1 motorway from the south of England to the north, stopping at a service station every few hours, I'm struck by the distinct change in accents in different locations – and this isn't just about how people sound, it's about the way they talk: their tone, intonation, cadence of dialogue and even cultural attitude. Social values are subtly different from region to region, country to country. All of this needs to be reflected in dialogue. The more detailed, specific and accurately observed, the more relatable the dialogue will feel.

We all speak with a subtly different accent, dialect, use of colloquial expression. Each regional accent has a slightly or extremely different cadence and use of language. People in different parts of the UK use different words for the same thing (different words for the bread roll: bap, cob, barm cake), and all of these different region-specific uses and phrases will add colour and distinctiveness to the way your characters speak. Find the rhythm, the music of the way each of your characters speak.

Foreign language

There is something to be learnt from our enjoyment of films or TV shows written in a language we don't understand and that is subtitled. When foreign-language stories on screen work for us (English-only speakers), and engage us, it's a reminder of how relatively unimportant dialogue is. Often we can enjoy stories told in foreign languages even more than we enjoy stories told in our own language. If the story and characters work, then the dialogue will work – even if we don't understand it, and in reading it, get fewer of the nuances of performance and emphasis in the way the dialogue is spoken. Because ninety-nine times out of a hundred, it's not about what is said, it's about what is going on under the surface of the scene – what is going on in what is *not* being said; and, as above, in us being able to appreciate the narrative arc and dynamic of the scene through the dialogue.

Some recent examples of foreign-language TV shows or films that are wonderful and demonstrate this universal language of storytelling for the screen:

* *Call My Agent!/Dix Pour Cent* (in the original French version with English subtitles) and *Standing Up/Drôle* – two great examples of shows that are completely engaging because of the quality of the characterisation and storytelling, regardless of language, both created by the brilliant Fanny Herrero.

* *Money Heist* (in Spanish), created and written by Álex Pina.

* *The Worst Person in the World* (in Norwegian), written by Joachim Trier and Eskil Vogt.

* The Jonathan Glazer film *The Zone of Interest*, in which all of the dialogue is in German – with some of the most brilliantly banal yet chilling lines of dialogue.

Watching foreign-language screen fiction that you enjoy is a hugely instructive process for screenwriters. Take a moment to analyse why certain scenes work for you, regardless of the fact that you can't understand the dialogue and are getting some of the sense of the scene through the subtitles. You might think this would seriously undermine your appreciation of the show, but somehow this is rarely the case – effective dramatic storytelling, however culturally specific, is, at its best, universal. If the dynamics of a scene work in one language, they will work in any language. What is of primary importance is the life of the characters, and the clarity of the dynamics of the story, scene by scene. If these work, the dialogue will work, regardless of what language it's in.

An ability to enjoy and appreciate subtitled foreign-language films is a helpful reminder of how film and TV narratives are primarily visual rather than verbal.

Connected to this, there is a certain type of film story where language is a particular issue: a story set in a country where English isn't the first language, but where all the spoken dialogue is in English. This often occurs, for example, in UK- or US-produced World War Two stories set in Europe (where German soldiers speak English with 'German' accents). Think about how you use language. Are you using it in a way that is artificial? Or are you treating it in a more realistic way? And how does this 'artificiality' affect the tonal approach of your storytelling?

Subtitles

Whether you use subtitles when characters are speaking in a foreign language (in a predominantly English-language story) is an important storytelling choice. Sometimes you won't want to have them; you will want the audience to experience a foreign language in the same way as the characters do (i.e. not be able to understand it). But if you want English subtitles under foreign dialogue, you need to write it into the directions.

There are also examples of writers using subtitles to strong comic effect to articulate the subtext of a scene or conversation. One of the best-known examples is in the film *Annie Hall*.

Texting, Messaging, WhatsApp, etc.

In the last few years, a whole other arena of on-screen dialogue has opened up. There is a lovely moment in the final episode of series one of *Only Murders in the Building* that pays off a moment set up in the opening episode: Steve Martin's character finally plucks up courage to send a text to a certain person. (I'm trying to avoid an unnecessary spoiler here!) It's a lovely, human moment that says so much about character in a few simple exchanges of words – all shown on screen. This is an example of hugely effective dialogue (and character interaction) – but all played on a phone screen.

Messaging is such a big part of most of our lives now, with a code, language, and social values all of its own. As with other forms of dialogue (and as stated above), having your audience read from a screen, using computer or phone text as exposition, can be problematic. But this variant of dialogue can also provide enormously rich, affecting and narratively powerful story beats. Think about how people communicate electronically, how this has become so integral and all-pervasive. This form of verbal communication should be an important element to consider in how you dramatise character and story in contemporary narratives.

Dialogue: Conclusions

While dialogue is clearly one of the most important elements of your screenplay, I often find myself advising writers, in trying to enhance the effectiveness of a scene, to avoid writing dialogue. In feedback to writers, one of my most common notes is 'Try not to tell your story in scenes of dialogue; instead tell your story visually. Tell your story through character action, through physical language, through make-up, costume and props.' Dialogue should almost be viewed as a last resort, only to be used when you can't find a way to tell the story of the scene solely through visuals and action.

In life there are certain moments where the cliché that 'there are no words to describe this' applies. This is also true of drama. At certain points in your story, dialogue won't be adequate. Only action – an image, a tableau, a physical exchange – will be able to express the emotional depth and specificity of certain situations. Dialogue can be wonderful, but its usefulness is limited. Another cliché that articulates this idea is that 'actions speak louder than words'. This is also as true of drama as it is of life.

There's a moment right at the end of Noah Baumbach's *Marriage Story* (2019) when Nicole reties the shoelace of her estranged, now ex-husband, Charlie. This small, domestic act is a poetic moment of spontaneous intimacy. No dialogue could have dramatised where Baumbach wants to leave the relationship at the end of the story more effectively and poignantly than this. Film and TV are full of these moments that transcend dialogue.

I read too many scripts where dialogue carries so much of the story, where characterisations and story sag under the weight of the exposition in the dialogue. This has made me value those scripts where dialogue is at an absolute minimum, as a lesson to writers on how it can be done and how wonderful purely visual storytelling can be. Examples include the long middle section of *Cast Away* (William Broyles Jr.); the J. C. Chandor film *All Is Lost*; the opening sequence of J Blakeson's *The Disappearance of Alice Creed*; sections of the brilliant film *Room* (Emma Donoghue); and so many scenes and sequences in *The Godfather* (Francis Ford Coppola and Mario Puzo).

There are enormously powerful moments in life and drama that are non-verbal – a spontaneous embrace, someone bursting into tears unexpectedly, the moment an argument becomes violent. Sometimes, dialogue just won't do, and your story will demand a non-verbal moment or sequence.

There are of course all sorts of different ways to write dialogue, all sorts of different styles of speech, from inarticulately colloquial, observed, relatable exchanges to the more formal: a well-organised, political, religious or patriarchal speech; a news report; a coach or CEO's rallying cry to his team; a private, internal monologue in voice-over; even direct address to camera. There is a place for all these variations of dialogue as an integral part of telling stories for the screen.

Used at its best – judiciously and economically – dialogue is a vitally important, powerful element of storytelling for the screen.

In Brief: Some Principles of Story, Character and Dialogue

* Leave your audience wanting more.

* Questions are what keep us hooked by story – not answers.

* Tell your story with clarity and simplicity.

* The best storytelling is incomplete – let your audience fill in the gaps for themselves.

* Your audience isn't interested in the writing – they're interested in the story. Keep the writer out of the story.

* Dramatic story is about conflict and, finally, the resolution of conflict.

* Dramatic story is about consequences, connections and connectedness, in a progression of escalating intensity. The way the story unfolds should feel both inevitable and surprising at the same time. Everything in a story should connect and feel interdependent.

* Dramatic story is about the tensions that arise from the conjunction of character and location.

* Dramatic story is about both establishing and then challenging the conventions, values and social parameters of your story world.

* The best stories explore universal truths and mysteries. The big ones – What is the meaning of life? And why do we die? – combine the absolutely specific with the universal.

* Political correctness is death to story. The converse – taboos and the forbidden – are the substance of story. Good stories are provocative.

* Story is character in conflict.

* Story is about character actions – like life, it's about what we do, not what we say…

* But it's also about the gap between what we say and what we do…

* And the gap between what we say and what we're really thinking or feeling.

* This subtext is at the heart of good storytelling. There should be a tension between what characters are saying to each other and what is really going on in a scene.

* Successful storytelling – whether drama or comedy – depends on the audience recognising a truth in the actions of your characters.

* Story is about big ideas. We need to be receptive to the stories that surround us every day in our normal lives.

* Whose story are you telling? Consider the perspective or point of view of your whole story and of its every scene.

* What the best stories have in common is a deep sense of humanity, explored with passion.

* Good storytelling is about dramatising the present moment. Your default should be that the scene is about the action between the characters in the moment of that scene, i.e. your story should happen on screen. Drama should feel immediate and urgent.

* So avoid scenes in which characters dispassionately discuss something we have already seen or that has happened in the past or elsewhere (off screen).

* In particular – do not repeat information for audiences.

* Tell your story with economy and focus.

* There is a subtle but important distinction between setting up something that you will later pay off (good), and flagging or signposting story events that are about to happen (bad). Too often, writers will 'mark' or signpost an event that is about to occur by having characters predict or anticipate that event; by so doing they remove the possibility of surprise from story.

* There is so much potential for variety and unpredictability in the dynamic of a three-handed or single-character scene compared to a two-handed scene.

* Detail is persuasive. Ground your story and your characters in specific, idiosyncratic, observed detail.

* Drama is about what happens when you put your characters under pressure or stress.

* Every life is a story. Every life contains thousands of different stories. It's all there, we just have to excavate and shape it: digging out the gold.

* Words versus pictures – this is the screenwriter's constant, ongoing, internal debate.

* Good writing is about accessing, then conveying, an emotional response to an event.

* Good writing is shocking, disturbing, challenging, surprising, unsettling. Life is extraordinary and good writing reflects this. The worst sin is to be boring. Be wild, be crazy, be unfocused and undisciplined – but be daring and never dull.

* Drama is about adversity – both internal and external strife – and meeting uniquely challenging circumstances. Ask the most difficult questions of your character.

* Time pressures are an important aspect of dramatic stories – the ticking clock.

* What questions are your audience asking of your character and their story?

* Does each and every scene change the status quo of your story?

* Character knowledge versus audience knowledge: how much does your character know? And by comparison, how much does the audience know? These questions profoundly alter the nature of a scene.

* Observe structure in all aspects of your own life, and think about how this can be transposed to dramatic storytelling, e.g. the start of the school year, the start of the calendar year… All these aspects of temporal structure have a place in stories.

* Dramatise your story without explaining it. There should be no writer's commentary. And in particular, don't have your characters commentating in dialogue on their own stories, e.g. 'I have a feeling this is going to be one of the most important evenings of my life.'

* Great art transcends the intellect and engages primal emotions.

* Character self-knowledge is death to story. People who are perceptive about other people aren't necessarily perceptive about themselves.

* Give every single one of your characters a story, an attitude, an agenda. Every character in a story needs to be a participant in that story, not just an observer.

* Make sure your characters are emotionally engaged by their situation.

* Avoid dialogue where possible – tell stories in pictures and actions. Facial expression, body language and character action are often more effective ways to dramatise character than dialogue.

* In both life and screen drama, dialogue on its own is woefully inadequate. We are all so much more than – or less than, or different to – what we say.

* Disguise exposition – through arguments, misunderstandings, jokes, awkwardness, lies, etc.

VI

Presentation

Introduction: Getting Your Story onto the Page

Note Whereas in the Craft section of this book I have largely talked about 'audience', from now on I will more usually refer, instead, to the 'reader', as this section is predominantly about how you present your work on the page, and then getting that work read and assessed: the first step on the road to having your ideas and scripts commissioned and then produced.

★ ★ ★

The way you present your script on the page is an important aspect of screenwriting; and 'presentation' also covers the quality and clarity of your writing.

As (screen)writers, all we have are words. Because screenwriting and film stories are so overwhelmingly visual, this essential and obvious fact is rarely discussed. But the difficulties of the medium – conveying through words how a story will play out on film – mean that the way screenwriters use words and language is of critical importance.

Ultimately the way you present your story material and the story material itself merge into one another.

What we write has to be capable of imaginative translation into three-dimensional, physical, on-screen action. Like all stories, screenplays should be open to interpretation, but a director coming to the script should not have to ask the writer what they mean, what their visual intentions are. We need to use words with care, purpose and confidence.

Write economically, sparingly – avoid long, dense, overwritten blocks of directions; or seven-page, two-handed dialogue scenes. Overwrite and your words lose their value and impact, and risk the reader losing faith in the story you're telling.

We all have our own way of writing, our own individual style and 'voice' (see pages 6–10). The more you write, the more you will understand your own strengths and weaknesses, and will learn how to play to your strengths.

But also…

Read screenplays

The more screenplays you read, the more you will understand about the possibilities and limitations of screenplay storytelling and formatting.

Reading good, successful screenplays will show you what's possible, it will inspire you, and importantly it will make you think about how to communicate your own story on the page and how not to. It will teach you the difference between what a good and bad script look like.

Professional readers and writers will have an instinctive understanding and appreciation of this – the right proportion of directions to dialogue; the right proportion of words to white space – the look of a page.

If the script consists of a series of ten-page dialogue scenes with very few directions; if there isn't much dialogue but several sections where there are three-page blocks of unbroken directions; if there is too much text on a page and the font is too small; if it isn't written in acknowledged, professional screenplay format; if it's not written in Courier 12-point, then a reader may have doubts when they start reading it.

> In the Further Reading section from page 306 you will find links to places where you can find scripts to read – the BBC Writers website, and my own site's script library.

Use screenwriting software

It's important that you write your screenplay using screenwriting software so that the layout and formatting is as close to perfect as possible. If you try to cobble together your screenplay using Microsoft Word, however well you mimic conventional screenplay format, your script won't look right. It will look amateur rather than professional. From a professional script-reader's point of view, this will be an immediate negative. This is one of the easier parts of the process to get right. Using screenwriting software will also make the onerous task of writing a screenplay very much easier for you.

The industry-standard screenwriting software, worldwide, is Final Draft. It's expensive but I'd say it's very much a worthwhile investment if you're serious about pursuing professional work as a screenwriter.

There are cheaper or even free alternatives available, e.g. Celtx, Highland 2, Script Reader Pro, Arc Studio, Trelby, and many others. It's worth doing your research and asking around to work out which software might work best for you. But the bottom line is – write your script using screenwriting software, not Word.

Presentation Considerations

Tell your story with clarity and simplicity

Your reader will be happy to go on the story journey with you if the quality of the writing is good – confident, dynamic, articulate, economical.

You need to make sure you are communicating your story clearly and comprehensibly.

Try to avoid clumsily phrased and poorly structured sentences – read through your work and edit it so that it's as well-written as possible. For example, in a script I read this direction, 'Sally gives a stern look at George.' Wouldn't this have read better as 'Sally gives George a stern look'? This may seem picky, but a script full of clumsily constructed sentences like this will not be easy or enjoyable to read.

Make sure what you write is fluent and clear, not overly florid and 'writerly' – e.g. don't use 'verdant' for 'green'.

Respect the language you're using. Avoid misuses such as:

* 'their' for 'there'
* 'loose' for 'lose'
* 'breath' for 'breathe'
* 'right' for 'write'
* incorrect use of apostrophes, etc.

You need to develop a feel for clear and elegant sentence construction in the directions.

Note Dialogue is a different matter – so much of the most effective dialogue is to some extent incoherent or inarticulate. (For more on this, see page 178.)

The reader experience should be as close as possible to the audience experience

As a writer, you need to recognise some of the subtle differences in how the reader and the audience experience your story. For instance, it is often harder for a reader to take on board five new characters all introduced for the first time in the same scene than it is for the audience. As a reader, we cannot see these characters in the same way as the audience can – as unique individuals. As a screenwriter, you need to guide the reader through the story helpfully, helping them to visualise these characters.

You need to write your script to make it as easy as possible for your reader to visualise how it will play – as on-screen action in their mind's eye. Watching a film is a visual experience – and reading the script of the film should attempt to replicate this experience as closely as possible within the acknowledged formatting of screenplays.

This is your challenge as a screenwriter, and the most important principle of screenplay presentation. Even if we all bring our own interpretations to the read, and we imagine your story in our own subtly different ways, write it as we'll see it.

Introducing characters

It's important when we first meet characters that you describe them physically. It's also important that the situation into which you introduce them is not visually neutral. The reader should learn something about this new character not just from your description of how they look, but also through their role within the scene, their behaviour and manner, the way you introduce them into the story – how, for instance, they enter the room, their attitude towards the other character(s), and particularly by what they initially *do* or say.

Introducing a new character into your film is about giving us some guide to their physical appearance, but also making this first impression impactful, distinctive and intriguing.

Imagine your script from the reader's perspective

As a writer of screenplays, it's important to think about the perspective of the person reading your script. The script is a blueprint for how to shoot the film, not like a novel, poem, newspaper or magazine article – forms to be read and enjoyed in their own right.

Reading a screenplay is harder than reading a novel. It's important that you recognise this and work to make your script as clear and easy to read as possible. Speaking as someone who has read many thousands of scripts over many years, it is dispiriting to read a screenplay that is hard to follow and understand.

Open your script on the protagonist

Unless you have a very good reason for not doing so, open the story with the character whose story it is. Sometimes, it's only at page ten that as a reader I begin to realise whose story this is – who we should be following. And many times I will then have to go back over those ten pages to reread them with a different perspective on the material.

Note There are of course many exceptions to this principle that work, but if you do give your character a long, slow build-up, keeping them off screen for some time at the start of your story, be sure this is what you're doing – that it's a deliberate story choice.

Distinguish between what the writer and director brings to the film

There are accepted conventions of screenwriting in distinguishing between what the writer and director bring to the script. As screenwriter, it's not your job to be specific about the way the film is going to be shot, technically. You shouldn't, for instance, describe:

* Shot size (e.g. 'extreme close-up').
* Camera moves (e.g. 'the camera pans slowly across the barren landscape').
* Camera angles (e.g. 'We look down from above at the car racing down the motorway').

This is the accepted convention of professional screenwriting – but it's worth saying that there are rare but allowable exceptions to this principle. There will be times when a certain camera move, angle, shot size, etc., will be absolutely integral to the story.

This distinction between the writer's and director's role also applies to things like writing in 'pre-laps' from one scene to the next (i.e. where the dialogue from the following scene pre-laps the end of the present scene). Some writers use this technique a lot – but you shouldn't, it's not your job.

Similarly, as a writer, you shouldn't write in cues for composed music (that is traditionally a decision for the director). Writing in diegetic music – that is, music played within the action of the scene – is of course fine (and something that isn't used as much or as effectively it could be in many screenplays).

In terms of dialogue, <u>underlining</u> or **emboldening** particular words to emphasise how the writer imagines the actor will deliver the line should very much be the exception – used very sparingly, if at all. In my experience, the decision about how the actor will deliver the line is rarely clear-cut or obvious. And any actor worth their salt will understandably baulk at being instructed by the writer how to stress a particular line ('I will *not* say the line like <u>*that*</u>!') Even just as a reader, I often find myself questioning the suggested use of particular emphasis in how a line should be delivered.

Film-making is a collaborative process, and a script that feels too prescriptive in its instructions to director, actors, designer, composer, etc., will often be regarded with suspicion. At the same time, though, so often the best screenplays sing off the page because of particular details and specifics, so this is a tricky balancing act for the writer. Here is a somewhat random but, in my opinion, insightful and humorous (and very specific!) character description from the unproduced *Boomerangs* by Sonya Desai:

```
A MAN, bearded, sits opposite them. His beard
covers so much of his face it's hard to tell if
he's in his 20s, 30s or 40s.
```

The more scripts you read, the better informed you will be when making these sorts of presentational decisions.

Guiding the reader

Also be wary of using excessive direction to the reader through use of grammar in the directions for action. A plethora of exclamation marks, *italics*, **emboldening**, CAPITALS, etc., to indicate how exciting, emotional or surprising a particular event is will very quickly elicit the response in the reader, 'It's your job to tell the story, it's my job as reader to decide for myself how exciting or otherwise it is, without you leading me by the nose, thank you.'

In some scripts, the writer will CAPITALISE certain words, words that they presumably see as IMPORTANT or IMPACTFUL in the directions. I suggest you don't do this. It will hold up the read, as the reader tries (and usually fails) to understand the rationale as to which WORDS are capitalised and WHICH aren't. (You see, it's DISTRACTING, isn't it?)

You have to allow the imaginative space for director, actors, designer, etc., to inhabit your script and bring their own skills, ideas and interpretations to it. The way you write your screenplay should invite and inspire this spirit of collaboration, while at the same time being utterly distinctive to you and expressive of your individual vision. The script is not a straightforward, prescriptive document for the director. Your directions should be clear without feeling dictatorial or restrictive.

Don't cheat!

What you write should reflect what we will see and hear on screen. Don't 'cheat' by giving your reader privileged information that won't be accessible to your audience. Doing this may make your script easier to understand for your reader but it will also raise difficult questions and considerations. The professional reader will think, 'Okay, so I know all this internalised background information that the audience won't know – how does that change my experience as a reader compared to the viewing experience of the audience?'

As a reader, this extra information will mean that you are experiencing the film in a different way to the audience, and this is unhelpful, misleading and confusing. If you're doing this as a writer, it demonstrates a fundamental misunderstanding about the purpose and intention of the screenplay – of enabling your reader to get as close to possible to experiencing your script as they would to the experience of watching the film. Here are some examples:

* Keep the character descriptions when we meet characters in the script for the first time to a simple physical description (e.g. `Trevor, 16, bad acne, tall with a stoop, scruffily dressed in a worn and dirty school uniform`). Don't be tempted to add,

for instance, `'the son of a single mother, he has severe self-esteem problems. On the quiet he is highly intelligent but uses it for acts of extreme but secret cruelty.'`

If you want to convey all this secondary information about Trevor, you will need to find a way to dramatise it on screen, rather than telling the reader something the audience will not at this point know.

* Don't include in scene headings unfilmable information like `'Two days earlier'`, or `'Several hours have passed since the last scene'`.

All of the above is privileged information for the reader, not accessible to the audience.

Writer's commentary

By which I mean: writers explaining the story or character actions, commentating on events in their story.

Leave out explanation and interpretation in the writing of the directions. We don't get this in the film and we don't want it in the script. This often feels like it unhelpfully gets in the way of the 'cinematic experience' that the reader hopes the read is going to be.

We don't want to know what the writer thinks about their story, we just want to experience it. The directions should present the on-screen action without explaining or commenting on it.

Ultimately, your reader is interested in the story rather than the writing. They don't want the writer and their ego to come between them and the story. So don't – also – draw attention to the writing with your use of language.

(There are occasional exceptions to this – astute or amusing observations by the writer about the story they are telling that sometimes brighten the reading experience – but they are *exceptions*.)

Similarly, we don't want to know what the character is (apparently) thinking in response to the events of the film, in straightforward explanations in the directions – this is more like novel-writing than screenwriting (e.g. `Eliza mulls this over in her mind's eye but we won't yet understand what her response means`). The directions should describe what we will be seeing on screen, nothing more, nothing less.

And the 'nothing less' is equally important. When we come into a new scene, we need the writer to set the scene so that we can visualise what and who we will be seeing on screen. It's unsatisfactory when we're reading a scene on the page and, halfway down the second page of the scene, a different character, whom we had no idea was present, suddenly speaks, thereby only at that point revealing their presence in the scene to the reader. This 'invisibility' of the character wouldn't be the case on screen – so it needs to not be the case on the page.

In the directions at the top of the scene, the writer needs to let us know who is present and what the location looks like.

Some principles for directions

In these clear and simple scene-setting sentences at the top of a scene are some of the trickiest storytelling decisions you will have to make as a writer.

There are several principles here that I think it's important to acknowledge:

> *The directions should feel active, dynamic and economical*
>
> As stated elsewhere (see pages 88–9), movement and dynamism are such important elements of story. Some writers preface a direction with 'We see…' Don't do this. It adds nothing and somehow takes the dynamism out of your writing. 'A car pulls rapidly to a halt' reads better than 'We see a car pull rapidly to a halt.' 'We see…' is superfluous and reminds us unhelpfully that this script has been written by a writer (when what we want to focus on is the story).

The information you give us (and what you decide to withhold) should be absolutely pertinent to the story and character.

The directions should focus primarily on the characters rather than the location or layout

Whenever in doubt, focus on the people rather than the furniture and setting. Over-detailed description of furniture and room layout at the top of the scene often feels deadening and will sap the energy and dynamism from your story. For example:

```
The dining room is modern and tasteful. Around
the large, mahogany dining room table are
six wooden chairs. The table is laid with
smart crockery and cutlery. There are several
tasteful prints and photographs on the wall and
large French doors lead into a mature, three-
acre garden. Philip appears around the door and
looks nervously into the empty room.
```

By the time I've reached the important human action of the scene (Philip looking around the door), I will have got bogged down in all this unnecessary information and my interest will have begun to sag.

Instead, the directions could read:

```
Philip appears around the door and looks
nervously into the large, smartly appointed
dining room. As he enters, he is alarmed to see
that the table is formally laid.
```

There needs to be a narrative, dramatic reason to describe the furniture and props in any detail: a reason that helps dramatise the actions of the characters.

> *Directions should be singular and precise – not plural or general*
>
> Be precise. The film can only show us one thing at a time, and the way you write directions should reflect this. Directions like 'Several people go into the room one after another…' feel unsatisfactory. How many is 'several'? Do we need to see this action of people going into a room repeated like this?

Elements of the Screenplay

These are the (main) elements as listed in the dropdown menu in Final Draft when you're writing your script.

Scene headings

The scene heading (otherwise known – in the US – as a 'slugline') will be written in CAPITALS and should contain –

1. `INT.` or `EXT.` (is this scene interior or exterior?) Sometimes – for instance in scenes in cars – the scene can be both: `INT/EXT.`
2. *Location*, e.g. `INT. BATHROOM` or `EXT. VICTORIA GARDENS.`
3. `DAY` or `NIGHT` – not evening, dusk, dawn, late afternoon.

A few tips about scene headings:

* If a scene is `EXT.`, you don't also have to write 'OUTSIDE' in the location (e.g. `EXT. OUTSIDE JOHN'S HOUSE`). `EXT.` means `OUTSIDE` – so this is needless repetition.

* Scene headings should be `CAPITALISED` but should not be **IN BOLD** or UNDERLINED.

* It is helpful to number scenes in the scene headings – this will make the dialogue between writer and script editor easier when referring to specific scenes. The only caveat is that these scene numbers will change

when you rewrite or restructure the script – but this shouldn't be an issue before the script reaches pre-production. At that point, scene numbers need to be locked off and any further changes tracked so that adjustments are flagged to all departments and factored into the budget and schedule.

Note You should always number pages. From time to time I will read a script without page numbers or scene numbers – which makes it very hard to have a dialogue with the writer about specific scenes or pages!

Action

In the UK, the 'action' is more normally referred to as 'directions'. This is the element that will immediately follow under the scene heading and may well punctuate the whole scene between sections of dialogue. Indeed, often scenes will consist entirely of action with no dialogue. The action (self-evidently) will describe the on-screen action – what we will be seeing on screen.

Getting this balance between action and dialogue right is such an important part of screenwriting. I think the term 'action' (as opposed to 'directions') is really helpful because ultimately it's this that should be described – this element should feel active and dynamic.

So often this is the most important part of the script (yes, more important than dialogue!) – the part of the screenplay that carries most of the story (yes, more than the dialogue!).

The more scripts you read (good and bad), the more you will develop an instinct for what needs to be included and omitted from the directions. It's so important that the directions are written economically and dynamically, with energy, momentum and narrative purpose. Everything in the directions needs to count as a significant part of your story.

You need to tell us (elegantly) who is present in the scene from the top (unless they enter the scene later). The reader needs to have a visual picture of what and who we are seeing on screen.

Scenes with no introductory directions between the scene heading and the dialogue should very much be the exception. There will be very few instances of scenes that don't require directions at the start. A script with a load of scenes that are all dialogue, no directions, rings an alarm bell for the reader. Film is a visual medium – and what we are seeing is as important or more important than what is being said.

Directions should not be abstract or cerebral – they should be physical and specific.

Character names

The name of the character who's speaking must always precede their dialogue. It's important that the character name you use is consistent throughout the script, so don't, for example, alternate between **PHILIP** and **PHILIP SHELLEY**. Stick with either one or the other, otherwise you will cause havoc for the first assistant director trying to schedule the shooting of your script, who will assume these differently named characters are two different people.

Often, a surprisingly tricky aspect of screenwriting is coming up with believable character names, without being boring and using lots of common, dull, featureless names – John, Paul, Mary, Sarah, Philip – apologies if this is your name!

Be careful to differentiate with character names. If, for instance, you have two important characters who are in many scenes together called Benny and Penny (they sound too similar) or Sam and Sally (they look too similar on the page), it can get confusing and frustrating for your reader – and, ultimately, for your audience. Names should be an important defining aspect of your character, and character names need to feel helpfully specific. (Nominative determinism is an interesting issue around character names!)

Avoid having too many unnamed, one-line characters – e.g. **POLICEMAN 1, 2, 3**; **PARTY GUEST 1, 2, 3**, etc. Generally this is a sign that you have too many speaking characters. Often these one-line characters tend to be uninteresting, under-characterised functions of exposition. Having the occasional unnamed character is fine but, in general, if you care about and invest in your characters, you will name them! Every character, however little of the script they're in – even if they only appear in one scene – should have their own story, their own sense of purpose within a scene. Having unnamed characters will suggest to the reader that these characters are flatly functional rather than three-dimensional and definitively individual.

If you find that you have a plethora of one-line characters who are only there to help ease the narrative mechanics of your scene, think about which characters you can conflate. Turning four one-line characters into a single character with four lines may enable you to create someone far more interesting – a character with an agenda, an attitude, a story – not just someone who's there to give your hero flat – even if essential – information.

Parentheticals

Sometimes used between character name and dialogue, these are so-called because they're in parentheses. This is an adjectival or adverbial indication for the reader and ultimately the actor (and director), of how the line is to be spoken, of the mood or attitude in the dialogue, e.g.:

```
              PHILIP
             (angrily)
     I'm not angry.
```

As touched on on page 201, often actors and directors are suspicious of parentheticals in the same way as they are with writers stressing particular words in dialogue. As a writer, you will probably imagine a line being spoken in a particular way – very loudly, tearfully, with a laugh, etc. But resist the urge to be prescriptive. As with line or word emphasis, actors will resist being told how to interpret a line and may well come up with an unexpected but brilliant reading of your line that is the opposite of your parenthetical suggestion – but equally valid. So write the line, and trust the director and actor to find the intention behind it in their own way.

Parentheticals, writer's commentary, indications of emphasis in dialogue – all of these will cut down on choices for the director and actors. Within the scene you have created, give the director opportunities for interpretation.

So parentheticals should be used sparingly and only when you feel as a writer that they are absolutely necessary and important in conveying your intentions, or specific character or story moments.

Dialogue

As with the other elements of a screenplay, the more scripts you read, the clearer an idea you will have about how much dialogue you need. For the professional (over-sensitised) reader, lengthy blocks of dialogue, many speeches over a page in length, many scenes over three pages in length, will immediately elicit scepticism.

Dual dialogue

This allows you to add overlapping dialogue – two characters speaking simultaneously. This can be effective but should be used very sparingly. If used too much, the overall effect may be that the audience won't be able to hear either of the speakers' lines.

Transitions

These are usually characterised by CUT TO on the right-hand side of the page, to indicate the ending of a scene – the cut from one scene to the next.

Whether you need to include a transition like this at the end of each and every scene is debatable. There is a danger that these transitions feel superfluous and repetitive. Many professional scripts do not include transitions at the end of each scene.

Where transitions can come in very useful is *within* a scene – to indicate a time-jump. Jumping time forward within a scene or setting is a valuable storytelling tool, and a deliberately jagged time-jump within a scene will be indicated by **JUMP-CUT TO**.

There are quite a few less frequently used variations to convey a transition from one scene to another, for instance: **SMASH CUT**; **DISSOLVE TO**; **FADE IN** or **FADE OUT**. But I suggest you use these very sparingly if at all – they are more normally seen as directorial rather than writing devices.

★ ★ ★

The way you present your story on the page is about dramatising with flair, focus and economy. There should be nothing extraneous in the way you write your story. Every single sentence should have a purpose, should connect to something else. And while the writing should not be literary and overly florid, it should be dynamic and purposeful.

Once You've Finished Writing

Proofread on paper, not on screen

Once you think you have finished your script, that it's ready to send out, print it out, sit down with a pen and read it through, looking for instances of lack of clarity and typos. You will see things on paper that you missed on your computer screen.

The objective read

Even the most complex and deliberately cryptic stories need to come off the page clearly. This isn't as easy to achieve as it sounds. Have you taken some key story or visual information for granted? Sometimes in meetings with writers, if I don't fully understand a scene, I will ask the writer to explain it to me. So often, once they explain it in conversation, I begin to understand what the scene is about – and I tell the writer that what is clear in their head is not clear on the page. The fact that they know what they mean doesn't mean the reader will automatically understand it unless they write it clearly and fully.

Sometimes it's only when the script is read by someone who is coming to it completely fresh that some very important and fundamental questions are asked about the lack of particular points of story information. For example:

* Why haven't you told us the gender of that character with the gender-neutral name? (Vivien, Lesley, Sam, etc.)

* Why haven't you found a way to tell me that this is set in the year 1992 rather than the present day?

* Why haven't you found a way to give us information about where this film is set?

A few instances of this sort of lack of expositional clarity in the writing can seem like disproportionately big hurdles to the enjoyment of the script for a reader.

It's incumbent on you at a certain point in the process to try your best to stand back from the script you've written and read it in the same way as this outside reader coming to it fresh, with a detached, objective eye. This is one of the hardest things to do as a writer, but it's really important. So once you think you have finished a draft of a script, put it away in the proverbial drawer for a few days, then come back to it with a more detached, objective point of view.

If this proves too difficult, it may be helpful for you to give the script to a trusted friend and ask them to read the script in this way. However, this is a hard thing to ask of someone – anyone doing this may not fully understand what they're supposed to be looking for and what they're not; and it may be that they give you a load of uncalled-for story or creative notes rather than concentrating on the script on a fundamentally expositional and presentational level. So, even if you do give the script to a third party to read, it's important to remember that the ultimate responsibility for making sure that your story is clearly and comprehensibly told is yours.

Sometimes writers, when given feedback about poor presentation, will excuse themselves by saying that this isn't their strength and that they haven't yet had the script professionally proofread. But proofreading is part of writing.

Rereading, correcting and honing your work is a huge part of the process. The 'first draft' you submit should be more like your tenth draft. Once you've written the first draft, you should go back to the script time after time, editing and improving wherever you can, reworking and sharpening the quality of the writing, questioning every line and action. Whether you're doing this for issues of storytelling or presentation will soon cease to be an issue – it's all part of the same process.

Titles

Titles are so difficult but so important. The best titles are memorable in their own right, tell you something of what the show is about, and feel tonally apposite.

Two of the best recent BBC comedy shows, in my opinion, have been *There She Goes* (Shaun Pye) and Tom Basden's excellent family comedy series, *Here We Go*. Even in writing that sentence, I had to go back to the internet to check I'd got both titles right. Both titles are vague, essentially meaningless, unmemorable, uninformative about what the shows are and tonally uninstructive.

A memorable, punchy title will be of enormous help in drawing deserved attention to excellent scripts and shows.

As with so many aspects of screenwriting, opinions about titles are always subjective and I'm sure you'll disagree with some of what I say, but I hope it stimulates you to think about the title of your own script and what makes for a memorable, attention-grabbing title.

* *Fleabag* feels specific and tonally reflective of the show.
* *Back to Life* (which, by the way, is a show I love) feels unspecific and unmemorable.

Titles need to be specific, interestingly odd and attention-grabbing, without being completely 'on the nose' (like *Snakes on a Plane* or *Cocaine Bear*).

* *The Shawshank Redemption* and *The Green Mile* are good titles.

* *Better Things* is a great show with a forgettable title.

* *The Day Today* was a great title – it told you everything about what sort of show this was, and it makes me smile every time I think of it because as a title it's just slightly silly.

* *I May Destroy You* is an excellent title – it perfectly captures the essence and tone of this wonderful show in its hints of power, submission, violence, revenge and ambiguity.

Successful Titles

Here is a list of titles to be debated over (a combination of real titles and titles I've invented) – all of which I think are pretty good:

* *Desperate Children*.
* *The Memory Police*.
* *Fuckwit* (swearing in titles is a cheap and easy way to grab audience attention while at the same time demonstrating street smarts!, like *The End of the F***ing World* and *Inglourious Basterds*).
* *Briefly Gorgeous*.
* *The Man Without Talent*.
* *Black Mirror*.
* *The Dumping Ground* (this title tells you so much of what the show is about in a way that feels emotionally resonant).
* *Micro Aggressions*.
* *Hate Crime* (interestingly ambiguous?).
* *A Boy and His Dog at the End of the World*.
* *Friday Night Lights* – very specific, and evokes what the series is about.

I think these titles would pique my interest in these shows or books (the real ones definitely did!).

Then there are quite simple titles, almost challenging in their straightforwardness – *Normal People*, for instance, or *Marriage Story*.

Perhaps I'm biased because I liked both of these shows – but with *Normal People* there seems to be an interesting, ironic question implied by the title: are these, in fact, *Normal People*? Similarly, *Marriage Story* feels like a statement in itself – this is the story of one particular marriage, even if it's possible to read from the title that this is a film about marriage in general (and ironically the film is actually more about separation than marriage). But I like the simplicity and confidence of this as a title. The Richard Linklater film *Hit Man* is a similarly clear but ironic articulation of what the central character pretends to be (but isn't).

Titles that include names often work well because they feel distinctive and specific (*The Disappearance of Alice Creed*, *The Miseducation of Cameron Post*).

Less Successful Titles!

* *Misbehaviour* – a 2020 film based around a Miss World contest from the 1970s, about gender politics (a really interesting story area). But unless you know this, you won't understand the pun ('Miss Behaviour'). As a title, it feels unoriginal, generic, and ultimately unhelpful in telling you what this is about.

* *Come Again* – a novel by Robert Webb. Brilliant novel, forgettable title.

* There is a whole genre of generally rather excellent, low-key, relationship-based, US indie films with bland, unmemorable titles: *What If* (2013), *Enough Said* (2013), *Begin Again* (2013), *Outside In* (2018), *Other People* (2016), *Shortcomings* (2023). These are all good films but I can never recommend them to anyone (until now!) because I struggle to remember the titles – none of which tell you anything useful about what they are.

* *The Way Way Back* (2013) is another great film with a poor title – annoyingly easy to confuse with another film, *The Way Back* (in fact two different films with this title – 2010 and 2020!).

* *The Godmother* – its antecedents are too obvious, and the first thing you absolutely know about this book is that it isn't going to be a patch on *The Godfather*. Titles that reference other, better-known titles like this almost seem to be saying – before you know anything else about them – 'This is not going to be as good as the show I'm referencing.' As a general rule, I think referring to or winking at more famous titles when naming your new show is not a good idea – it instantly makes your script a hostage to fortune, inviting comparisons with shows that are memorably good.

* *Colin from Accounts* seems to have polarised opinion as to the virtues of its title. Personally, I think this is an excellent title – the unlikely juxtaposition of a quirky romcom with such an apparently superficially dull title makes me smile. The humour and understated irony of the show is reflected in the title. However, I know others have taken it more literally – and come to the conclusion that such an apparently dull title must surely presage a dull show.

So, are there any conclusions to be drawn? Only that the best/most striking titles feel specific rather than generic, in the same way as the best screenwriting is specific rather than general. But also that a weak title is no indicator of weak content – plenty of brilliant shows have poor titles. But a memorable title can really help make your project stand out.

If a script has a title that grabs me, I'm more likely to start the read with enthusiasm.

More examples of (what I think are) strong, distinctive titles:

* *Bridgerton*
* *Better Call Saul*

- *Yellowjackets*
- *Cheaters*
- *Killing Eve*
- *Derry Girls*
- *Happy Valley*
- *Gentleman Jack*
- *Last Tango in Halifax* (an exception to the rule of 'winking at' a more famous title!)
- *The Essex Serpent*
- *Apocalypse Now*

VII

Supplementary Screenwriting Documents

Pre-script Documents: Treatments, Outlines, Beat Sheets

All of these documents are points on the journey to writing a script – and are guaranteed to make even the steeliest writer's heart sink a little. But as writers, you need to learn to embrace them, even if you can't quite get to love them! If you can enjoy the process of creating these documents, it will be an enormous help to your success (and creative fulfilment) as a screenwriter.

One issue is definition. There are so many variations of these documents – both in what they get called, and in their function – and the various names seem to mean different things to different people.

It is really important that you know why you're writing these documents, and who you're writing them for. Every single drama-producing indie and film company, every producer and development executive, will have a different brief, a different agenda, often a slightly different approach. Make sure you know what you're being asked for. Once you've convinced a producer or script editor that your idea is worth pursuing, you need to know what they're looking for in every draft you write.

In particular, you need to distinguish between:

* *Selling or Pitch documents* (written pitches, treatments), written to convince potential employers of the power of an *idea* that you want them to commission you to write up into a script.

And:

* *Development documents* (outlines, beat sheets, etc.), which are documents that you write once a producer has committed to a story idea, developing it on the path towards first-draft script commission. These are mainly for your benefit as a writer – in planning the story, structure, tone and content of your script – but they're also for your producer or script editor to track how the story is developing and help you with their input and suggestions.

They're important!

Once, as a screenwriter, you've written one or more cracking spec screenplays that have started to get you noticed, and potential employers and literary agents have read the scripts and want to meet you, these shorthand documents (everything that isn't a script) are of vital importance to your building and sustaining a career.

From a professional point of view, it's really important for writers to get their heads around the idea that they need to nail the skill of writing these pre-script documents. They are the gateway to script commissions and an income! In developing and building your story through a pitch, outlines, beat sheets and scene-by-scenes, you'll be more easily able to take on board big story, conceptual and structural changes, to experiment with the way you tell the story, than if you were doing the same thing with a finished script.

Writers are generally less emotionally attached to an outline than a script, and so find it easier to omit what may not be working and try out new ideas, to experiment with both content and form, to try out radically different narrative and structural changes.

I have come to realise over the last few years – working with so many wonderful writers – how good these documents can be at their best. There have been several outlines written for the Channel 4 screenwriting course that I have enjoyed almost as much as a brilliant script. At their best, outlines can be gripping, exciting, emotive pieces of visual storytelling that give a clear indication that the script that follows is going to be equally wonderful.

I haven't yet read an exciting, excellent outline that doesn't become an exciting, excellent script.

On the other hand, written pitches for your idea – the first step – shouldn't be viewed as pieces of structured storytelling in the same way as outlines and scene-by-scenes are. Writing a pitch is a very different skill to writing a screenplay. As skilled screenwriters, you need to be equally adept at writing brilliant pitches and outlines.

Pitching: Verbal and Written

Pitching – both written and verbal – is an essential part of your work as a screenwriter. Even when producers know your work as a writer and are keen to work with you, they will want as much evidence as they can get that your story or project is going to be brilliant, before they take that big financial step of commissioning you to write the first draft of a script.

This means that a significant part of your life as a working screenwriter will *not* be writing scripts – but pitching (verbally and in writing) ideas, and then developing them further in response to a production company's feedback.

While the way you shape the stories you're going to pitch is dictated by all of the same principles you use to write your screenplays, there are skills that you need for pitching that are very different to those for screenwriting.

An introduction for screenwriters into what pitching is and what it means for you as a writer in the UK often comes from initiatives at events like the Studio21 drama series competition and the London Screenwriters' Festival, where selected writers have to get up on stage in front of an audience to do a one-minute verbal pitch – a performance – of their idea. This unique form of torture bears no relation to the reality of how you will use pitching to gain work in the UK TV and film industries (but, arguably, is a way to get your projects in front of a lot of potential buyers).

Generally speaking, your verbal pitches will take place in a room with one or two other people as part of an informal conversation. You won't be expected to 'perform' your pitch, just to discuss your ideas and hopefully interest the listener enough for them to want to ask particular questions and start a conversation around the idea.

During the last twenty-five years, I have been sat on the other side of the desk from hundreds of writers pitching. The actual word 'pitching' is rarely used in this context. More often, the prompt will be along the lines of, 'Are there any particular ideas you're thinking about at the moment that you'd be interested in sharing with us?' In fact the industry in general is suspicious of screenwriting 'jargon'. In most instances people actually working in the business will get twitchy if you start talking in the language of screenwriting manuals.

Don't 'perform' your pitch!

From personal experience, on the occasions when a writer has clearly memorised their pitch and gone into a form of performance to articulate it, my overriding response is to be a bit freaked out by how a normal, informal conversation has suddenly been turned into a more formal performance that brooks no interruption.

When it's just the two of you in a room together, this feels a bit weird; and more often than not I become transfixed by the performance aspect of the pitch and find myself failing to actually listen to what is being said – which has been hijacked by *how* it is being said.

To some, there is a negative connotation to the word 'pitching' (just as there is about 'networking' – more on which on pages 262–3), which is normally to do with this performative aspect. But let me be clear about this: the pitchee – the person you're pitching to, the potential employer – likes a performative pitch as little as you the writer do. We don't want to be 'pitched at', we want to have an informal, spontaneous conversation about your ideas.

This isn't to say that there is never a time or place for more formal pitching. For example, there will be instances when a writer has pitched or discussed an idea with a producer or production company. The producer likes this idea, contacts the broadcaster (or in the case of film, a financier) who they think will 'get' the idea, and asks for a meeting at which this idea can be aired, bringing you the writer along to this meeting to pitch it.

In this instance, the stakes have gone up a notch from the initial meeting, although at this stage you will also have the support – moral and hopefully practical too – of the producer with the shared vested interest in helping you prepare for this meeting. But often in this situation a producer may say, 'Just pitch it to the broadcaster (or commissioning exec or funder) the exact way you did to us.' Suddenly what started as an informal discussion with a producer threatens to turn into a formal pitch in front of a room full of people.

So you will have to be braced for the occasional situation where there is no escape from the formal pitch. Even in this situation, however, nine times out of ten, the broadcasting exec will feel similarly to the producer with whom you initially discussed the idea, and will want the meeting to feel as informal, discursive and organic as possible.

The producers and commissioners involved in decision-making about whether to put money into a project will more often than not feel more positively towards it if they also feel (through conversation and development of the idea) that they are at least a small part of the creative drive behind the project.

So, rule number one for verbal pitching: if at all possible, make it a conversation, a normal, social interaction, not a performance.

The context of the pitch

One important thing to remember as a writer coming in to meet a script editor, development executive or producer, is that you're there because they're interested in your writing, they feel positive about you as a writer and are potentially interested in working with you. What they are looking for are those common areas of interest they may share with you, to be reassured that working with you is going to be creatively productive and enjoyable. So you as a writer need to be doing almost as much listening as 'pitching' in this situation. And remember: you're there because they like your writing, they already feel to some extent invested in you as a writer.

The quality of the idea

I can't stress this particular point strongly enough: it is never about how well you perform or articulate your idea, it's about the quality of the idea. A good idea can survive a bad pitch, but a bad idea pitched with skill and thorough preparation is still a bad idea.

In any potentially stressful meeting, interview or pitching situation like this, I would always suggest that you make notes in preparation and have them to hand during the meeting. You shouldn't use them if you don't need to, but it's a helpful security blanket to know that you do have them if your mind suddenly goes blank. No reasonable person will object to this. In my experience, seeing a writer come to a meeting or interview with notes that she or he refers to, is a positive and encouraging sign that the writer has thought about the meeting in advance and has prepared well.

But I would advise you in a meeting not to read your pitch verbatim from your piece of paper (or phone notes). As above, this will give it an unhelpful feeling of 'performance' and will often turn a conversation in which producer and writer are connecting on a personal, creative level, into a situation where meaningful communication suddenly ends. If you're reading your pitch, it will be very hard for you to make it feel spontaneous and lively. You will lose eye contact and therefore your ability to 'read the room' and respond to the non-verbal communication coming back from the other side of the desk. Normal, conversational eye contact is important – just as it is in any conversation. I've also been in meetings where a writer will open up their laptop and read from this. This can feel like the laptop screen is some sort of physical communication barrier between you and the writer.

Meetings and written pitches

Then there is the question of whether you bring along a written, printed, (normally one page) version of the idea/s you know you're going to be verbally pitching, to hand over to the pitchee if they're interested. This is a tricky one. I would advise you generally to bring these along, but not to make the decision to hand them over (or even admit to having them!) until the end of the meeting.

It may be that in conversation the idea has changed, grown, or headed in a direction you hadn't anticipated pre-meeting, and that as far as this producer is concerned your written version is now obsolete. It may also be that by the end of the meeting you have decided that this is not someone you want to work with!

Copyright and ownership

There are also issues of ownership and copyright to consider. It may be that you leave behind two or three written ideas and the producer then gets back to you or your agent saying that they aren't in fact interested in pursuing any of these ideas – in which case you may feel a little uneasy about having handed these documents over to them when you know you are now going to be pitching them to other producers.

This whole area of 'copyright theft' is a tricky one.

In my long experience of the industry, the instances of a producer cynically stealing other writers' ideas and either passing them off as their own or handing them on to another writer are mercifully rare.

What does happen sometimes, however, is that very similar ideas arise or are developed at the same time by different companies or writers. There is something in the ether or zeitgeist that means this happens frequently.

It may also happen that a producer loves the idea you pitch but not the way you pitch it, or the way you want to tell this particular story – but that they may, some time later, then develop a similar idea with a different writer, even though it was you who planted the seed of that idea in the producer's mind.

Is this theft? Not exactly, but it's undoubtedly a morally murky area. One of the things you need to acknowledge as a writer is that the basic idea is one thing, but how you personally dramatise it is quite another. Ideas in themselves are important – but the clincher is what you as a dramatist bring to this idea.

It's good to remember that once a producer buys your idea, it technically becomes their property rather than yours. Often, while it may not make obvious financial sense, it can make creative sense to explore your options in some depth with a producer before you commit to a financial arrangement over a project – with all the issues of ownership that that entails.

But as a writer, if you're lucky enough to have a series of general meetings with indies, you need to keep a record of each of the ideas you introduced in each meeting and you (or your agent) need to follow up so that you have a definitive record of which project that company wishes to pursue with you and which they don't.

You should also understand that, until they make a financial commitment to you and option that project, you are free to pitch it wherever you want (although obviously it's not wise for you to promise verbally that you won't do this if you're going to).

Trust

I think the important principle to abide by in these initial creative encounters with producers and other potential employers is that you should act in good faith towards them. Trust them, be generous to them, and understand that they will do the same with you – and continue to do so unless and until they give you genuine reason not to do so (which in my experience is very rare).

A starting point of a lack of trust in producers, and a paranoid fixation with protecting the copyright of your idea at all costs, feels unrealistic and unnecessary. Generally, this will mark you out as an amateur rather than professional writer. The industry operates (initially, before the contractual negotiation begins) on a basis of trust; and I think this should be your default position as a writer.

One of the keys to your success as a professional, working writer is an ability and willingness to get ideas out of your head and into the real world where people might want to pay money for them.

This is another area where your own or your agent's research and background knowledge will come in handy. No independent production company worth their name will want to have a reputation for stealing ideas or treating writers badly. It's a small, gossipy industry and we all speak to each other. Bad practices are talked about.

Pitching: essential elements?

It is so easy to get hung up worrying about all the different elements that can go into a pitch, for instance: the big idea at the heart of your project; its USP (Unique Selling Point/Proposition); an idea of how the three-act story plays out in a sentence or two; your protagonist; something about what defines the central characters, the relationships between them and the big story question that confronts them; the antagonist of your story and how they interact with your protagonist; the tone of your story – the style and tone of how you will write this story to make it feel unique and compelling?; the genre or combination of genres that you're using to dramatise this story; your unique, personal take on this story, and what it means to you; useful comparisons to other shows…

I could go on. All of these elements are worth considering and have a place in certain pitches. But I want to debunk the idea that there is some sort of foolproof template to make sure you do full justice to your idea in a short pitch. Just as there is no foolproof structural template for your script, nor is there one for the pitch. In my experience, if you as a writer try to cover all of these questions with a universal structure or template, you will get lost in the detail of your pitch, you will lose sight of the wood for the trees, and your pitch will come across as overstuffed and lacking focus. You need to find the most effective form and approach for each particular idea.

These opinions have been formed by many years of running courses in which I invite a room of twenty writers each in turn to pitch their idea in a maximum of one minute (or even sometimes thirty seconds).

Often, the shorter the pitch, the better, because the brevity of the pitch forces you to distil your idea down to its essence, and forces you to remind yourself what excited you about the idea in the first place. And this is what we want to know: why do *you* think your idea is a good one? What excites you about this idea?

If you can distil your brilliant idea down into a single page that is going to excite producers, it is more likely to get read and taken seriously than a speculative twenty-page document.

If you have a huge checklist of elements you hope to include, the pitch begins to feel more like a shopping list than an idea you love, as you neurotically try to cover every single base.

Another thing to avoid in a pitch (whether verbal or written), in my experience, is a detailed plot chronology, particularly if you haven't pre-empted this with any context (whether that context is narrative, character or tonal). The pitches that are hardest to get excited about or make sense of are the ones that fall into the rhythm of…

> …and then they all go outside and they see a car passing so they go back inside and three hours later another car passes so they troop out again but not before they've had a big meal but when they're outside again they start to fall asleep… Oh did I tell you they had a big meal, that's why they fall asleep but meanwhile Minny is still hiding in the attic. Oh yes, I should have said, Minny is the youngest child who has been hiding in the attic for the last two years. Where was I? Oh yes, so they're now all outside again, waiting for cars and now it's dark…

This sort of stream-of-consciousness, unfiltered, unedited and unskilful regurgitating of plot is so hard to listen to because you have no anchor in the story, no sense of *why* the writer is telling the story. Don't get bogged down overexplaining the rules of your story world.

Character is more important than plot. Why should we care about the character at the centre of your story? What is the human or emotional connection between your characters and the audience? (For more on this, see pages 66, 67 and 93 and the chapter from page 126.)

The incomplete pitch

Throw out a hook, don't try to tell your pitchee the whole story.

What you are trying to do (and this applies to both verbal and written pitches) is convey to the pitchee your excitement in the idea you're pitching, your passion and conviction, the reasons why you think this project will be brilliant. Your pitch can never (and shouldn't try to) be the complete package. What you should be trying to do is start a conversation – interest the pitchee enough in your idea that they will want to ask questions and invite you to fill in some of the gaps, get a conversation flowing around this starting point of the pitch.

Seeing a pitch as a complete package in itself, to which the answer is either yes or no, is not, in most instances, helpful to you the writer, or realistic.

The most important aspect of your pitch is your belief in it. This is so often the thing that attracts the person you're pitching to – your enthusiasm must communicate itself.

Pre-meeting research

Your ideas should be coloured by who you're pitching to. When you're invited in for a meeting about your work as a writer, research into the people and company in question is invaluable.

The people on the other side of the desk may be reluctant to acknowledge this, but a writer articulating intelligently and specifically why they like shows the company has made is very helpful. It is the first indication that this may be a working relationship that could be fruitful. It is also flattering: everyone likes their work being positively recognised. Obviously, you should only do this if it's genuine, but don't be backward in coming forward if you have genuinely nice – and interestingly specific – things to say about the work of the people and company you're meeting. And the better you know their work, the easier you will find it to choose which ideas you pitch to them.

What's your story?

This is of vital and fundamental importance. Is your story the sort of one-line pitch that will make other writers say, 'Of course! Why didn't I think of that?'

Find stories that you believe are compelling, gripping and enthralling. If you do this, then it's quite hard to go wrong. Conversely, if your one-line pitch, your logline, is unexceptional, if you're unsure about it as you pitch it, then it's very hard for the pitching to go right – in other words, it doesn't matter how well-written any document is, if the essential story premise isn't exciting and if you don't have real confidence in it, it will be a huge uphill struggle all the way through the process.

Particularly as a new writer without a screen credit, your ideas have to be exceptional. You are competing against Sally Wainwright and Jed Mercurio, Richard Curtis and Abi Morgan, so your ideas have to be really outstanding to justify a producer backing you – a new writer without any track record.

Know what genre your story is

What genre does your story fit into? How are you subverting this familiar genre? How does this story idea fit into the history of that genre? What are you bringing to the genre that is fresh and unexpected?

Be clear about what it is in the story that excites you, and the tone you are aiming for. (For more on genre and tone, see pages 48–54.)

The form of the written pitch

There are all sorts of different ways to write and structure a pitch. You have to find the form that brings out the best in your particular story idea.

Here are some examples of different forms of effective, enjoyable written pitches that I have read:

* One that opens with a half-page dialogue exchange between the two central characters.

* A pitch in which 90 per cent was description of a single, short sequence that set up the whole story powerfully and emotively.

* Characters themselves pitching their own story or describing themselves in their own words.

* A pitch written in the form of a scene in which a writer pitches an idea to a producer.

* One describing how the writer came across this story: how someone told the writer this story, and their personal connection to it.

Written Pitches – Some Technical, Detailed Points

* It's always a good idea to submit your documents as PDFs.

* Include title, writer's name and contact details.

* Font size – no smaller than 12-point. Documents written in fonts smaller than that, with long, dense blocks of text, are instantly discouraging for the reader. Your pitch documents need to look uncluttered and have plenty of white space.

* This isn't an exercise to see how much text you can cram into one page, *but*, as a general principle, make the document as short as possible while still feeling that you are doing justice to the project.

- ★ Layout, paragraphs and formatting – print your page off and think about how it looks. Is it welcoming, well laid out and professional-looking?

- ★ Fonts – without going over the top with a font that is absurdly showy, make sure that your font is clear and interesting to look at. 12-point Calibri, for instance, just looks a bit... boring. (I realise this is highly subjective! But think about what font you can use to make the document as engaging and easy to read as possible.)

Deliver content

It's always important to really deliver on the story front – to demonstrate through story events and character action just how exciting, moving, emotive, etc., this is going to be (rather than just writing, 'This is going to be the ultimate emotional roller-coaster – exciting, moving and emotive...'). Deliver, don't tease. And if your story has the most wonderful narrative twist or reveal, tell us what it is. This isn't the place to hold back.

The less-good pitches deal in empty promises. It's a good idea to convey your sense of excitement as a writer in a project, but it needs to be backed up by hard evidence.

So, if you're pitching a comedy, your one-page pitch has to be funny. And similarly, drama pitches need to be inherently dramatic – and that's tough.

Pitch decks

This is a phrase that is used more and more frequently. A 'pitch deck' implies a visual element to your pitch, to complement the text. You need to be judicious in your use of images. You need to be convinced that the images you use genuinely add to the richness of the story, that they elevate and improve the overall pitch. Sometimes the use of pictures and photos can feel unhelpful – for instance, when you give us a photo of a famous actor alongside a character description. Often, this will both rob the reader of the ability to imagine the characters as they want to from how you've described them, and will lead to judgements such as 'You should be so lucky that that pictured actor would be available or interested!'

As with every aspect of the story, the imagery you use needs to feel distinctive and utterly specific to the idea – not just generic images used to break up the text and make the presentation easier on the eye.

But key images can express the essence of your pitch poetically, economically and powerfully.

Visual details

What you remember or take away from the best one-page pitches is often a telling, memorable visual image that defines the lead character, story or tone – the image you might find on the film's poster. (I am talking here about images described in the writing, although this can also apply to actual images.)

As with every aspect of screenwriting, planting a memorable signature image in the reader's mind is one of the keys to reinforcing the power of a story or character.

References and comparisons

References to other shows can be very useful if they feel specific and illustrative. For instance, I worked on a project that the writer described as '*Fargo* meets *Local Hero* meets *Happy Valley*', which really helped me understand what he was trying to achieve – even though the project actually has a tone and character all of its own.

Sometimes, though, these sorts of references become a hostage to fortune. If you're referencing a brilliant show, there has to be an equivalent touch of brilliance and originality in your pitch.

Writer's agenda, and theme

With one-page pitches and treatments, it's often helpful to open with some sort of overview that expresses the idea as succinctly and persuasively as possible, and that states your agenda as a writer for pursuing this project, and something about the story's themes – what it's about.

The hardest pitches to read are those that are pure plot with no sense of tone, context or writer's approach. The plot and characters – the substance of the story – will be far more accessible if we read them knowing why you as a writer are telling this story, what you bring to it, and why it's a story you *need* to write. It's all about context.

And remember, you're not just pitching an idea, you're also pitching yourself as a writer to some extent – justify why you are *the* writer to tell this story. At this time, when producers are looking for an ever-increasing diversity of voice and story, this connection between the writer and their material is important. It's great to get a sense of the writer's conviction and passion for the story they're telling, their emotional investment in their own characters and story. The writer's relationship to their material is key.

Character biographies

I would suggest as a general rule that you don't write separate character biography lists within a short pitch document. You shouldn't have room to do this. Try to introduce the characters within the context of the story, the idea. The tone and context of your story should do the job of introducing and illuminating your characters. Reading lists of characters with one- or two-sentence biographies often feels like information overload; it's hard then to see how all of these characters will fit into the story.

Loglines

The logline can broadly be described as a one- (or at most two-) sentence description of the story of your project. This can (and probably should) be part of your pitch, and is something that you should be constantly returning to and honing as you develop and write up this project.

If you can excitingly encapsulate the dramatic potential of your idea in a single sentence, that is a powerful selling ploy. It will persuade potential employers not only that this is an exciting proposition, but also that you as a writer have a clear handle on exactly what story you want to tell.

The world is full of loglines – every time you scroll through Netflix, BBC iPlayer, etc., one-line pitches are there to grab you. It's indicative of how hard it is to come up with compelling loglines that even many of these projects that have been made, marketed and had millions of dollars spent on them, still don't have persuasive loglines! (For more on loglines, and some examples, see pages 40–1.)

Pitching – sealing the deal

This is a business. Producers' development budgets are very limited, and they need to be really confident about an idea before they spend money on it. They have to believe that your idea is going to cut through the huge quantity of ideas being developed all across the UK and is going to stand out for commissioning executives. Be realistic – your ideas have to be AMAZING. And you have to have that strong belief in them.

In relative terms this is the best time ever for new writers to be trying to get original shows made. High-profile, authored shows are being commissioned from brand-new writers who have never had a credit, in unprecedented numbers. Don't get me wrong, it's still incredibly difficult, but it feels like the TV and film industries are willing to 'take risks' on brand-new writers in a way that wasn't the case previously. It seems now to be much more healthily about the quality of the material regardless of the profile of the writer.

And this is something that is brought home to me at the end of every year's 4Screenwriting. There is an industry feeding frenzy for the best writers – in fact, recently, *all* the writers. As writers who have all written an outstanding spec script, if they have good ideas, these ideas will be picked up by producers.

Here are some examples of writers who have had their own, authored shows greenlit quite soon after finishing the Channel 4 screenwriting course:

* Charlie Covell – *The End of the F***ing World* (Channel 4).
* Paul and Michael Patrick Clarkson – *Red Rose* (BBC).
* Adam Usden – *Zero Chill* (Netflix).
* Anna Symon – *Mrs. Wilson* (BBC).
* Theresa Ikoko – *Grime Kids* (BBC).
* Catherine Moulton – *Code of Silence* (ITV).
* Grace Ofori-Attah – *Malpractice* (ITV).
* William Mager – *Reunion* (BBC).
* Camilla Whitehill – *Big Mood* (Channel 4).

And feature films:

* Theresa Ikoko – *Rocks* (2019).
* Kitty Percy – *She Will* (2021).
* Archie Maddocks – *Gassed Up* (2023).

Recently, a very good literary agent called me, wanting to take on more clients because she can't keep suggesting the same oversubscribed people, and asking for suggestions.

So the indications I get from the industry are that if you are a talented, hard-working writer, there are real opportunities.

And if you are genuinely enthusiastic about the idea you're pitching, and believe in it, you will pitch it well. It's not supposed to be a complete package – it's just supposed to pique interest and initiate a conversation and questions about the idea.

A successful pitch works when you cannot help but communicate your excitement about the story you're telling. That's what everyone wants to hear. In many ways, this is a confidence business – one of the key factors in persuading someone of the virtue of your project is your own confidence and belief in it.

Recently I read a three-page pitch outline of a brand-new idea by one of the writers I am working with. When I got to the end, even though I was alone, I laughed out loud with pleasure at how good it was. When I told the writer how much I'd enjoyed it, she told me how much she'd enjoyed writing it – this enjoyment shone through in the writing.

Do try your pitch out on other people before your meeting. You can learn so much from other people's responses, even from their facial expressions. Clarity is all-important – there is nothing more off-putting than not being easily able to understand the pitch. Get your trial listener to tell you if they understand the idea. But you shouldn't have to ask the pitchee – if they like it, they will inevitably tell you. Good stories are universally appealing.

You have to believe that the ideas you're pitching *need* to be made, and that they will be the best films, or shows on TV. And you need to be able to explain why you are not only the best but the *only* person to write this particular story. Communicate your passion, inspiration, distinctive vision. What are your strengths as a writer? What can you bring to this story that no other writer can? Why is this your story? What is personal to you about the story? Why are *you* the writer to tell this story?

Because in the case of all of those greenlit projects that are being made, the writer and producer will believe all of this and will have persuaded the commissioner or financiers.

Get into the mindset that you are going to be constantly sharing your ideas. Don't hide your stories away.

As screenwriters, you need to work hard at creating this portfolio of knock-out ideas. For professional writers who have written really good scripts, who are in a position where their spec script has started to open doors for them, there is an industry of indies out there – development executives, script editors, producers, and literary agents – competing with each other to find these good ideas.

So you need to be constantly, consciously looking for stories that you want to tell. How do you access these stories? Turn to page 11!

Some Written Pitches

Here are some examples from one-page pitches, which demonstrate how they can work at their best...

In this case, in expressing the themes – the writer (Sarah Page)'s agenda:

> SPOILED *is about generational responsibility – should we leave the world a little better than we found it, should we do everything we can to ensure our children have a better future than we had? Should parents give up their savings, or even their dreams, to help their kids succeed? But what if the kids then, in turn, do the same for their children?*

A clear, economical expression of something that seems to be quite zeitgeisty, but also universal. And the story itself – about a father trying to protect his son, after the son has been responsible for killing a pedestrian in a road accident – clearly dramatises those themes.

Here is writer Anna Symon articulating her agenda for telling a story:

> THE CONTRACT *is about the takeover of the British state by multinationals such as G4S and Serco. Although entirely fictional, it is inspired by real stories and the result of intensive research.*
>
> *Between them, G4S and Serco not only provide a vast swathe of the UK's security services (running prisons, immigration, Olympics security, etc.), they are also increasingly involved in health and care provision. As the state is slowly run down, the government will become increasingly subservient to these corporations. Quite simply, one day soon, the country will not be able to run without them.*
>
> *These multinationals have tentacles that stretch into all of our lives. Who are they accountable to? If things go wrong, where does that leave us, the users of these services? It's certainly in the interest of these global providers to keep any 'blunders' under wraps. Running old people's homes and hospitals is big business; providers seem to be willing to go to almost any length to keep their contracts. Are these companies, like the*

> *banks, now simply too big to fail? Will they — with the government's help — do* anything *to continue to serve us?*

I think the writer passionately and articulately expresses her reasons for writing this thriller. There is a strong political agenda and a clear sense of moral indignation — which instantly made me buy into this story.

Questions to Ask of Your Idea and Pitch

Context and presentation are nothing without a knockout idea. Here are a few questions to ask of your idea (and process), to work out whether the project you're considering is worth taking further:

* How/why is the idea exciting to you? Are you conveying this?
* What is your emotional connection to the idea?
* What is your personal connection to the idea?
* Why are you the best/only writer to tell this story?
* Does the way this pitch is written convey your unique style/voice/take as a writer (the conjunction of story and voice)?
* What is the inspiration for this idea?
* What does your idea tell us about the world today?
* What is unique about this idea?
* Is your idea inherently dramatic/comic? And is this inherent drama/comedy encapsulated in the pitch?
* If this is a comedy, is your pitch funny?
* What is/are the key image/s for your pitch?
* Are you laying it all on the line — not withholding key story moments, important reveals and/or twists?

- ★ What is the human/emotional connection between your characters and the audience?
- ★ Is your idea expressed with total clarity and economy?
- ★ Who are you pitching it to? Are they the right people for this idea?
- ★ Have you researched the people/company you're pitching to?
- ★ Have you made preparatory notes for this meeting?
- ★ Does your short pitch document look appealing and professional on the page?
- ★ Can you find a distinctive, entertaining, illuminating way of pitching your story?

Story Documents: Outlines, Beat Sheets, or Scene-by-Scenes

Developing an idea

Following a successful pitch, once a producer has bought into your idea, you'll begin to work together on development documents. As a script editor or producer working on a new project, much of the critical development process with the writers is the work they do pre-script – initially pitching and discussing the idea, writing that idea up into a one-page document, and then beyond that into an extended written outline for the film or series as a whole, and then into a detailed beat sheet of the first episode.

For production companies with limited development budgets, this process of developing an idea before a full script commission is critical. It can remove some of the financial risk of paying a script fee – because screenwriters are typically paid only 10 per cent of their script fee for (often several drafts of) this initial outline.

The fact is that as a professional screenwriter in the UK you will need to be constantly developing a fund of new ideas, and once you interest a producer or development executive in these ideas, you need to be prepared to work on them in pitch, outline, treatment or 'series bible' form (see Glossary), in order to win a script commission.

Learning from the best…

…is a problem because really great examples of these documents are hard to come by. Unlike screenplays, they don't seem very often to make their way onto the internet for public consumption.

I'm not exactly sure why this is – except for the fact they're so very hard to get right! And because, even more than screenplays, they're just seen as a step towards something else, rather than documents to be read for their own sake.

> In the Further Reading section of this book, on page 308, there is a link to the Script Library on my website – this is a rare place where you can find a collection of outlines to read.

Visual, dramatic storytelling

For me, the most important principles of writing effective outlines, beat sheets or scene-by-scenes are to write visually and explain nothing. The outline has to work in the same way as the script. It needs to dramatise the story and leave interpretation of the story action up to the reader.

When writers fill outlines with explanations of character motive, it gets in the way of the story action, and defeats the purpose of the document – which is to show how the story is going to be dramatised. So, dramatise; don't explain.

A TV Pilot Episode Outline

This is a sequence from a six-page outline written by Regina Moriarty for the first one-hour episode (forty-six minutes excluding adverts) of a Channel 4 three-part serial – i.e. the final story document created by the writer before she wrote the first draft script:

> *Laurie and her son George sit in the headmistress's office. They have three black eyes in a row. Laurie looks totally numb. They listen to a recording George made of a group of boys shouting ferocious abuse at him. The headmistress shifts uncomfortably in her seat. She tries to turn the recording off but can't. The abuse escalates. She pushes at the buttons trying to turn it off. The volume increases. George turns it off.*
>
> *The flustered headmistress says it's not acceptable to record other pupils without their knowledge. She talks about procedures, protocols and counselling. She says that she thought Laurie was 'on the same page' as the school on this matter and is frankly surprised that they would jeopardise the mediation process in this way.*
>
> *As they leave, Raymond Raisin, who is the size of a man, is sitting outside the headmistress's office. He makes a gun gesture at George's head as they pass and mouths 'snitch'.*
>
> *Laurie and George drive home in silence.*

I like many things about this bit of outline – it is a shining example of how these story documents can work at their best. When I first read this, I was hooked. I was immediately engaged by the two lead characters, Laurie and George, and I wanted to know what would happen next. Even this short section gives a clear example of the slightly heightened tone – drama with a hint of dark comedy, but all rooted in a recognisable reality.

This section shows how the story will cut from scene to scene and these cuts energise the storytelling effectively – for example the cut from Raymond Raisin's threat to the silent car journey.

The headmistress's office scene shows a strong sense of original, comic, visual storytelling (the three black eyes in a row) and an appreciation of character dynamics within a scene (the headmistress 'shifts uncomfortably in her seat' and can't turn off the tape recorder). There's a pleasing irony to the way the child, George, has the status, controls the technology – and therefore the scene. And the characters' emotional states are dramatised rather than explained.

PART TWO
THE CAREER

Introduction

'WE DO NOT ACCEPT UNSOLICITED SCRIPTS' is what the industry seems to say most loudly to new writers trying to break in.

From the Clerkenwell Films website (a TV and film production company that has a brilliant record of nurturing and working with new writers):

> We only read material which has been submitted to us via a recognised literary agent and are unable to accept any unsolicited scripts or treatments.

So you look at literary agent websites, such as Casarotto Ramsay & Associates...

> Please note that any unsolicited scripts, treatments or other reading materials sent to us will be deleted unread.

In other words, for budding screenwriters, the TV and film industry in the UK is set up to look like a closed shop.

The point of this section of the book is to demonstrate that this appearance isn't the reality. In fact there is a whole community of people – script editors, producers, development executives, literary agents – whose job it is to look for and work with new writing talent.

What these companies and agencies fear is that if they had an 'open door' policy, they would be swamped with more scripts than they could ever read; and that receiving scripts and so many different stories would leave them open to accusations of theft and plagiarism.

Breaking into the industry as a screenwriter isn't easy. But everyone now working as a screenwriter had to go through the same process, and plenty have broken down the doors.

This section of the book is about how you find your place in the industry, gain that initial foothold, and then sustain your writing and turn it into a long-term career. Without the skills and practices outlined in this section, craft and your skills as a dramatic writer have little meaning. The two go hand in hand and are equally necessary.

The life of a professional, working screenwriter asks a lot of you, particularly in that tricky combination of two very different skillsets.

On the one hand you need to live inside your own head and be happy spending solitary hours in front of your computer screen living vicariously through your characters and their stories.

But then you also need to be the sort of person who likes getting out and about, meeting people in the industry, discussing and pitching stories, and working collaboratively with many different people to try to bring projects to fruition. And then working equally closely with many different people as a project nears and then enters production.

These two 'personas' feel like very different personality types. To be a successful writer of drama, the most important thing is your ability to write (obviously!), *but* it is worth remembering that there is this whole other side to your work as a dramatist that shouldn't be underestimated.

That is: the aspect of marketing yourself and your work, getting your work in front of the people that matter, getting yourself in front of the people that matter, and making sure you are the sort of person that other people want to work with. Broadly speaking, all the aspects of being professional and focused about your career that are the same the world over in any business.

But writing is a very particular craft, and very often the sort of people who become writers aren't the sort of people to whom 'networking' and related business activities come naturally.

INTRODUCTION

These two sides of a screenwriter's life aren't quite mutually exclusive – but they call on two very different sides of your personality, and require different skills.

This section is going to concentrate on the career side of your work as a screenwriter.

It's important to state that this whole section is predicated on one big, important idea – that you are going into this process of trying to break into the industry with at least one outstanding spec, calling-card script in your locker – and hopefully two or three. These scripts are your initial currency as a screenwriter. They are the units by which the industry can begin to assess you and engage with you as a writer.

I
Breaking In

Screenwriting Training

How or even whether you train as a screenwriter is a big, contentious question. There are many different opinions about the best way to train, but I think the bottom line is that there is no single, conventional way in to working as a screenwriter, and that every single writer has their own unique story of how they broke in.

Here are a few of the different options for how to train:

* Formal screenwriting education – there is an ever-growing list of BAs and MAs teaching screenwriting, dramatic writing or more broadly creative writing.

* Short courses – week-long, one- or two-day courses in screenwriting.

* Theatre – a lot of writers who enter screenwriting have a background as theatre writers.

* Short films are also seen as a very good training ground for longer-form screen stories.

* Other forms of writing and media – journalism, documentary film-making, podcasts, novel writing, etc.

* Online courses. There are more and more of these courses, either short – e.g. one-hour masterclass-type talks and Q&As – or longer courses that run over weeks or months but take place entirely online.

* Self-education – using the almost infinite resources of the internet, screenwriting books, reading scripts, and watching film and TV.

This career section will touch on all of these possible routes to entry, but here I'd like specifically to go further into the pros and cons of longer degree and post-graduate courses compared to shorter, less formal, less academically based courses.

Longer university courses – BAs and MAs

As I've mentioned above, there are now a lot of university courses in screenwriting, or more broadly in dramatic writing and creative writing. A lot of these courses and the institutions that provide them have strong, long-standing reputations.

What these courses can give you is the framework and environment to look deeper into screenwriting with like-minded people, to build up a portfolio of work that you can then take out into the industry. Being in this sort of protected environment for a year or three, being encouraged and pushed to write scripts – this is the main value of this sort of course. Some of these courses are more 'industry facing' than others. Some will help introduce you to potential employers in the industry, to help prepare you for work afterwards, others less so.

Many of these courses are run by experienced industry professionals with first-hand experience of working in the industry as screenwriters, producers, script editors, etc. And sometimes, even if the core teachers are from a more academic than professional screenwriting background, the courses may include many sessions and classes run by visiting guest lecturers from the industry.

If you're thinking about doing a university degree (usually three years) or postgraduate course (usually one or two years) in screenwriting, it's important that you are clear about what you are looking for from the course, what you want to come out of the course with at its conclusion. Try to find out about or even talk to ex-students from that particular course – try to find out who and how many have gone on to do significant work in the industry, who exactly teaches on the course, and what their practical industry experience is. Find out exactly what work you will be doing on the course, how many scripts, and what sort of scripts, you will be asked to write on it.

The one thing you can be certain of is that no one in the industry is going to be interested in what university you attended or what mark you got in your degree. They will, initially, assess you solely and purely on the quality of the writing in your spec scripts. They will not be impressed by or interested in your first-class degree. Academic grades have no relevance to industry success.

If, like me, you work on the other side of the fence and have observed many writers over the years breaking into the industry, you will develop opinions about the virtues of certain courses over others. For instance, at this moment, probably the most highly regarded long-term, academic/formal screenwriting training in the UK is the MA course at the National Film and Television School (NFTS). There are quite a few examples of writers from this course who have made a big impact as working writers in the industry. One of the elements that seems to be particularly strong with this course is the importance they give to introducing their writers to potential employers and agents, showcasing their students' work – the course's direct links to the industry.

The potential drawbacks of university BA and MA courses are:

* The overly academic nature of some of the courses. Some of them may be more about academic theory than the actual practice of screenwriting. Fine if that's what interests you, but this sort of course will have limited application to industry realities – to helping you actually becoming a professional screenwriter.

* Linked to the above, teachers who have no real industry experience, or a lack of quality guest speakers and teachers. All of these courses are only as good as the people running them and teaching on them.

* The lack of connection between academic success and industry success. You may work very hard to try to achieve first-class honours, but this may have no application to the sort of scripts that will get you noticed

in the industry. The criteria by which university teachers may assess or grade your work will potentially be very different to the value industry professionals put on it – and this has the potential to take your writing in unhelpful directions.

* The financial cost. This is clearly a major factor, particularly in this day and age, where there is such limited state support for higher education.

* The time commitment. If you devote three years to a course that doesn't give you what you'd hoped for, that is a major minus.

(Here is a blog from my website by Lily Shahmoon on exactly this subject: script-consultant.co.uk/ma-or-not-ma-training-for-dramatic-writing-lily-shahmoon)

Shorter courses

There is a huge and ever-increasing range of shorter courses – both in person and online.

I have to confess my own personal bias (and vested interest) as I have run so many short courses over the years and have seen many writers who have used these courses really effectively as part of their career strategy; and I've seen these courses act as a small stepping-stone on their path to real screenwriting success. Most of the courses I have run have been one or two days. But there are also longer courses that are spread over weeks or months (perhaps for one evening a week).

Some of these courses are run out of universities – but are perhaps more obviously practical rather than academic, compared to some of the formal BA or MA courses.

For these shorter courses (as with the longer ones), you should do your research. Do the teachers have genuine industry experience? Does their track record reassure you? Are you clear about exactly what you're getting for your money? Does the course have impressive testimonials? And can you get word-of-mouth recommendations from people who have done the course?

One example of this sort of course that has stood out for me in recent years is 'Writing the Pilot' – a ten-day course from the NFTS, run by Peter Ansorge, who has significant and impressive experience as a producer and TV drama commissioner over many years. On the course you get to write a TV drama pilot script in the room over these ten days, sharing your work and giving feedback to the other writers in the room.

I think this is an outstanding example of a short course. This is mainly because of the number of excellent scripts that I have read over the last few years that have been written on it, but also because of the many positive testimonials I've been given about it.

It seems to me that this is the ultimate practical course, in that you will come out of it having written a full-length TV pilot script, written in an environment that is both challenging and supportive.

These are the sorts of courses that you should be on the lookout for – courses that distil a huge amount of learning into a short, intense period; and out of which you will emerge with something very tangible.

Here are some other examples of shorter (online) screenwriting courses in the UK that look promising (links can be found in the Further Reading section, from page 306):

* 'Story for Screenwriting: Advanced Structure', from John Yorke's Story website.

* Jed Mercurio's course 'Writing Drama for Television', via BBC Maestro.

* The series of screenwriting courses from the Masterclass website.

What these online courses obviously won't give you, which in-person courses will, is that all-important social interaction with your peers – the importance of which can't be overstated.

However you approach it, educating yourself about screenwriting is incredibly important. One thing the most successful screenwriters have in common is the way they obsessively immerse themselves in the craft of storytelling for the screen.

As a screenwriter you should always be reading scripts, watching as much as possible and thinking about the shows you watch, why they work, why they don't work. So many of your introductory chats with potential employers will be about story (any story, not necessarily yours), what you've both read, what you've both watched and what you both think of it; why some shows work, what there is to enjoy in them, and how the shows that you don't think work could have been improved. This immersion in the craft is something that will be ongoing. But as a screenwriter breaking in, one of the most important things is simply to demonstrate your love for, and fascination with, the craft of screenwriting.

There is no substitute for reading a lot of screenplays, watching a lot of film and TV, and making both of these habits for life. (And if this feels like a burden rather than the treat it is, then screenwriting isn't for you.)

> Links to all courses mentioned in this chapter, and more, can be found on the Further Reading section from page 306.

Competitions

Screenwriting competitions are one of the main acknowledged entry routes into professional screenwriting. I think it's important to differentiate between the competitions and courses that pay you, the writer, and those that you have to pay to enter.

In the UK, the two main organisations that run paying courses and competitions are BBC Writers (and their many initiatives), and the Channel 4 Screenwriting course, 4Screenwriting (which I initiated and have run for the last fourteen years).

It goes without saying that I think both BBC Writers and 4Screenwriting present brilliant opportunities for breaking into the screenwriting industry, for getting your name on the map as a screenwriter to be reckoned with. But because so many people know about these schemes, a lot of people will enter and – however brilliant your script is – the odds of breaking through via these schemes are not good. 4Screenwriting usually receives around two thousand scripts from which we choose twelve writers. And the BBC Writers Drama open call regularly receives more than four thousand scripts.

You need to be in this for the long-term to achieve success. Significant success sometimes takes a number of years to get to. Often we invite writers onto 4Screenwriting at their fourth or fifth attempt – there is nothing more persuasive than a writer who enters year after year with different but equally promising new scripts. When you are deciding between two different writers, one of whom you've read five scripts by, one only one script, that range and evidence of determination is persuasive. So be philosophical and realise that however good your script is, the odds are stacked against you with these big broadcaster initiatives.

And think laterally. By all means enter these more high-profile entry points, but find other competitions and initiatives where your odds are better and where you could stand out (e.g. regional schemes). For instance, in 2024 Channel 4 also ran a scheme dedicated to writers based in the south-west and north of England, and Scotland.

And then there are all the competitions that charge you to enter. I would advocate approaching these initiatives with a healthy dose of scepticism. Some of them exist to exploit screenwriters' hope and dreams; and even winning or placing will have little wider meaning for your screenwriting career.

So do your research, make sure the competitions you enter are reputable, that there is a list of previous winners with something of a track record, and that they are not extortionately, disproportionately expensive to enter.

Some reputable screenwriting competitions (in the UK at time of publication):

* BAFTA Rocliffe – there are several different versions of this every year.
* The Studio21 script-writing competition.
* Edinburgh TV Festival New Voice Awards.

There are a *lot* of US-based competitions. Some are worth entering (e.g. the PAGE awards), some not. I think you should be very judicious about which ones you choose to enter. You can spend a lot of money entering competitions that have little relevance to your career as a UK-based screenwriter.

Also look for the growing number of broadcasters and independent production companies who run initiatives and bursaries for new writing talent – for example ITV Studios, Dancing Ledge Productions, Imaginary Friends Productions, Sky (their table-reads and other initiatives), Bonafide Films, Kudos, Left Bank Pictures, etc.

> Links to competitions and opportunities can be found in the Further Reading section from page 306.

CVs and Interviews

With experience of the tens of thousands of entries over many years of the Channel 4 screenwriting course (and the Greenlight Screenwriting Lab in Ireland), I have developed strong opinions about CVs and interviews.

CVs

The script is always the first and most important consideration. It's only if the script is promising that we read the CV.

Writers' CVs should of course be primarily about their writing and their achievements in writing. But you should also include interesting life and work experience. If you think it's going to convey a positive impression then include your academic achievements and qualifications – where you were educated.

Information about other work (other than writing) is often interesting and helpful. As a general principle, include anything that makes you come across interestingly and might have an influence on your writing (e.g. writers who have backgrounds as a doctor, lawyer, social worker, police officer, etc., often have very interesting and particular stories to tell). Interesting, colourful life experience will inform your writing.

Your CV should tell us where you are from and where you live and work. Most writing courses and initiatives want to have as broad a range of writing voices as possible – whether that's about where you live and come from, your age, gender, sexuality, politics, ethnicity and specific interests and passions – anything about you that is distinctive and influences your writing.

Try to avoid the generic (e.g. 'I enjoy reading, exercise and going to the cinema'), and also the CV that tries too hard to be different, kooky, witty, irreverent. Too often, this looks like an unconvincing cover for a lack of substance.

Your CV is in effect a pitch. It's your chance to tell us who you are, what makes you unique, what you're good at, your writing achievements, and how your background, lifestyle and work impacts on your writing. And like the best pitches, your CV should be as short as possible and as clear as possible.

You should be constantly honing and improving your CV as you build up life experience and writing credits.

You should also have a selection of subtly different CVs for different opportunities. The CV you submit for 4Screenwriting, BBC Writers or any other opportunity should be uniquely geared towards that specific application. (Sometimes actor-writers submit their standard acting CVs. This merely conveys to me that they are more interested in or serious about their acting than their writing.)

The layout should be clear and relatively simple. Sometimes an over-designed, multicoloured CV is hard to read and points up the writer's attempt to cover up a lack of significant and persuasive content through flashy design!

Ideally, CVs should be sent as PDFs, as these feel more like finished, professional documents. (There is more chance we will be able to open the document, and also we can't mistakenly reformat them!)

One thing I'm a bit dubious about in CVs is the personal-profile blurb you often get at the top nowadays, about the applicant's personal qualities, often along the lines of:

> *An exceptionally focused, creative and self-driven, aspiring screenwriter with a passion for storytelling. Self-motivated and committed to creating original and innovative stories with the ability to work under pressure and to strict deadlines. I am a very open-minded person and seek inspiration for my stories through various channels of research. I enjoy a challenge and I am always interested in undertaking new projects in whatever genre that might be, to further develop my skills and knowledge of the film industry.*

Avoid blurb like this that feels generic rather than individual. This takes up significant space without telling the reader anything very specific or helpful.

Similarly:

> *MY QUALITIES – Ethical – Perceptive – Reflective – Intuitive – Helpful – Adaptable – Punctual – Empathetic – Conscientious – Reliable – Organised.*

When you've read three or four of these similar, blandly positive sections, they merge into one enormous, amorphous blancmange. *Don't* include this section on your writing CV! (Unless, that is, you're going to subvert it in an entertaining, creative way that tells the reader something specific and memorable about you – there's a challenge.)

I simply skip over this sort of information to get to the real substance, the stuff that tells me something particular about who you are and what makes you unique as a person and a writer.

A 'Personal information/About me' section at the top of your CV is a good idea in principle – just make sure it is distinctive and has impact.

Interviews

For the first three years of the Channel 4 screenwriting course, entry was entirely dictated by script and CV – there were no interviews. This was a mistake. From the 2014 course onwards, we have interviewed prospective writers. We generally interview about thirty-five writers for the twelve places.

Holding interviews has significantly improved the overall quality of the writers we have on the course. It is also one of the aspects of the course that has brought home to me how screenwriting success is not only about how good you are at writing, it's also about how you run your career, how organised, focused and ambitious you are. I think this is the thing that the course has taught me most strongly – that it's not enough to be a hugely talented screenwriter. There is so much more to screenwriting success than that, and that is what the whole of the second section of this book is about.

Before we held interviews we used to have a (very occasional) writer on the course who just didn't flourish. Either they weren't well enough organised – they missed deadlines, didn't respond to notes, didn't return phone calls – or they had too many other commitments and didn't put the necessary time and work into their course script. Or else we discovered once they were on the course, that they just weren't that interested in TV drama. Or they were too difficult to get on with on a personal level – lacking in courtesy, consideration, etc. Or that the script they had written to get onto the course was the only script they were really interested in writing, and they weren't interested in developing further as a screenwriter.

I should add that all of these issues are incredibly rare. But they have definitely become even rarer since we started interviewing prospective course writers.

So why do some writers stand out in their interviews from other writers?

I generally send out an email to the writer interviewees with a list of things we'd like to talk to them about – about their writing work so far, about the script they submitted to the course, about ideas they'd like to explore in the script they write on the course. Something along the lines of: 'We'd like to talk to you about your submitted script, your other writing work, why you want to come on the 4Screenwriting course, and ideas you may be considering for the script you would write on the course, if chosen.'

So one of the big things we're looking for is that the writer has prepared for the interview and thought about the questions in advance. It's not a good sign if the interviewee seems to be surprised by and unprepared to answer any of these questions we've told them in advance that we're going to ask them (which happens).

But I also usually try to ask at least one question that I haven't flagged up in advance, e.g. what TV and films they have watched recently, what writers they particularly admire and why, what they think of recent Channel 4 drama output – nothing very left-field, but it's good to get a sense of their passions and of how thoroughly they study the craft of screenwriting.

The course interview is so valuable as a reflection of how the writer might get on after the course, in general meetings with production companies. So much of the initial work of breaking in as a writer is sitting across the desk from a development executive or literary agent, talking about yourself and your work; finding out about the production company and what they make and are looking for – and being able to get on with people you're meeting for the first time when the stakes are high for your writing career.

This isn't easy – and writers who come to the 4Screenwriting interviews are invariably nervous. It's about how you channel your nerves, how you handle this situation.

For instance, I'm always impressed by writers who come with written notes to hand. Sometimes, when I ask what they have been watching on TV recently, some writers will (apologetically) resort to reading through their list. I don't think this is anything to apologise for. This shows that the writer has prepared conscientiously and has anticipated this question. I'd far rather have someone refer to their list and then pick out their highlights than the person who says, 'No, sorry, my mind's gone blank…' (For some reason this is the question that tends to make people forget everything – until they've left the room!)

I sometimes get emails from writers after the interview, apologising for not answering a question how they wanted and emailing me with how they wish they had responded. Again, I always think this is an encouraging sign – it shows the writer's desire to get on to the course and that they do think deeply and interestingly about screenwriting.

I think in interview, writers (well, all people!) worry too much about how they're 'presenting' instead of really focusing on the questions.

As part of their preparation for the 4Screenwriting interview, the best candidates have clearly anticipated all the likely questions they may be asked and prepared a response to all of them.

There is no getting over the fact that something like the interview for 4Screenwriting may be thirty of the most significant minutes of your screenwriting career – and that's enough to make anyone anxious. All interviews are, to some extent, formal, artificial, unnerving situations. Part of the skill of the interviewee should be to come to terms with this, get past the artificiality of the situation and just concentrate on answering the questions in the way you want to, making sure you're getting across what you want to get across.

I think research and homework always helps. If you are genuinely well-prepared, you are less likely to be nervous (or at least likely to be less nervous!).

On a basic human level, interviewers will be looking for people who are comfortable as themselves – who are able to give a good impression of themselves in this undeniably difficult setting. Be yourself, demonstrate your self-confidence, being comfortable in who you are, rather than thinking you need to impress us by projecting an image of the sort of person you think you need to be to get on to the course.

Your Network: Writing Groups, Peers and Support, Community

Writing is by its very nature a solitary and isolating pastime, which is why it's so important to find and form a network of your writing peers – others who are on the same path as you, who will understand and be interested in your experiences and in sharing work. It's vital that you form your own, or find an already-existing writers' network.

You need to be able to thrive living in your own head – but mitigate this by regularly talking to other writers.

It will also prepare you for interface with the industry, and teach you to get used to talking about yourself as a writer, and about your work. It will also arm you for responding to notes and suggestions, which is such an important part of your writing career.

We all need our own network of fellow writers – to share the loneliness and difficulties of writing; to give support when times are tough; and for them to be interested and engaged in your work in the same way as you should be supportive and interested in theirs. Your generosity towards other writers will be enjoyable and it may well pay off in turn, in their generous responses.

It will be so helpful to you as a writer to have regular meet-ups with fellow writers whose company you enjoy and with whom you can swap work and opinions. Above all, this will give you something you desperately need as a writer – deadlines! If, for instance, you meet up once a month, you will use this as a deadline for producing new work monthly to share with your writing group. Writing groups like this can be invaluable in supporting and sustaining you through many years.

It can also be helpful to swap notes about people you're working with or want to work with; and, importantly, for finding out about opportunities. But above all, it's great to have a trusted network of fellow writers with whom you can meet regularly and swap work and give each other feedback. Having your own writers' group who are committed to meeting regularly and sharing work is invaluable.

There is a blog on my website (script-consultant.co.uk/writing-groups) about one such group that grew out of a session I ran at the London Screenwriters' Festival in 2014. Lisa, Amanda and the two Charlottes outline here exactly how helpful writing groups can be in sustaining and nurturing your writing.

Networking

'Networking' is something of a dirty word in any industry, often interpreted as a sort of compromised, disingenuous version of socialising. But I think it's really important that you find the positives in networking, however you choose to label it. The premise underlying this suggestion is that, however good your script is, you're always far more likely to be hired to write something by someone you've already met than by someone you've never met.

The working relationship between writer and producer or script editor is often intense, and you get to know each other almost unnaturally quickly. So if the producer in question has already met you and feels there was a rapport, that you're going to get on and that communication between you is good, they're more likely to hire you.

So you need to try to *meet* as many potential employers as you can. Although I hope this goes without saying, while pursuing this idea professionally, there is a fine line between professional ambition and courtesy on the one hand, and desperate pushiness on the other hand. Don't be that (admittedly very rare) writer who pins you in a corner, invades your personal space and won't let you get out until they have spent five minutes on a rehearsed pitch monologue. You shouldn't view events where 'networking' is an option purely as an opportunity to pitch yourself and your work. You should be as prepared to listen, to enjoy meeting other people, as to be making an impression on them. This sort of professional social event will be made a lot more palatable for you and everyone if you are as generous at listening, as willing to hear other people's stories, as you are at telling your own.

This networking aspect of your life as a professional writer has to be constantly ongoing, in the same way as your writing has to be. You can't spend six months concentrating furiously on the networking side and then think you're done. You have to be able to enjoy this side of the business, and make sure you're constantly putting yourself and your ideas out there. Take the opportunities when they present themselves.

When I was an actor (a long time ago!), my strengths (if I had any) were comic. I had the opportunity to go to a party and drink with *The Young Ones* crew and cast after the shooting of a studio episode (my wife acted in two episodes of the show). We discussed it and persuaded each other it would be a good idea not to go because of a lack of confidence, fear of going into a room of well-known actors. As a budding but very unsuccessful actor whose only talent was for quite broad comedy, this was probably the worst career decision I ever made. So, do as I say not as I do (did)!

It's a cliché, but often the most important connections you can make are not at the formal events but in the bar afterwards. This is something I've learnt from years of running the Channel 4 and other screenwriting courses. I always try to include a post-course social event because this is so often where the meaningful, long-term connections get made, rather than in the formal setting of the course itself.

However good you are at writing, if having a drink with your fellow writers and industry professionals is your idea of hell, it will without doubt negatively impact on your career potential. (And I'm not saying here that you have to be a big drinker. Alcohol is absolutely not an essential part of the equation!)

You need to be prepared to put yourself out there, to take your writing career seriously, to be comfortable with being ambitious; to value yourself and your work. It's about confidence – your own confidence and instilling confidence in others about you and your work.

And you also need to find the way to enjoy this process, to find the positives in it. For the most part, I think the people working in the film and TV industries are a remarkably affable, nice, interesting group of people.

Many of your conversations will be about TV, film and writing, with other people who share your interests and often your taste. Most of the time this not only has the potential to be professionally beneficial but is also very enjoyable.

Selling yourself and your work

As a writer, or budding writer, it's likely that this idea of 'selling yourself', like 'networking', will have negative connotations for you. But, in this industry where judgement is so subjective and unquantifiable, the writing is both a confidence business and a business of (often radically divergent) opinions.

An example from a writing competition panel on which I sat: I was struck by how myself and the two other judges, all reasonably experienced and well-qualified, were in complete disagreement in our assessments over which were the 'best' of thirty scripts. As a script editor, literary agent and writer respectively, we were all coming to them with different baggage, agendas and taste.

As writers, you need to think about why you have the right to tell your own stories and expect other people to be interested in them. Not an easy question to answer, but you nevertheless need to own your work, have the ability to get behind it, and articulate why you think it is or could be brilliant. You need to be able to demonstrate your belief in your work.

This is such an important part of the business, because so much work is generated through conversation. You need to be able to enjoy and thrive in this process; and at the same time you need to be able to say no sometimes, to hold out for what you believe in when there are conflicting and unhelpful opinions.

You need to have the skill of a diplomat. It's not just about the words on the page, it's about your qualities as a collaborator and communicator.

If a script editor or producer is working with someone whom they find difficult – if they're uncommunicative, shy, grumpy, prickly, oversensitive, arrogant, whatever – the difficulties of the working relationship will be exacerbated by the intensity as they work to develop a script under the pressure of knowing that there are immovable dates looming, when a crew of dozens of people will be paid to translate the script into film.

The business of being a writer and of establishing and sustaining a career in the industry has changed over the last few years with the pandemic and increased use of apps like Zoom and Microsoft Teams. A lot of general meetings are now held online rather than in person. Apps like Zoom have their pluses and minuses – they are great for enabling more communication between writers and potential employers, regardless of location. But they also have their limitations for things like detailed script meetings. It's just not possible to read mood and body language online, to read the room, in the same way as in real life. And somehow you get to know people quicker and more easily in real life than you ever seem to be able to do on Zoom, etc. It's harder to initiate and have those random icebreaking conversations that you might have if face to face in the room.

But what these apps have done is to open up the industry to those who do not live in one of the big urban centres, who live away from the main hubs of production companies and agents.

Events

An important part of making these connections that are going to benefit your career is finding events where you might meet your peers, your fellow writers, and also learn something about the craft or industry. I'm talking about film screenings followed by a Q&A; public talks by screenwriters and film-makers; book signings; screenwriting or literary festivals; film festivals, etc.; and more broadly, film and theatre trips. The more dramatic writing you encounter, the more you will learn about the craft.

Here are some organisations within my London-centric orbit that hold events of interest to screenwriters:

* BBC Writers.
* BFI (including the London Film Festival, BFI Flare, the BFI Future Film Festival).
* BAFTA (including the BAFTA Rocliffe New Writing Competition).
* The Royal Television Society.
* Creative Skillset.
* Creative England.

* London Screenwriters' Festival.
* Writers' Guild of Great Britain.

And there are many, many others – groups and organisations all over the UK that hold events of interest to screenwriters. A few more examples:

* Edinburgh TV Festival.
* Northern Ireland Screen.
* Screen Yorkshire.
* New Writing North.
* New Writing South.
* Arvon Foundation.
* Scottish Screenwriters.

Not only will these events stimulate your creative imagination, they are also a really useful way to meet like-minded creatives and potential employers.

And there is a vast and growing plethora of film and literary festivals around the UK and the world: *Guardian* talks, writers' and artists' events, events at universities, theatres, bookshops, etc. These are all great ways to get away from your computer and out into the world, to meet other writers and stimulate your writing perspectives and imagination.

Champions

Having even one or two people within the industry who act as 'champions' for you or your work is incredibly valuable. These champions can help you build and sustain your career as a screenwriter. The world of UK TV and film development is small, and we all talk to each other. Recommendations from people in the industry whose judgement you trust are incredibly valuable and powerful.

These relationships with industry people are a vital, sustaining element in building your career as a working screenwriter. It really doesn't take that many people in the industry who love your work, and are keen to hire you, to help you sustain a career over many years.

Whether people in the industry like your scripts enough to want to meet you and discuss the possibility of working with you is a reliable indicator of the quality of your script – an indicator that you need to be sensitive to and listen to. If you think your spec script is good enough to send out, but no one is biting – if it is not getting you any traction or attention – then you need to listen to this. If the script isn't opening doors for you, then you need to accept that it's not yet strong enough, and you need to either rework and improve it, or write another script.

Readings and showcases

There are a number of individuals and small organisations who organise readings of scripts and other showcases of new dramatic-writing work. It can be really valuable to showcase your script in this way, either through one of these organisations that have access to a pool of talented actors, or through your own initiative.

The ability to set up and arrange showcases of your work is another very good reason to form relationships and communities with your fellow writers. When organising something like this, think about what is going to attract potential employers and agents – the range of different work being showcased, the time and location of the event, the calibre of the actors, the professionalism with which the showcase is presented, and the persuasiveness and specificity of the marketing.

Social media and Zoom have made this sort of showcase so much easier to organise, and also so much easier to persuade important industry people to engage with.

Do your research

The world of TV drama and film is expanding and changing at an unprecedented rate. As a writer working in this industry, it's up to you to be aware of all the potential opportunities out there. You need to be looking at where you fit in and what opportunities you should be trying to take.

For example, the ever-changing and growing number of dramatic-writing competitions; the ever-changing and expanding number of production companies; and then more general trends – which streamers and broadcasters are commissioning in the UK, and what exactly they are looking for at any one time.

All of these production companies and broadcasters share this information online – it's up to you to find it and use it to your advantage.

This work of researching the industry and identifying opportunities is a vital, ongoing part of your work as a screenwriter.

Friend of a friend of a friend

You may well find that, without realising it, you know people who work in TV or film, or you will know people who know people. Use them shamelessly. If they don't want to help, they will say no, and you can move on. But in my experience, people actually like to be asked for your help – it flatters them – and they will be impressed by your ambition and initiative.

Contacts are all-important. Scour your brain and your address book for potentially useful contacts – people who know people in the industry to whom they can introduce you. It's so important to initiate and arrange face-to-face meetings with people who work in the industry or have industry contacts who can be helpful to you.

Offer to buy people a coffee in order to spend an hour or thirty minutes picking their brain. The more targeted and specific your approach, the more likely it is to succeed.

Other Media

I talked earlier (on pages 253–4) about the huge number of script submissions received by the more high-profile script competitions. There are a few obvious, attractive potential entry points into the industry for screenwriters, but these will all be oversubscribed. So it's important that you think laterally, think more creatively about other ways of breaking in. Telling stories in different media is another way of engaging with potential employers. For instance…

Podcasts

There are now a huge and ever-increasing number of podcasts. There is so much scope within the broad umbrella of podcasts for telling stories in interesting and unexpected ways, for demonstrating your initiative, your creativity and your abilities as a storyteller (even your interest in, enthusiasm for, and insights into the craft of screenwriting).

For instance, UK production company Brock Media have made two series of podcasts showcasing the work of dramatic writers: *Never Told* and *Eerie*.

I worked on a series of dramatic monologues as podcasts some years ago (tributepodcasts.co.uk). For some of the writers who wrote these monologues, they were both an enjoyable outlet for their dramatic writing, and also opened doors for them for screenwriting work, acting as a showcase that introduced potential employers to their work.

Theatre

There is a long history of writers starting in theatre before breaking into screenwriting. In the UK there exists a far stronger – and more visible – new-writing culture in theatre than there is in TV and film. Many TV and film producers and development executives look to theatre as a source of new-writing talent. This new-writing culture is particularly strong in London – with so many small-scale theatres that specialise in new plays by new writers – but there are many impressive national and regional theatres also doing this work.

There are countless theatre-writing awards and competitions in the UK, some of which come with very healthy prize money. Here are a few:

* Bruntwood Prize for Playwriting.
* Verity Bargate Award.
* George Devine Award.
* Papatango New Writing Prize.
* Alfred Fagon Award.
* Theatre503 International Playwriting Award.
* Nick Darke Award.
* Women's Prize for Playwriting.

…and many others.

Audio and radio

Radio is another rich area of dramatic writing. There are many storytelling parallels between writing for radio and screenwriting. While the BBC has historically been the biggest producer of radio drama in the UK, independent producers like Audible are now also offering more and more opportunities for writers in audio drama. Several Channel 4 screenwriting course alumni have had exciting, original dramatic writing commissioned and made by Audible. And many audio drama productions are made by independent production companies for the BBC, Audible and other broadcasters. Some examples of these independent audio production companies include Goldhawk Productions, Wireless Theatre and Allegra Productions.

There are also quite a few competitions and awards for audio drama in the UK, such as the Alfred Bradley Bursary Award, the Imison Award, the Tinniswood Award, and the BBC's International Radio Playwriting Competition.

Short films

Short films are another very common route into the industry, historically for directors to showcase their talents, but also for writers. Writing short films is a very particular, niche part of the craft of screenwriting – but both short-film scripts and, particularly, produced short films, can be a really effective 'calling card' for new writers.

Short-film scripts are also a great starting point for new writers looking to write their first scripts and to develop their craft. I know of many examples of short films (both scripts and finished films) that have alerted people in the industry to new writing talent.

Two of the best-known examples of short films that have showcased a writer or director's talent and have then gone on to be made into full-length feature films are, in the US, *Thunder Road* (written and directed by Jim Cummings), and in the UK, *Boiling Point* (written by Philip Barantini and James Cummings – no relation!), which has spawned not just a feature film but also an excellent four-part BBC TV series.

There are also several annual film festivals and competitions that are specifically for short films, e.g. Aesthetica Short Film Festival in York, Glasgow Short Film Festival, and London Short Film Festival, among many others. And nearly all of the major feature-film festivals also showcase the best new short films.

For budding screenwriters, short films can be a brilliant stepping-stone on the path to longer-form scripts.

Other writing

If you want to break into screenwriting, then I think many different forms of writing can potentially help you make that leap. There is so much demand for new content and new talent that producers are increasingly looking for content from so many different sources.

JOURNALISM

There is a long tradition of journalists moving into screenwriting, several of whom have been on the Channel 4 screenwriting course. The disciplines involved in journalism are very translatable to film and TV, in particular developing an eye for a challenging, inherently dramatic story, and finding real-world stories that could work as drama.

NOVELS

There are so many examples of writers like David Nicholls, who has a background as a script editor and screenwriter, and now works predominantly as a novelist, but who also regularly writes both original screenplays and adaptations.

Steven Bochco, David Wolstencroft, Gillian Flynn, Nick Hornby, Emma Donoghue and Charlie Kaufman are all examples of writers who have written both novels and screenplays (both original screenplays and adaptations of their own novels).

GRAPHIC NOVELS AND COMICS

More and more graphic novels are being adapted into TV and film – *The End of the F***ing World* (Charles S. Forsman/Charlie Covell), *The Walking Dead* (Robert Kirkman/Frank Darabont), *Shortcomings* (Adrian Tomine), *Kick-Ass* (Mark Millar, John Romita Jr./Jane Goldman, Matthew Vaughn), *Scott Pilgrim vs. the World* (Bryan Lee O'Malley/Michael Bacall, Edgar Wright) and *Bodies* (Si Spencer/Paul Tomalin).

BLOGS

Substack, WordPress, Squarespace, or whichever platform works for you – but they all make it relatively easy to get your writing in front of people. If you have something to say in blog form, this can be a great way to share your writing, introduce readers to your 'voice', to talk about everything and anything. It doesn't necessarily need to be screenwriting-related. If you have something to say and write well and entertainingly, blogs can act as a great showcase for your writing. If readers enjoy what you have to say on this platform, I would argue that they are then far more likely to engage with your screenwriting.

DOCUMENTARY FILM-MAKING

This is a fertile training ground for screenwriters. As with theatre and audio, there are so many crossovers and parallels between screenwriting and documentaries in the way stories are created and constructed. This is another area where there are many examples of people who have moved from one to the other over the years, proving equally adept and interesting in both forms (directors like James Marsh and Nick Holt).

POETRY AND SONGS

Less obvious stepping-stones to screenwriting perhaps, but similarly, if people like your writing in these forms, they are more likely to want to read your screenplays.

★ ★ ★

It's hard to sustain a career solely as a screenwriter. There are so many great examples of writers who write equally brilliantly between different media (Jack Thorne, Dennis Kelly, Alice Birch, Lucy Prebble, debbie tucker green, Abi Morgan, Inua Ellams). Your work in one medium will invariably spark interest and ideas for other media.

Social Media

Social media can be a very powerful tool for screenwriters in the whole networking, self-publicising part of your work. Important professional relationships can be initiated via social media.

There is some understandable reluctance about engaging with social media, but I think you can have the best of both worlds. You don't have to be personally, actively involved to be able to make use of the resources social media offers – namely information about opportunities, reading views from influential industry figures, and hearing what writers have to say about their work and the industry. You need to choose who you follow carefully. If you follow certain accounts, people you trust or rate, the list of who they are following can in turn be very helpful to you. It's important to keep an eye on social media trends – it's a constantly evolving world – for instance, I may have added Bluesky, a more recent Twitter/X alternative, to this list.

X (TWITTER)

I do think it can be very beneficial to be active on X (formerly known as Twitter, and that's what I'm going to keep calling it here!). The one piece of advice I would always give, though, is that you are always positive there. Don't negatively criticise shows and writers on Twitter. It's a public forum, anyone can read it. Negatives on social media often lack the nuance or irony you'd hoped would be inferred, and people may not receive your negativity happily. If people know of you as a writer but don't actually know you, your criticisms will be the only thing that defines you for these people, so be careful!

I feel like I have been introduced to, got to know, or even continued relationships with people through Twitter in a way that is both enjoyable and very useful. As writers, creating generous, enjoyable, personal content on Twitter can keep you in the minds of the people on the platform who can hire you or have influence in the industry.

As with my earlier caveat about not being the person at networking events who shows no social awareness (see page 262), I'd say the same about Twitter. If you use it shamelessly and excessively for unapologetic self-promotion, it may be counterproductive. Your personality will come across through your tweets, so think carefully about what you say and how much you say. Think about what you tweet and why. For instance, I think there is nothing more helpful than recommending scripts, shows, films, etc. Gleaning recommendations from people you trust is social media at its most helpful.

Twitter in particular can be very powerful in helping to cultivate your network and find out about events and opportunities you'd otherwise not know about. Twitter is a great way to identify like-minded people in the industry. It's a weird and rather wonderful thing that if you follow and enjoy someone on Twitter, when you actually meet them face to face, it's a whole lot easier, and you already have loads to talk about with them.

I also think that Twitter can be creatively helpful and energising. There are so many thoughts, opinions and stories there that may spark your interest and creativity.

FACEBOOK/META

I feel more ambivalent about Facebook. I have always found the social/professional crossover harder to negotiate! I think where Facebook can be very helpful is in its Groups. Being a part of groups of fellow writers, sharing information about craft and industry – particularly closed, private groups – can be an invaluable resource.

And again, whether through Groups or through your normal Facebook feed, if you are connected to the right people, you will find out about events and opportunities that you wouldn't find out about elsewhere.

WHATSAPP

Similarly, being part of a closed group of creatives on WhatsApp can be a really helpful way to swap ideas, anecdotes, information; to keep in touch with your fellow writers.

LINKEDIN

...can feel a little dry and impersonal compared to Twitter and Facebook. But again, if you are connected to the right people, if you work on building up your connections, it can be very useful in introducing you to people who can be of assistance professionally – in informing you about jobs and opportunities, and in enabling you to spread the word about your own work and successes.

TIKTOK

TikTok allows you to go viral and to reach people beyond your immediate circle more than any other social media app. I often see creatives doing call-outs for cast and crew on TikTok and getting really positive results. It's also a great place to share your own writing and connect with screenwriters of all ages, all across the world, who you might not have had access to otherwise. As an app used primarily by younger generations, it might also be really helpful for screenwriters who are writing for or about Gen Z and now Gen Alpha.

The weird thing about TikTok is that, despite it being the app where you are most likely to go viral and be exposed to a large audience, it's also the app that people tend to be most vulnerable on. The app where people tell you the most about themselves. It's a strange but fascinating incongruity. Millions of TikTok users don't follow or aren't followed by their immediate real-life friends and family.

This vulnerability and openness that is displayed on TikTok is unique, and I would imagine it is really wonderful for screenwriters who are either looking for stories to tell or wanting to share already written stories and get feedback. TikTok at its heart is a grassroots storytelling app.

INSTAGRAM

Instagram is more of a visual medium, but it's still a place to connect and keep up with people you meet, to promote what you are doing and comment on things you have seen. While it would be abnormal to post about a recent achievement or career promotion on TikTok, it would be pretty normal on Instagram.

I'd suggest having your full name visible on Instagram so that people who might be interested in you can find you, and I'd also suggest being a public account if you want to use Instagram for screenwriting business opportunities.

II

Sustaining a Career

Strategy: Making the Most of the Opportunities

In the world of film and TV drama, the switch from no success or recognition at all to having to fight off meetings and offers can happen very quickly. The industry is quite small, and producers and script editors are constantly swapping notes on writers. If you get on to one scheme like BBC Writers, if a couple of people read and love your script and spread the word, you may suddenly find you get all sorts of other offers.

You need to make sure you're ready to take advantage of these opportunities when they do come along.

And if you're putting yourself out there and working hard at writing scripts, generating ideas and meeting people, and nothing is coming of it, then you need to be able to stand back and re-evaluate why things aren't happening for you and work out what you need to do differently.

There is an industry of people actively, hungrily looking for new writers, and if you're working at it but not breaking through there will be a good reason for it – but perhaps one that the potential employers are too polite or cowardly to tell you. At the same time, you need to be sure that you are receptive to constructive feedback about how you can improve your chances of success.

It's important from time to time to stand back from the everyday process of writing and ask yourselves bigger questions: why do you write? What do you want from your writing? What are your ultimate ambitions? Your dream job? Then you can refocus what you're doing so that you're continually aiming for what you want. You need to keep reassessing where you are and work out where you want to be. You need to set short-term goals (the next hour, week, month) and longer-term goals: Where do I want to be in five years' time? Who do I want to be working with? What sort of shows do I want to be writing on?

It's so easy to get caught up in the day-to-day business of keeping on top of all your tasks that sometimes you lose sight of what you want to achieve in the longer term, of remembering what your strengths are, what you ultimately want to achieve with your writing, both creatively and in career terms.

And make use of your peers – have these sorts of broader, strategic conversations with your trusted fellow writers, and your agent if and when you have one.

General Meetings

The initial results of people in the industry reading and enjoying your spec/calling-card scripts will be 'generals' (general meetings). Once you've written two or three outstanding spec scripts and people in the industry are starting to take notice of you, you will get a lot of meetings and you need to be ready to take advantage of what these meetings offer.

This is something I particularly think about at the end of each year of the Channel 4 screenwriting course – how that year's writers can make the most of these general meetings. If writers have written an outstanding script on the course, they will be invited to a lot of general meetings. One writer from the 2022 course told me that in the nine months after the end of the course, he had around sixty general meetings with different production companies, some in person, some on Zoom.

What are general meetings for?

Some new writers have expressed their puzzlement about the purpose of these meetings. The general meeting is something of a gateway into the industry (once you have managed the tricky task of getting your outstanding script in front of the people that matter). If a producer, script editor or development executive gets in touch and offers to meet up for a cup of tea and a chat – for a general meeting – this is *not* just about a cup of tea and a chat!

No script editor is going to want to meet up with you unless they genuinely like your writing and are keen to work with you. So take these meetings seriously. Understand that a busy script editor or development executive isn't going to initiate a meeting with you unless they're seriously impressed by your writing. Us Brits like to downplay things and you have to be adept at reading the subtext of what is said.

These meetings have the potential to be the start of a twenty-year working relationship for you as a writer with that particular development executive and production company. So much of your career is about developing working relationships with those people who 'get' you as a writer, the people who like you and your work, and will continue to champion you for years if not decades. I can't overstate how important these industry champions will be to you.

This initial meeting will be to sound you out – to make sure you and they are roughly on the same wavelength, that you come across as professional and conscientious. Most importantly, they want to know what ideas you might like to write about, and to see if there's any common ground between your interests and theirs – and within the sort of story areas the people who run that indie or production company are interested in making.

Come prepared

Don't rock up waiting to be impressed. You need to have done your homework, researched the person you're meeting and the company they work for (and even the companies this particular script editor *used* to work for) and have opinions about the shows made by the company you're going to see. This doesn't necessarily mean you have to be glowingly positive about every show they've ever made, but come with constructive, engaged opinions about the TV or film they have been involved in working on.

Clearly the most important thing as a writer are your scripts. But once people have read and liked your scripts, there are so many other aspects to the work.

So much of the business is about working relationships. In particular, when you're working on a greenlit show with deadlines that are non-negotiable, the pressure to deliver can be quite intense (although let's keep perspective: this isn't life and death, it's just film or television). Even on 4Screenwriting, on which writers have five months to go from initial one-sentence pitch to at least the second-draft script, the pressure is real – and much of what the course is about is seeing how writers cope with this, whether they thrive or not in a collaborative environment, working with script editors who are often asking difficult and searching questions of their stories.

The bottom line is that the people who are going to hire you not only need to believe you're a talented writer, they also need to know that you're hard working (i.e. you've done your research); that you're genuinely interested in (even obsessed by) the process of creating stories for film and television; that you watch a lot and enjoy talking about it; that your opinions about dramatic writing and screen stories are constructive, engaged and enthusiastic.

Note This doesn't mean, I think, that you have to be 100 per cent positive about everything you talk about. We all learn a lot from the shows we think don't work as well as the ones that do – as long as your critiques come from a place of enthusiasm rather than bitterness and general negativity!

You need to come across as someone who genuinely loves television, film and storytelling. Think about your favourite writers and favourite shows.

Keep lists, study the way the industry works, where opportunities lie and how things are changing (TV and film are in a constant state of flux).

Above all, we all want to work with people whom we get on with. This certainly doesn't mean you have to become bosom buddies with the people you work with, but being generally courteous and communicative counts for so much. I'm occasionally surprised by writers who don't follow the normal courtesies of any industry: replying graciously (or replying at all) to emails; responding to notes constructively, even (or particularly) if you don't agree with those notes.

Any script editor worth their salt will welcome a constructively combative debate about story and script notes. What we find less easy to deal with is a lack of response, or writers who say they agree with all the notes in a meeting but then don't actually address them in the new draft of the script.

So much of the success of a writing career is predicated on your ability as a writer to communicate yourself and your ideas in person, in meetings and by email; about engaging with the industry and the people who have the potential to employ you constructively, conscientiously and generously. Remember, you will be hired by people you have met and got on with or who have received a positive reference about you, on top of the fact that they like your writing.

A two-way relationship

At a certain tipping point when you have got to know quite a few people in the industry and know who you want to work with and who you don't, these people will start coming to you with their ideas. Sometimes it's smart as a writer to be receptive to ideas that companies are bringing to you – this is an advantageous position to start from – when the company is trying to persuade you of the virtue of their ideas rather than the other way round.

The company or script editor will already have an emotional or vested interest in the idea, and you will be leaping on board the momentum that has already been built up in-house without having to initially persuade them of the virtue of your idea. Hopefully the ideas that companies bring to you will already be informed by their knowledge of what is likely to get commissioned at that particular moment and by their knowledge of your strengths and interests as a writer.

Even if a general meeting goes well, it may be that you don't hear back from a particular company or development executive for some time – even a matter of years. But I have heard many instances of writers hearing back from a company, say, two or three years after this initial meeting, when they do have a project that they think might be right for you. In the meantime, find ways and excuses to keep this relationship going – perhaps email to congratulate this script editor or producer on a show they've made that you particularly enjoyed, or get in touch to update them about your own progress and successes. It's important to keep the relationship active, to make sure this person still has you in mind. But be careful that this doesn't tip over into nagging or harassment – it can be a fine line!

Literary Agents

The writer and literary agent relationship

For many un-agented writers, there is an idea that having an agent to represent their interests will instantly transform their writing fortunes. Literary agents can be incredibly helpful to you as a professional (or aspiring professional) screenwriter, and once you are making money and working regularly, you will undoubtedly need an agent.

But it's important, I think, not to see getting representation as the be-all and end-all. It is a helpful step along the way, but I would advise you not to get too hung up on this particular step. Once you are ready to have an agent, you will get one. But there is a huge amount that can be achieved without an agent. And any agent worth their salt will be keener to take you on if there is already wind in your sails, interest from several sources in you as a writer; and if you can demonstrate that you are not only already heading in the right direction but also that that you have initiative, have made some significant professional contacts and are working hard on your own behalf to knock down industry doors.

Not only will they want to see that you're a talented writer – that they like what they read on the page – agents will also want to know about you as a person. They will want to meet you and hear your thoughts about your work and where you want to go. They will want to be convinced by your interest in the world of film and TV, your passion for the craft and your ability to engage with potential employers in the room.

They will want to hear about the contacts you have already made, the successes you have already had. The best agents correctly see their relationship with clients as long-term. They want to feel confident about investing in you as a writer – investing their time in introducing you to their industry contacts, persuading them that you are a risk worth taking. The best agents will be prepared to lose money on you in the short-term in the hope that this will pay off in the long-term. This is a relationship based on trust – their trust in your hard work and determination to succeed; your trust in their commitment to you.

Finding the right agent

So it's vital that you sign on with an agent who you feel 'gets' you as a writer, recognises and is excited by the strengths of your work. Your agent should demonstrate to you a genuine passion and enthusiasm for your writing. After all, that is what they will be having to do on a daily basis on your behalf to potential employers.

Often, when an agent declines to take you on, it's based on nothing more than their gut response to your writing. The best agents feel, quite rightly, that they really need to connect to your writing on a personal level to be able to represent you. Sometimes, no matter how strong your scripts are, for whatever reason your writing won't click with a particular agent – so try to be philosophical about this. If an agent doesn't 'get' your work, there's no real point in trying to persuade them.

The perception is that it is so hard to find an agent, because agents receive so many applications, so it's tempting to throw yourself on their mercy – to put them on a pedestal. Don't do this. It's not helpful to you and it won't make you a more attractive prospect as a client.

Instead, remember and keep reminding yourself that your agent works for you, not the other way round. Try to meet a number of agents, take your time about making a choice, and do your research – talk to other, represented writers, find out who writers recommend. Also talk to people within the industry – development executives, script editors, producers. Find out which agents they rate highly. These are the people your agent will be talking to, so this is key.

And when you go to meet an agent, don't treat it like a job interview. You should be asking them at least as many questions as they ask you. Challenge them – what can *they* do for *you*? Ask them, what will be the benefit of having them as your agent. If they don't like this approach, they're not the agent for you.

Don't necessarily say yes to the first offer of representation, but meet as many agents as possible – get a wider sense of who's out there and find out how they're different. The more agents you meet, the more understanding you will have about who can best represent you. And let them know that you are meeting as many agents as possible and that you will be taking your time making a decision. Playing 'hard to get' will only enhance your value!

Remember also that it may take a while to secure the right agent. Often agents will read a script, like it, but ask you to come back with your next spec script. If you think this agent is right for you, don't let this put you off. Agents aren't going to say this if they're genuinely not interested. And sustaining a career in the long-term will mean continually writing new spec scripts. In fact, even once represented, some agents will encourage their clients to keep writing spec scripts regularly over the course of decades so that they have scripts that represent those writers' talents, that are new and feel fresh.

Think about representation from an agent's point of view. What is attractive about you to them? Why might they want to represent you? What evidence can you give them that people are likely to want to hire you, that you're going to make money for them?

All agents have their strengths:

* Some are brilliant editorially and will give you excellent guidance on your scripts and pitches, giving you notes and feedback to make them as strong as possible before they send them out on your behalf.

* Some are most comfortable with contracts and driving a hard bargain, and you know they will always get you the best possible deal financially and protect your financial interests on any project.

* Some are great allies and supporters, (almost) a friend, who always has time to talk you through a problem, is always there as a supporter or a shoulder to cry on.

* Others, conversely, are more businesslike on the phone, harder both to get hold of and to talk to. But they are brilliant at representing your interests with producers, getting you a meeting for that project you are desperate to be considered for.

* There are some agents who have more industry clout than others, this is really important. It doesn't matter how nice your agent is, how sympathetic, if they don't have some clout in the industry – if potential employers aren't going to listen to them.

In what ways can an agent make the most difference for you the writer? If you're entering into an agreement for TV, for example, the basic Writers' Guild contracts do not cover rewarding the writers for other possibilities, i.e. if someone else wants to take it and turn it into a movie; it gets another series; sells elsewhere, etc. Big, potentially important issues need to be negotiated by an agent, to protect writers, right at the start of the development process.

At an early stage of development of a project, you need an agent even more than further down the line, because you need someone to negotiate terms of contracts even though the money at this stage is small. You need an agent who will make sure you're protected because you don't want to be taken advantage of – for example, if you have a break-out hit, you don't want to have given away all your various rights in the project for very little.

Writers' Guild contracts will only deal with repeats and residual payments, they don't give you any potential writer's share of the producer's profit, so this is a big part of agent negotiations.

Agents will generally charge their clients 10 or 12 per cent commission.

Approaching agents

It's really important to do your research. Find out who agents represent; make sure they represent some writers who mean something to you, whose work you enjoy. Try to talk to their clients or industry people who know them for any inside information about how they work and how well-regarded they are in the industry. All of the reputable agencies have their own website, with listings of each agent within that agency, their clients and their clients' CVs. Take your time, look through these lists, aim for the agents whose client lists excite you, agents whose clients' work you like, and be specific about this when you contact them. An agent will be more likely to engage if they feel that you've done your research and are approaching them for very specific reasons that you can articulate. No agent is going to be impressed by a blanket, mass 'Dear Sir/Madam' mailout.

The bottom line is that most good agents will only consider new clients if they come with a personal recommendation from someone in the industry that they know and respect. If you're not yet in a situation where someone's willing to do this for you, then perhaps you're not yet ready to have an agent.

Think about an agent's profile within the industry, but also within the agency where they work. For instance, you may be taken on as a client by newer, younger agents within the bigger agencies (Independent Talent Group, Casarotto Ramsay, Curtis Brown, United Agents, The Agency) – agents who have just made the move from being assistants to more senior, experienced agents, to creating their own list of writers. These newer agents often provide the best of both worlds – the clout of a larger agency with all the contacts and industry credibility they have, with the hunger and excitement of someone trying to make a name for themselves in the industry. Sometimes, as a new writer going with a senior agent with starry clients, you can get a bit lost. If your agent is dealing with several big-name clients, they may not have the time to devote to introducing you to the industry, no matter how much theoretical goodwill they have (this isn't always the case – it's horses for courses and every individual case is different).

It could alternatively be a good idea to be represented by an agent in a much smaller company who has a smaller list of clients and therefore will have the time to give you.

In the UK, look at the PMA website (thepma.com). Any reputable agency is on there, and that'll give you a list of the agents worth considering.

The writer–agent relationship should be viewed as something that ideally will be long-term. You can be with the same agent for your entire writing career, so it's essential that you don't go with the person who looks great on paper but who you dread phoning because you find them hard to talk to, terrifying, or just don't have that personal connection with. Above all, don't go with someone who you don't get on with on a basic level. They don't have to be your best friend, but you need to be able to be professionally honest with them, you need to feel they are someone you can talk to. There may be a slight trade-off here if they aren't your natural ally but are doing a great job of getting you work, but be very careful about this trade-off. If you find them hard to talk to, there may not be a viable, long-term future to the relationship.

What should you expect from your agent?

Once you have an agent, don't sit back and think they will now do everything (except the writing, obviously!) for you. It's so important to continue to use your own initiative in reaching out to the people you want to be working with, in forming your own professional connections. Hopefully your agent's work will complement your own work in making important contacts.

I have seen or talked to many writers about the best and the worst of these agent–client relationships. I have come across several instances of an agent 'letting a client go', and this seriously damaging the self-confidence and therefore the work of a writer.

A writer I worked with was taken on off the back of the script they wrote on the 4Screenwriting course by a senior agent in one of the most reputed UK literary agencies – success!

A year later, this same writer contacted me to say they were at a low ebb professionally. Initially encouraged by their new agent to do so, the writer had sent them several written pitches and two new spec scripts over the course of several months – but after some initial emailing back and forth, and a few meetings arranged for the writer by their agent, the agent had now not been in touch for several months.

The writer had sent several polite emails asking for a response but had heard nothing back. By the time the writer had got in touch with me they were feeling not only thoroughly disheartened but also rapidly losing faith in the quality of the work they had sent the agent, and at a complete loss as to what they could now do to further their career and make use of the momentum coming out of the course.

This was from a really excellent writer, someone who had been selected from thousands to be on the course because of an excellent stage play. They had already written other stage plays that had deservedly received a lot of positive attention, and had then written an outstanding TV pilot script on the course. It frustrated me to see how their confidence and indeed work prospects had been significantly impaired by this non-relationship with the new agent.

I encouraged them to confront the agent with a polite but honest email about their frustration at this lack of response. They did so, and quite quickly received a polite but non-negotiable email from the agent saying that they were no longer able to represent this writer.

The writer then approached another agent who had originally offered them representation at the same time as that first agent. They are now happily represented by this second agent, with confidence and work prospects restored.

I have seen several instances of writers who are represented by theoretically good agents, agents with some clients who are doing very well, agents who have excellent standing and reputation in the industry, but whose working relationship with this particular client has gone stale.

Writers talk to me about their emails and phone calls not being returned and how their self-worth as writers takes a hit because of this. In many of these instances, I can see how these writers try to convince themselves that it makes sense to stay with these agents because the agent's name looks good on their CV – that they, the writer, are perceived more positively in the industry because they are with this particular agent. But I can see how their agent's lack of interest in them and their work eats into their creative energy, how it undermines their own belief in their work.

If they are working hard on new ideas and scripts, sending them on to their agents to send out to producers, and the agents just sit on this work with no response for weeks or months, it will undermine what they are doing as a writer.

The credibility and value the agent's name gives you within the industry is never worth it if this same agent is demonstrating a lack of belief in your work by not engaging with you. In this situation I think it's always best to get out, even if you have no other agent to move on to.

This is tricky because the world of film and TV in the UK is small. Agents talk to each other, they swap notes and (quite rightly) discuss working practices, etc. As a writer, it's understandable that you don't want to leave an agent without having another one lined up. I would say, though, that if things aren't working out with your agent as you'd hoped they would, you need to have that conversation with them; and if they don't respond positively, then you should move on. Staying with the wrong agent in a relationship that has run its course will do you as a writer no good.

Anecdotally I was also told of a successful writer who makes a point of changing agents every five years, to make sure the spark doesn't go out of the relationship. I can see the rationale of this, but it's not ideally what you should have to be doing.

What should your agent expect from you?

I don't want to give the impression that this is a one-way street. I have had conversations with agents who have worked very hard for clients but through no fault of the agent, the writer isn't thriving in the industry. In these instances, where the agent feels they have done all they can for the writer but things aren't happening, it's also probably best for the relationship to end.

There are writers of real talent who aren't as successful as their talent suggests they could be – pushing back on notes, proving intractable on seemingly unimportant creative issues, delivering late, not responding to emails, etc.

This should be an area where your agent can be very helpful to you, the writer. If a producer or employer has a perception that there are professional difficulties in the working relationship, it makes sense to convey these concerns to the agent (although probably only after they have tried to iron out these issues face to face with the writer).

The agent should have a broader knowledge of their client and how professional relationships have worked more generally over time. The agent should know if this is a regular pattern or if there is something particular in this working relationship causing it to have problems.

Is it a particular problem caused by particular issues with this project, or is this a more deep-seated, recurring issue with this writer? If it's the latter, you need to listen very carefully to the feedback your agent is passing on to you and address the issue.

Notes, Feedback and Collaboration: Working with Script Editors

Notes

Creative, professional collaboration – and in particular how you as a writer respond to notes and feedback – is such a huge aspect of successfully sustaining your career as a screenwriter.

The incongruity of notes is that, pretty much without exception, *notes will always hurt* but, creatively, personally and professionally, you need to find a way to take notes and to use them to the benefit of your work. This is actually one of the keys to having a long-lasting and successful career as a screenwriter. It's also one of the most difficult aspects of the job.

Putting your work out into the world – having it constantly judged, assessed and picked over – is hard. Professional screenwriting requires courage. You need to find ways to protect yourself through the process of notes and feedback, to survive and ultimately to thrive.

The big thing to remember as a writer is that ultimately the script editor or producer (or whoever is giving you notes) is on the same side as you. Their intention with the notes is to help you make the script the best possible version of itself, and to help it become a script that will get made.

As a writer you need to find the virtue in – or at least the intention behind – notes. Even if a note is bad, you need to find the motivation and understand the reasoning behind it. The best notes sessions are conversations. As a script editor, I find the best way to discuss issues in scripts is to ask a writer questions. Often a note is about something I (as script editor) don't understand. Simply asking the writer their intention will often result in the writer articulating their own solution to the issue without it coming across as a negative or a criticism.

As a general principle of note-giving, I think it's really important (perhaps counter-intuitively) to focus on the positives in a script – acknowledging and analysing the things that work well. Often this will provide the solution to what works less well.

But you will, as a writer, get difficult notes – notes that betray a lack of understanding of the script or the sense of a scene; notes that you feel strongly will make the script less good; or notes that address a potential issue in a way you don't agree with.

The more written notes you receive, and the more script meetings you attend as a writer, the more strategies you will develop for dealing with these issues.

This all sounds very negative. At its best, the notes process can be a huge positive. On screenwriting courses, I get immense satisfaction from new writers articulating their gratitude for the input of their script editors on their projects. Year after year, many of the writers make a point of publicly thanking their script editors for all the help they've given them, acknowledging that their scripts would not have been as strong without the expert input and suggestions of their excellent script editor.

It's important that writers learn to be open and receptive to notes. It doesn't matter who gives a note or when – if it's good, if you genuinely feel it's going to improve your script, then use it. Both a script editor and a writer's aim is the same – to make your script as good as it can possibly be. It's important as a writer to remind yourself of this, if and when there are disagreements. Good script editors will openly accept a writer's pushback or disagreement – but on both sides, as in any relationship dynamic, it's important to show sensitivity and courtesy in how this is done.

The suggestions of the best script editors should aim to be as technical and analytical as possible. Many of the notes I give are guided by principles of storytelling in which I passionately believe, based on a quarter-century of reading, viewing and note-giving.

As a writer, there are so many different aspects to this all-important relationship. Being able to articulate your ideas clearly and interestingly is vital; as is responding positively to notes and feedback. This means being a good listener, making sure you understand the feedback you're getting, and responding creatively and dynamically. It *doesn't* mean 'obeying' every note and responding robotically.

The writer–script editor dynamic should be a creative conversation. Writers need to learn how to make the most of the good notes they're getting and how to respond to notes they're not so sure about. Sometimes the least satisfactory response is the literal addressing of every note – it's all about you as a writer understanding the principle behind the note and addressing it in such a way that you make it your own.

It's about behaving professionally – dealing with each other with courtesy and consideration; working hard; always being communicative about what's possible and what's not; delivering on time, or communicating clearly why and when this isn't possible.

As a script editor, however technical I try to be, notes are always to some extent personal: motivated by my own unique perspective and taste, and feeding back on a writer's very personal take and approach. Scripts, particularly the best ones, are always deeply personal. So from both sides of the process, there is ego involved. And where ego is involved, the script editor has to tread carefully and with sensitivity.

Above all, I have to respect the bravery and the process of the writer. One of the most valuable experiences I ever had to prepare me to work as a script editor was writing my own script, giving it to a screenwriting evening class and receiving their almost universally negative feedback. I can't remember exactly what was said but I can remember the complete lack of positives and the feeling of humiliation and affront I had. I was ridiculously oversensitive, I'm sure, but the discomfort of that evening stood me in really good stead for subsequent script-editing.

A writer's ability to engage with producers, script editors, directors and their assorted suggestions is a key part of your career and whether you can flourish in the industry. A professional TV dramatist *has* to find a way to not only survive but thrive in this collaborative creative environment.

This certainly doesn't mean being a pushover and politely and meekly agreeing to address every single note whether you agree with it not.

As writers, the sort of people you want to be working with are those who you feel will add value to your script, who will come up with ideas that will enhance your vision of the story, help you to make it an even better version of the script you originally envisaged.

There will be times when you will have to be politic, bite your tongue, nod sagely, tell the crap note-giver that their note is 'really interesting. I'll think about the best way to do address that.'

> I have recently been working with a writer who has a background as an excellent development executive and script editor. The script I worked with him on was his first professional TV screenplay, and extremely good it was too. He was a delight to work with, but when he didn't agree with a note I was giving him, he'd say, 'That is such a good note, thank you!' This was very disarming, and it wasn't until the third or fourth draft, when I saw that he was quietly ignoring certain notes, that I caught on!

The one big takeaway, I'd say, is: be very careful who you work with. Work on finding your champions and allies in the industry, the people who 'get' you as a writer and your work.

My working life as a script editor and producer has educated me in the highs and lows of life as a writer – the sensitivities of the writing process – both through observing (and being involved in!) massive arguments and bust-ups, but also through moments of great creative satisfaction. For instance, seeing writer Neil McKay watching the first cut of one of his episodes of *Medics* (1994–95), a story about post-natal depression. The lead character was brilliantly played by a very young Samantha Morton, and it reduced him to tears. It was a pleasure to observe him enjoying the power of his own writing, and how a brilliant actor had elevated it even further.

At the same time, I can't overstate both how difficult the response to notes can be, and how important it is that as writers you find a way to be receptive and creative in your responses – but also philosophical and thick-skinned about some of the less sensitive or helpful feedback that over the course of a career you will inevitably receive.

You need to find a way to navigate this process, not to let it damage your confidence and passion. Sometimes this involves sleeping on a note or set of notes, not firing off that enraged email but reviewing it the next morning (and more often than not, being relieved that you hadn't pressed the 'send' button!).

The fragility of story

Good story is delicate. Protect it! It is easily destroyed. If you feel that something is working, maintain your belief in it and only lose or change it if you feel the change you're making is genuinely improving the script.

There is nothing more dispiriting than going through a development process and coming out the other end with the observation that the first-draft script was better than the tenth-draft script. In my experience this doesn't happen very often, but it's important for both writers and script editors to learn the lessons from a development process like this that goes wrong. When a good draft is turned into a less good draft by a rewrite, it is deeply frustrating.

One of the most important parts of a script editor's job is helping a writer to identify what works and is successful in a draft. And as a writer, you need to learn to understand and value the particular strengths you have and the moments in your scripts that stand out – and that you need to fight for. (But pick your battles!)

Writers' rooms

Working in writers' rooms is an ever-growing part of a screenwriter's work in television (the writers' room model seems to operate less often in the development and writing of feature films in the UK). More and more of the writers I have worked with in the last few years have got their first credit on a broadcast show through working in a writers' room.

Unlike in the US, the UK industry lacks a clear, structured, universal approach to writers' rooms. Each production company, each development or production project, each producer, will tend to use writers' rooms differently, to run them over different lengths of time, with different numbers or combinations of staff (e.g. sometimes all writers; sometimes a combination of writers, executive producers and script editors). Most writers' rooms will be run by the lead writer. As a newer writer being brought into a writers' room, the set-up will vary. Sometimes you will be guaranteed to write at least one episode of the show you're working on, sometimes there are no guarantees at all.

This rise in frequency of the writers' room approach to writing and creativity emphasises even further the need for screenwriters to thrive in a collaborative working environment, to be able to articulate their ideas passionately and persuasively, and to enjoy working alongside other creatives.

For writers, there is a need for these rooms to be run efficiently and transparently, so that there is a nurturing, enabling ethos at work, and everyone feels included and able to make speculative, left-field (even bad!) suggestions without it counting against them.

Love the craft

A passion for the craft, for the work of other writers – watching, reading, enjoying – will sustain and inspire you. Don't be insular, keep enjoying other people's writing.

Writers need a process, an appreciation of craft, some technique to fall back on. You can't sustain a whole career on instinct. You will learn as you go – there is nothing so instructive as seeing your idea go on a journey from initial pitch through script development to production and onto a TV or cinema screen. But the new screenwriter must be hungry to learn and make use of the myriad resources and people out there who can help.

We are all still learning with every new script or production we work on, the shows we watch and the scripts we read. Every screenwriter, but particularly a new screenwriter, needs to be hungry to learn; to keep investigating their craft, experimenting and pushing boundaries; and learning collaboratively, in discussing story, and how to dramatise it, with their peers and work colleagues.

Process, longevity and sustainability

So much of being a successful working writer is about having the ability to keep going back to the well. Keep generating stories, enthusiasm and the necessary creative energy. So much of this is about your own, individual process – about creating the right circumstances for creativity, finding the time and space to enable you to produce content.

This is also about finishing your work. So many writers when giving advice to new writers stress this simple idea – finish what you've started. Once you have a first draft down and completed, you have overcome a massive hurdle, and you can then go on to the next stage of the work – reworking, honing, improving what you already have. Psychologically, this is so much easier to deal with than the blank page, whatever the quality of this first draft.

Vomiters versus plotters

The excellent script editor Hilary Norrish identifies the writers she has worked with as one of two kinds: the vomiter and the plotter. In my experience, the vomiter thinks less about structure as they spew out their first draft – it's more of an instinctive, visceral process; whereas the (extreme) plotter will plan out everything in detail, scene by scene, beat by beat in outline form, before they commit to writing their first-draft script.

The TV drama industry errs on the side of favouring the plotter – any producer with a limited development budget wants as much evidence as they can get that a script is going to be brilliant before they commit the (relatively) big bucks on commissioning a script. (For more on this, see page 218.)

In my experience of working with some wonderful but new writers, on several occasions I have been almost certain that a script is going to be brilliant from the evidence of a detailed outline. On these occasions I have enjoyed reading that outline almost as much as the first draft script.

This has been an education for me – I have learnt the importance of doing the preparatory work of honing your concept and story premise and working through the story development before committing to script.

And this is the way the industry works – because it makes financial sense.

On the other hand, I have worked with plotters who put too much emotional investment into their outline, and are so committed to it that they won't take notes – refusing to countenance changing or experimenting with their structure once they have done this structural work.

> On a new ITV drama series on which I worked, I remember meeting with the lead writer in a café so that he could talk me through his structure for the all-important series one, episode one, scene by scene. The pitch must have taken an uninterrupted hour as this writer talked me though his story, scene by scene, act by act – with three ad breaks all thought through carefully.
>
> The pitch, and the amount of time and attention to detail he spent on it was enormously impressive, and there were many elements of the story that were brilliant.
>
> But when he got to the end, my immediate and instinctive response was that the first two (of four) acts (i.e. the first half of the episode) were backstory, not actual story and drama – and that he should cut these first two acts, hit the ground running by starting his episode where he was now starting act three, and rethink the second half of the episode.
>
> The look of pain he gave me as I made this suggestion is imprinted on my soul, because over the next few weeks and many meetings and discussions, he refused to budge, and the relationship ended in tears!
>
> For me, this was an example of the worst of 'plotters' – someone who plans so assiduously that they will brook no discussion of their story.

On the other hand, 'vomiters' are often more able to retain their equanimity in the process of script development, because the speed and lack of certainty with which they splurge their first draft enables them to come up with one that is more surprising, fresh and original. It also means that generally they are more open to viewing their first draft as a basis for discussion and reworking, rather than something that is set in stone.

As writers, we all need to develop and find our most helpful and productive working processes. Where do you fit between these two contrasting processes?

What you need to discover is what modus operandi works best for you. This will become clearer the more writing you do, and your process may vary depending on the nature of the story you are telling (e.g. is it a story that needs a lot of preparatory research?).

You also need to think about where and when you write best. Make writing an everyday habit, find ways to make it a part of your daily routine. Are you the sort of writer who needs to be tucked away in their own special, private room with complete silence to thrive? Or do you work best in a public space – in a café or on a train? Find what works best for you, but carve this space into your day, make sure your writing time is sacrosanct and protected. Value your talent and your career. You need to be organised, focused, calm, persistent and ambitious.

Career: Conclusions

There is no single, conventional way into the industry as a writer. Every writer is unique and has to find their own way of making their mark. Different writers appeal to different companies and producers. Each writer not only has their own taste and attitude but also their own process.

It has been exciting to see certain writers whom I met at the start of their careers explore narrative and tonal landscapes that didn't seem to exist in film and TV before these particular writers explored them. Pioneers in writing for the screen like Nida Manzoor (*We Are Lady Parts*, *Polite Society*), Charlie Covell and Theresa Ikoko. And there are many others who I feel sure will make their own unique mark as screenwriters in the years to come.

You need resilience, but you also need positivity. Go into each new working relationship in a spirit of trust and generosity, see the best in the people you work with (until proven otherwise!). They are all working towards the same goal – to make the script and show as good as it can possibly be.

If you can't puff your chest out and tell the world you're a writer, and believe that your work is good enough to be taken seriously by people in the industry, then you make it very hard for potential employers to take you seriously.

Don't apologise for yourself or your work. Demonstrate your self-belief, communicate your strengths as a writer – if you can't do this, no one is going to do it for you. Above all, it's about finding a way to enjoy this social side of the business. This is an industry full of people with similar interests to you, all of whom want to make the best, most exciting work they can. What's not to like about that?

Your writing has to become an integrated part of your life, you have to make space in your life for it. It can be incredibly time-consuming, so you need to carve out this time. And you need to develop exercises (see pages 14, 22 and 53 for some examples) – fun ways to keep your writing fresh, to keep coming at story from unexpected, even artificial angles and approaches. Above all, you need to be constantly striving to find the ways that keep you enjoying your writing.

Afterword

There is no secret formula to good writing. It's about conveying your passions, about helping us come together to celebrate the joys and mysteries of life in all its horror and glory. When a piece of writing hits the sweet spot and pulls you into its characters and its story, there's nothing better. It transports you to somewhere profound and wonderful.

All of the above has been an attempt to help you do that, to help you tap into your deepest feelings and passions, to write with commitment and joy, and then to find the right home for your work as a writer.

It has been my profound pleasure to work with so many wonderful writers over the past twenty-plus years, and see so many of them go on to achieve deserved and spectacular success.

But it has also been a great joy to work with the less obviously successful (so far) writers, to get to know them through their work (it's impossible not to reveal yourself as a person through your writing) – and I look forward to working with many more of you in the coming years.

This book has tried to describe and define a number of storytelling 'principles'. One of the most important things to remember is that all these principles are exactly that – they're not 'rules'. These principles are negotiable, even ignorable. But I think it's important that you recognise these principles before you subvert them. And subversion is actually a key principle in itself. If you slavishly follow all the story principles, you will produce a perfectly formed script that is without surprises.

AFTERWORD

Being a screenwriter involves a constant inner dialogue with yourself. The more you think about how story works, the better a writer you will become.

You need to keep thinking about the sheer multiplicity of stories. You will be inspired and energised and mentally refreshed by watching and reading screenplays, indeed any dramatic narratives, any stories at all. You need to keep developing, moving forward, changing, and testing yourself as a writer.

Avoid any script 'expert' who claims to know the secret formula of effective storytelling for the screen.

Instead, rejoice in the fact that the creation of story is such a strange, mysterious, unknowable process. Revel in the experimental. Try to find all sorts of different ways in, come at story and character from different angles, try odd, unexpected techniques and exercises to find the creative starting point for your story.

Despite domination of the film industry by industrial-scale blockbusters and franchises, in my view, the really exciting, enjoyable and enduring work is done by singular writers with a singular vision – writers who have something to say and want to say it in the way only they can.

* Sally Wainwright with *Happy Valley* and *Last Tango in Halifax*.
* Shane Meadows with *This Is England* and *The Virtues*.
* Jed Mercurio with his genre-busting shows like *Cardiac Arrest* (1994), *Bodies* (2004) and *Critical* (2015).
* Jimmy McGovern with his extensive catalogue of must-see TV films, series and serials – from *Cracker* to *Hillsborough*, *Bloody Sunday* to *Broken* (2017) and *Time* (2021). None of these shows are written to a formula, they all feel like they're carved out of his heart.
* Dennis Potter with *Blue Remembered Hills* and *Pennies from Heaven* (1978).
* Vince Gilligan with *Breaking Bad* and *Better Call Saul*.
* Matthew Weiner with *Mad Men*.

* Michaela Coel with *I May Destroy You*.

* Lucy Prebble with *I Hate Suzie*.

All of these shows are groundbreaking, utterly original, and could only have been written by the writers who wrote them. Aim high – aim to write the scripts that only you can write.

Ultimately, screenwriting, like all good writing, is about having the courage of your convictions – saying, 'Fuck it, this is what I want to say and how I want to say it. This is what I believe in, so you can take it or leave it.' Your passion, your sheer enjoyment of the story you're telling will communicate itself on the page.

Good luck – and happy writing!

Further Reading and Resources

There are so many excellent books about screenwriting and dramatic writing in general. Here is my own personal list, which is highly subjective and by no means comprehensive.

There are two books of the collected lyrics of Stephen Sondheim – *Finishing the Hat* and *Look, I Made a Hat*. Both books are interspersed with Sondheim's commentary and observations about lyrics and songwriting, and in his insights and wisdom there is so much application for screenwriting and dramatic writing more generally.

On Directing by David Mamet – yes it's called *On Directing*, but it actually has some of the best insights of any book into the craft of screenwriting, particularly about telling stories through the cuts between scenes.

Adventures in the Screen Trade by William Goldman – more autobiography than screenwriting manual but packed full of good stuff nonetheless.

Image, Sound and Story by Cherry Potter – particularly Part Three: 'The Creative Process and Telling Your Own Stories'. There's a really good section in here on 'Free-writing' – the other side of the process from the formulaic, structure-heavy 'rules' in some of the (less good) US screenwriting books.

Story by Robert McKee – not as good as listening to the man himself – his three-day talk is a brilliant performance – but there are a lot of really perceptive, fascinating ideas here. Also a lot of stuff you probably won't agree with…

Screenwriting: The Art, Craft and Business of Film and Television Writing by Richard Walter – quite a basic introduction to screenwriting technique but very good nonetheless.

The Pitch by Eileen Quinn and Judy Counihan – one of the very few UK books specifically about pitching, treatments, etc., and by people who work in the industry and know from personal experience what works and what doesn't.

Conversations with My Agent by Rob Long – gives a really good insight into the working life of a successful US writer. And it's very funny.

Monster: Living Off the Big Screen by John Gregory Dunne – a fascinating insight into the work of a US screenwriter.

Do the Right Thing by Spike Lee – as well as the screenplay, the book contains Lee's journal about the writing and making of the film.

Going Mad in Hollywood by David Sherwin – autobiography by the writer of *If* (1968) and *O Lucky Man!*

Difficult Men by Brett Martin – fascinating insight into the creative processes on some of the best US TV (HBO, AMC, etc.) drama series.

Into the Woods by John Yorke – very readable examination of how dramatic storytelling works, from someone who's worked at the sharp end of UK TV drama for the last twenty-five years.

The Art of Screenplays – A Writer's Guide by Robin Mukherjee – Robin's first-hand experience of writing for UK TV drama shines through. Practical and pragmatic but more importantly, creatively inspiring.

The Science of Storytelling by Will Storr – an alternative – and very perceptive – look at the fundamentals of story.

Playwriting by Stephen Jeffreys – a brilliant guide to writing for the theatre, much of which has huge relevance for screenwriting.

Little Miss Sunshine Screenplay and Notes by Michael Arndt. The screenplay is a joy and Arndt's notes are brilliant.

Online Resources

script-consultant.co.uk – my own website takes pride of place! I have been writing blogs about screenwriting since about 2010 (and there are many other resources).

guru.bafta.org – an inspiring wealth of TV and film industry interviews, talks and insights.

www.bfi.org.uk/learning-training – the place to find out about all of the BFI's resources for screenwriters and film-makers more generally.

www.bfi.org.uk/funding-industry – information about BFI funding.

scriptnotes.net – *the* podcast for screenwriters with a huge back-catalogue of episodes.

BBC writers: www.bbc.co.uk/writers – an invaluable resource for UK screenwriters.

The Writers' Guild of Great Britain: writersguild.org.uk

Personal Managers Association: thepma.com – including the definitive list of the UK's literary agents.

Screenplays

www.bbc.co.uk/writersroom/scripts – a brilliant resource of scripts of produced TV and radio drama and comedy shows.

script-consultant.co.uk/script-library – my own library of unproduced scripts, outlines and one-page pitches.

www.chrislang.co.uk/pitches-storylines – one of very few places where you can find examples of UK screenplay outlines.

Competitions/Opportunities

www.thetvfestival.com/tv-foundation/new-writers-collective

www.thetvfestival.com/tv-foundation/new-voice-awards

netflixscreenwriters.co.uk

seriesmania.com/en

redplanetpictures.co.uk/the-red-planet-prize

www.bafta.org/supporting-talent/rocliffe

https://www.studio21.com/script

Training / Courses / Education

rts.org.uk/education-and-training-pages/education-training – information about training and funding from the Royal Television Society.

nationalcentreforwriting.org.uk/free-resources

leverageedu.com/blog/best-universities-for-screenwriting-in-uk

www.whatuni.com/degree-courses/search?subject=screenplay-writing

www.masterstudies.co.uk/MA/Screenwriting/UK

www.thecompleteuniversityguide.co.uk/league-tables/rankings/creative-writing

www.findamasters.com/masters-degrees/london/scriptwriting/?fogiEYM4Evoo

nfts.co.uk/screenwriting

nfts.co.uk/writing-tv-pilot

www.johnyorkestory.com/course/story-for-screenwriting-advanced-structure

www.bbcmaestro.com/courses/jed-mercurio/writing-drama-for-television

www.masterclass.com/categories/writing-3

Industry News/Journalism

Deadline: deadline.com

Broadcast: www.broadcastnow.co.uk

Drama Quarterly: dramaquarterly.com

Televisual: www.televisual.com

Miscellaneous Links

www.hollywoodreporter.com/movies/movie-news/writer-roundtable-aaron-sorkin-emerald-fennell-kemp-powers-radha-blank-and-sam-levinson-on-the-journey-to-get-their-stories-to-screen-4133498

London Screenwriters' Festival: youtube.com/user/scriptplusuk/videos

Acknowledgements

Thank you to:

Matt Applewhite for commissioning this book and for his encouragement and support.

Sarah Lambie for the insight, positivity and conscientiousness with which she edited this book. After my years of editing other writers, she made it a real pleasure for me to be on the other side of the experience.

Sophie Wilson for her excellent and generous feedback and encouragement.

So many people who have helped and supported me over the years – to those all-important people who gave me my first breaks into the world of dramatic writing and script-editing – Tony Dinner, Robin Hooper, Laurence Bowen and, in particular, Gwenda Bagshaw, to whom I owe so much.

Camilla Campbell for allowing me to run the Channel 4 Screenwriting Course; and everyone in the Channel 4 drama department who has been so kind and engaged in their support of the course since then.

So many producers and script editors with whom I have enjoyed working over decades. And two people I never got to thank, rocks of the TV screenwriting world, generous, funny, brilliant and sadly missed: Muirinn Lane Kelly and Sharon Bloom. RIP.

The (literally) thousands of writers who have been both brave and generous enough to share their work with me, and from all of whom I have learnt something – thank you.

Amanda Duke, Charlotte Essex, Nick Flugge, Andrew Lynch, Lisa McMullin, Regina Moriarty, Hilary Norrish, Sarah Page, Claire Rowlands, Lily Shahmoon, Anna Symon, Charlotte Thompson – for very kindly allowing me to quote from their work in this book.

And finally, thank you and undying love to the most important people in my life always: Cindy, Hannah, Jake, Bertie, Eliza, Lee, Molly – and Monday, Maccabee and Leonie.

P. S.

★★★

The author and publisher gratefully acknowledge the reproduced extracts from the following works:

'Four Quartets' in *Collected Poems 1909–1962* by T. S. Eliot, 'The Mower' in *The Complete Poems* by Philip Larkin, and *Succession: Season Two: The Complete Scripts* by Jesse Armstrong, all published by Faber and Faber Limited and reprinted with permission. *A Handful of Dust* by Evelyn Waugh, published by Penguin Books. *Only Murders in the Building* (*Episode 1*) by Steve Martin and John Hoffman, co-produced by 20th Television, Rhode Island Ave. Productions, Another Hoffman Story Productions, and 40 Share Productions.

The publisher will be glad to make good in any future editions any errors or omissions brought to their attention.

Glossary

ANTAGONIST   The central oppositional character in your story.

BACKSTORY   Information about what has happened before your on-screen story starts.

BEAT SHEET   A detailed document outlining the action of the story, written before the script.

CALLBACK   Reference to an earlier story moment/event.

CALLING-CARD SCRIPT   An uncommissioned script, written to showcase your writing.

CAPTIONS   On-screen text to give the audience additional story information.

CHARACTER ARC   The narrative journey of your character over the course of the story.

CLICHÉ   A common, overused storytelling element.

COUNTERPOINT   The relationship between different, contrasting elements in your story.

DEUS EX MACHINA   A big, unmotivated story device that is introduced at the end of your story to artificially tie up the loose ends.

DEVELOPMENT EXECUTIVE   (Normally) an in-house script editor, who initiates and develops new projects for their production company.

DEVELOPMENT SLATE   The list of projects being developed by a writer or production company.

DIEGETIC MUSIC/SOUND   Music/sound that exists within the world of the story, and is audible to the chracters (as opposed to composed music cues).

DRAMATIC PROPOSITION   A brief description of the dramatic dilemma, the conflict, that will make your story propulsive and compelling.

DRAMATURG   is to theatre what the script editor is to TV.

EXPOSITION   Story information.

FINAL DRAFT   The industry-standard screenwriting software.

FLASHBACK   A scene/moment that interrupts the chronology to take us back to an earlier moment in the story.

FORM   The shape and structure of your story.

GENERAL MEETING   An introductory meeting between writer and script editor/development executive/producer.

GENRE   The story conventions, the specific form, within which your screenplay operates (e.g. horror, romantic comedy, whodunnit, farce, etc.).

GREENLIT   Used to describe a show that has got the go-ahead for production.

HOOK   A storytelling technique designed to alert the audience's attention to what might happen; to create intrigue, suspense and a promised answer to the question you are setting up.

INDIES   Independent production companies.

LITERARY AGENT   An agent who represents screenwriters.

LOGLINE   A pithy, persuasive summation of your idea in a sentence or two.

MOCKUMENTARY   A fictional story presented in the style of a documentary.

MONTAGE   A sequence of brief scenes/images cut together, usually to music or voice-over, that carry us through a particular section of the story.

MOTIF   A repeated narrative element/image that reinforces the theme of your story.

NOTES   Written feedback from producer, script editor, development executive, etc., for the next draft.

ONE-PAGER   A one-page pitch of your project to try to attract potential producers.

OPTION   The payment of a fee to a writer by a producer or production company to allow them an exclusive right to try to sell an idea, project or script for a limited length of time before the rights in this project revert to the writer.

OUTLINE   Usually a pre-script development document for the writer to develop their story before writing the script.

PILOT EPISODE   The opening episode of a new drama series.

PITCH   A persuasive articulation, verbal or written, of your idea.

PITCH DECK   A pitch containing visual elements.

PRECINCT   The story setting, usually for drama series (e.g. police station, hospital, law courts).

PRE-LAP   The beginning of dialogue from a new scene that comes in at the end of the previous scene.

PRODUCER   The person who develops, initiates and is responsible for making the show.

PROTAGONIST   The central character who drives your story.

SCENE   A contained unit of story, usually within a single location.

SCENE-BY-SCENE   A detailed document that lays out the action of the screenplay scene by scene in shorthand form, without dialogue.

SCRIPT EDITORS   The people who work on productions with overall responsibility for the scripts.

SEQUENCE   A series of scenes that tell a particular part of your story.

SERIES BIBLE   A long document that contains all the relevant information about an established television drama series for new writers working on the show.

SHOPPING AGREEMENT   The fee paid to a writer by a producer or production company to allow them a non-exclusive right to try to sell an idea, project or script for a limited length of time before the rights in this project revert to the writer.

SLUGLINES   The term used in the US for scene headings in the formatted screenplay.

SPEC SCRIPT   A 'speculative', as-yet-uncommissioned, script or screenplay.

STATUS QUO   The current, existing state of affairs in a story.

STORY BEAT   A unit of story action within a scene.

STORY PREMISE   The basis, the heart of your story idea, described in one or two clear sentences.

STORY WORLD   The setting, society or environment within which your story exists and which helps to define the values of your story.

SUBTEXT   What is happening underneath the surface meaning of your scene.

TAGLINE   A witty, brief, provocative hook/sentence usually written for the eventual poster or to try to sell a project.

TONE   The mood, atmosphere and story conventions of your screenplay.

TREATMENT   A longer document about a film or TV project, usually written to try to gain a producer's interest, and which can vary in length from two to twenty (or more) pages.

TROPE   A common, recognisable element of story.

VOICE-OVER   Dialogue spoken over on-screen action.

WRITERS' ROOM   A dedicated space in which writers discuss, develop and create story, usually for TV series.

Index of Names and Titles

127 Hours 136
24 108
4Screenwriting, 234, 253–4, 256, 259–60, 281, 289; see also Channel 4
(500) Days of Summer 50

Abbott, Paul xviii
Abigail's Party 30
About Time 67, 155
Adeyemi, Abraham xxvii
Aeronauts, The 10
Alamo, The xxiv–xxv
Alcott, Louisa May 155
Alfreds, Mike 175–6
Alice in the Cities 35
All Is Lost 136, 189
All the President's Men 51
Allegra Productions 270
Allen, Jim xxv
Allen, Woody xxiv, 7, 35, 50,154, 188
Amazon Studios 131
American Beauty 102
American Graffiti xxiv
Anatomy of a Fall 103
Angela Black 93
Aniello, Lucia 146, 160, 163
Annie Hall xxiv, 7, 35, 50,154, 188
Ansorge, Peter 252
Anybody's Nightmare 107
Apartment, The 50
Apocalypse Now xxiii–xxiv, 217
Apple TV+ 64
Armstrong, Jesse xxvi, 10, 38–9, 152, 155, 178–80
Armstrong, Lance 144–5
Arndt, Michael 34, 35, 53, 84–5, 89, 95–6, 130, 155
Arrested Development 155

Arvon Foundation 266
Assistant, The 42
Attanasio, Paul xxvi
Austen, Jane 4
Austin Powers 49

Baby Reindeer 103
Bacall, Michael 272
Back to Life 213
BAFTA 254, 265
Bagshaw, Gwenda xviii
Baldwin, Frank 36
Ball, Alan 36, 91, 102
Band of Gold xviii
Barantini, Philip 36, 138, 155, 271
Barber Shop Chronicles xxvii
Baruwa-Etti, Dipo xxvii
Basden, Tom 37, 213
Battsek, John 31
Baumbach, Noah 50, 189, 215
BBC xviii, xxv, 4, 36, 46, 49, 63, 75, 87, 108, 114, 121, 131, 138, 213, 234–5, 252–4, 256, 270–1
BBC Writers xviii, 197, 265, 278, 253–4, 256, 265, 278
Bear, The 37–8, 153, 155
Beatles, The xxiv, 21, 65
Beaufoy, Simon 136
Begin Again 215
Being There 139
Bendjelloul, Malik 28–9, 121–2
Bennett, Alan xxv, 56
Beresford, Stephen 36
Berg, Peter 118, 214
Berges, Paul Mayeda 7
Besson, Luc 36
Betrayal 54, 108
Better Call Saul 157, 216, 304
Better Things 214
BFI 265

Big Mood 235
Bikeriders, The 104
Birch, Alice 273
Black, Helen 46–7
Black Mirror 9, 214
Blakeson, J 88, 96, 136, 160, 189, 215
Blick, Hugo 56
Blinded by the Light 7
Bloody Sunday 304
Blue Remembered Hills 304
Blue Ruin 36
Bodies (2004) 13, 304
Bodies (2023) 30, 272
Bohemian Rhapsody 65
Boiling Point 36, 138, 155, 271
Bonafide Productions 255
Born Free 154
Bos, Hannah 12
Bowen, Laurence xviii
Boyhood 35
Boyle, Danny 136
Brassed Off 36
Breaking Bad 150, 157, 304
Brexit 14–15
Brickman, Marshall xxiv, 7, 35, 50,154, 188
Bridgerton 216
Brittany Runs a Marathon 131
Broken 304
Bronstein, Ronald 135
Brooker, Charlie 9–10, 214
Brothers, The 36
Brown, Gordon 148
Broyles, William, Jr. 64, 83, 97, 136, 189
Brydon, Rob 56
Bryon, Nathan 35, 50, 86
Burn Burn Burn 53
Burns, Scott Z. 32

INDEX OF NAMES AND TITLES

Butch Cassidy and the Sundance Kid xxiii–xxiv

Call My Agent xxv, 187
Cardiac Arrest 13, 304
Cast Away 64, 83, 97, 136, 189
Casualty 36
Chadha, Gurinder 7
Chandor, J. C. 136, 189
Channel 4 xx–xxi, xxvi, 4–5, 14, 44–5, 219, 235, 241, 253–5, 258, 259, 263, 270, 272, 279; *see also* 4Screenwriting
Chazelle, Damien 35, 145–6, 152, 159
Cheaters 47, 217
Cheney, Dick 29
Chibnall, Chris 55
Chin, Jimmy 28–32, 124
Christie, Agatha 4, 35
Clarke, Alan xxv
Clarkson, Paul and Michael 235
Clerkenwell Films 246
Coalition 14–15
Cocaine Bear 213
Cockfields, The 37
Code of Silence 235
Cody, Diablo 35
Coel, Michaela 214, 305
Colaizzo, Paul Downs 131
Cold Pursuit 36
Colin from Accounts 216
Columbo 35, 150
Come Again 215
Comer, Jodie 55
Coming Up 5
Confession, A 39
Contract, The 237–8
Coogan, Steve 161
Coogler, Ryan 82–3
Coppola, Francis Ford xxiii–xxiv, 36, 64, 139, 155, 189, 216, 217
Coppola, Sofia 29
Covell, Charlie xxvi, 28, 30, 214, 235, 272, 300
Coxon, Lucinda 154
Cracker xviii, 304
Creative England 265
Creative Skillset 265
Criminal 61, 101
Criminal Justice 101, 150
Critical 13–14, 304
Crook, Mackenzie 12, 79, 135
Crown, The 29, 155
CSI 35
Cubitt, Allan 36, 77, 153, 161
Cummings, James 36, 138, 155, 271
Cummings, Jim 271

Curtis, Richard 50, 67, 69, 154, 155, 229
Curtis Brown 287

Dancing Ledge Productions 255
Daniels, Sarah xviii
Darabont, Frank 36, 136, 214, 272
Davies, Russell T xxvi–xxvii, 8–9
Day Today, The 214
Days of the Bagnold Summer 30
Dead Set 9
Deep Water 32
Derry Girls 217
Detectorists 12, 79, 135
Dickens, Charles xvii, 4
Difford, Chris 26–7
Dinner, Tony xviii
Disappearance of Alice Creed, The 88, 96, 136, 189, 215
Disney+ 42, 153
Dix Pour Cent 187
Docter, Pete 105
Dog Day Afternoon 36
Donoghue, Emma 83–4, 189, 272
Downs, Paul W. 146, 160, 163
Drake, Nick 154
Drôle 187
Duel 36
Dunkirk 36
Duplass, Jay 29
Duplass, Mark 29, 215

EastEnders 155
Edinburgh TV Festival (New Voice Awards) 254, 266
Edmundson, Helen 39
Eliot, T. S. 109
Ellams, Inua xxvi–xxvii, 273
End of the F***ing World, The 30, 214, 235, 272
Enfield Haunting, The 36
Enough Said 215
Ephron, Nora 15, 35, 50, 154
ER 36
Eric 96–7
Essex Serpent, The 217
Euphoria xxv
Evans, Simon 75
Exorcist, The 36

Fall, The 36, 77, 153, 161
Fargo 232
Father of the Bride 155
Fetters, Will 51–2
Fields, Joel 153
Film 4 xvii
First Film Foundation xvii
First Signs of Madness 55

Five Days 108
Flanagan, John 107
Fleabag 103–4, 213
Fletcher-Jones, Surian 44
Fogel, Bryan 32
Flugge, Nick 47–8
Fontana, Tom xxvi
Forrest Gump 139
Forsman, Charles S. 272
Four Quartets 109
Four Weddings and a Funeral 69
Friday Night Lights 118, 214
Friedkin, William 36
Friends 155
Fruitvale Station 82–3, 87

Gadd, Richard 103
Gassed Up 235
Gentleman Jack 82, 104, 135, 146, 217
Gervais, Ricky 104
Gerwig, Greta 35
Get Back 65
Get Out 36, 54
Gilligan, Vince 150, 157, 216, 304
Glazer, Jonathan 187
Godfather, The xxiii–xxiv, 36, 64, 139, 155, 189, 216
Godmother, The 216
Golaszewski, Stefan 37, 155
Goldhawk Productions 270
Goldman, Bo xxiii–xxiv, 135
Goldman, Jane 272
Goodfellas 79, 102
Graduate, The xxiv
Graham, James xxvi–xxvii, 14–15, 36, 138, 153
Graham, Stephen 36, 138, 155, 159–60, 271
Granada TV xvii–xviii
green, debbie tucker 273
Green, Kitty 42
Green Mile, The 36, 214
Greenlight Screenwriting Lab 255
Grime Kids 235
Growth 47–8

Hacks 146, 160, 163
Haggard, Daisy 213
Handful of Dust, A 175–6
Hanks, Tom 64, 83, 136, 139, 154
Happy Valley 81, 117, 127, 153, 157–9, 161, 217, 232, 304
Harari, Arthur 103
Hard Day's Night, A xxiii–xxiv
Hare, David 148
Harold and Maude xxiv
#MeToo 42

INDEX OF NAMES AND TITLES 319

Haubman, Lawrence xxiii–xxiv, 135
HBO 30, 69, 91
Head, Sally xviii; *see also* Sally Head Productions
Heat 36
Help xx, 10
Here We Go 37, 213
Herman, Mark 36
Herrero, Fanny xxv, 187
Herskovitz, Marshall xxvi
Hillsborough xx, 304
His Dark Materials 100
Hit Man 215
Hitchcock, Alfred 19
Hittman, Eliza 41–2
Hoffman, John 42–4, 188
Holt, Nick 273
Homicide: Life on the Street xxvi
Honess-Martin, Jacqui 36
Hooper, Robin xvii
Hopkins, Anthony xvii
House of Ife 153
House Through Time, A 29
Howards' Way 37
Hughes, Gwyneth 108
Hurwitz, Mitchell 155
Hustle 51–2

I Am Sam 68
I Care a Lot 160
I Hate Suzie 39, 305
I May Destroy You 214, 305
Ibini, Matilda Feyişayo xxvii
Icarus 32
Ikoko, Theresa xxvi–xxvii, 235, 300
Imaginary Friends Productions 255
In Bruges 66
Incredible Kitty Fisher, The 45
Inglourious Basterds 214
Inspector Morse 70, 153
Ireland, David 50
Ishiguro, Kazuo 135
ITV xviii, 4, 14, 39, 55, 107, 114, 235, 299
ITV Studios 255

Jackson, Michael 33
Jackson, Peter 65
Jacobs Morgan, Matthew xxvii
Jaws xxiv
Johnson, Boris 146
Johnson, Kristine 68
Jordison, Sam 7–8
Joyce, Rachel 135

Kamen, Robert Mark 36
Kantor, Jodi 50
Kaos 28
Kay, Adam 14, 104, 162
Kay, George 61, 101
Kelly, Dennis 273
Kick-Ass 272
Killing Eve 217
Kiln Theatre 184
King, Stephen 36, 136, 214
Kirkman, Robert 272
Knight, Steven 53
Kohan, Jenji xxv, 136
Kramer vs. Kramer xxiv
Kranz, Fran 45
Kudos 255

La Plante, Lynda xviii
Ladybird 35
Lakhani, Chandni xxvii
Lang, Chris 153
Larkin, Philip 27–8
Last of Us, The 30
Last Tango in Halifax xxv, 157, 217, 304
Lawn, Declan 16
Lawrence, Bill 36
Leaving Neverland 33
Left Bank Pictures 255
Lehman Trilogy, The 39
Leigh, Mike xxv, 30
Lenkiewicz, Rebecca 42, 50–1
Lester, Richard xxiv
Levinson, Richard 35, 150
Levinson, Sam xxv
Levy, Andrea 99
Leys, Kate xviii
Liar 93
Life and Death in the Warehouse 46–7
Life in Ten Pictures, A 121
Line of Duty 77
Link, William 35, 150
Linklater, Richard 35, 215
Liotta, Ray 102
Little Miss Sunshine 34, 35, 53, 84–5, 89, 95–6, 130, 155
Little Women 155
Living 135
Loach, Ken xxv
Local Hero 232
Locke 53
London Film Festival 265
London Screenwriters' Festival 220, 262, 266
London Short Film Festival 271
London Weekend Television xviii
London's Burning 36

Long Good Friday 36
Love Story 50, 79
Lovers, The 50
Lyle, Ashley 46, 217
Lynch, Andrew 164–5
Lyttelton, Oliver 47, 217

McCarthy, Cormac 12
McCarthy, Tom 51, 105
McCartney, Paul 65
McClain, Johnathan 59
McCulloch, Andrew 107
McDonagh, Martin 66
McGee, Lisa 217
McGovern, Jimmy xviii, xx, 8–10, 36, 38, 87, 136, 185, 304
Machin, Barbara 63
McKay, Neil xviii, 15, 295
Mad Men 304
Maddocks, Archie xxvii, 235
Magee, David 67
Mager, William 235
Malpractice 235
Man Called Otto, A 67
Man on Wire 33
Mandel, Emily St. John 12
Manhattan xxiv
Mann, Michael 36
Manzoor, Nida 300
Manzoor, Sarfraz 7–8
Marion and Geoff 56
Marley & Me 154
Marriage Story 50, 189, 215
Marsh, James 33, 273
Martin, Steve 42–4, 155, 188
Mass 45
Massini, Stefano 39
Matafeo, Rose 49
Maternal 36
Materne, Taylor 51–2
Meadows, Shane 7, 10, 159–60, 304
Medics xviii, 295
Melia, Tom 35, 50, 86
Mellor, Kay xviii, 91
Memento 108
Merchant, Stephen 104
Mercurio, Jed 13–14, 38, 77, 93, 229, 252, 304
Mercy, The 32
Mid-Morning Matters 161
Millar, Mark 272
Miller, Suzie 55, 86
Misbehaviour 215
Miseducation of Cameron Post, The 215
Missing, The 93
Moffat, Peter 101, 150
Molly 164–5

Money Heist xxvi, 16, 42, 187
Monty Python's Flying Circus xxv
Moore, Graham 59
Morecambe and Wise xxv
Morgan, Abi 96–7, 229, 273
Morgan, Peter 29, 155
Moriarty, Regina 241–2
Morris, Felicity 45
Morton, John 183–4
Morton, Samantha 295
Moulton, Catherine 235
Mrs Wilson 235
Mum 37, 155
Murdered by My Father xxvii
Myers, Mike 49
Mystery of Edwin Drood, The xvii

National Film and Television School (NFTS) 250
National Theatre (London) xxvii; see also NT Live
Nelson, Jessie 68
Netflix 28, 61, 101, 234, 235
Never Rarely Sometimes Always 41–2
New Writing North 266
New Writing South 266
Newman, G. F. xxv
Newsroom, The 9
Niccol, Andrew 136
Nichols, Jeff 104
Nichols, Peter xxv
Nicholson, William 31, 124
Nickerson, Bart 46, 217
Night Of, The 150
Nighy, Bill 89, 135
Nolan, Christopher 36, 108
Nolan, Jonathan 108
Normal People 16, 131, 215
Norrish, Hilary 126, 298
Northern Ireland Screen 266
Norton-Taylor, Richard 184
Notting Hill 50, 154
NT Live 55
Nuts in May 30

Oborne, Peter 146
Ocean's Eleven 36
Office, The 104
Ofori-Attah, Grace 235
O'Malley, Bryan Lee 272
One Flew Over the Cuckoo's Nest xxiii–xxiv, 135
One Life 154
Only Murders in the Building 42–4, 188
Orange Is the New Black xxv, 136
Östlund, Ruben 124

Other People 215
Outfit, The 59–60
Outside In 215
Owens, Lisa 30
Oz xxvi

Page, Sarah 237
Paines Plough (company) xvii
Pakula, Alan J. 128
Palm Springs 50
Paramount Pictures xvii
Patel, Vinay xxvi–xxvii
Patient, The 153
Patterson, Adam 16
Peele, Jordan 36, 54
Pegg, Simon 54
Penhall, Joe 12, 35, 53
Pennies from Heaven 304
Percy, Kitty 235
Peterson, Bob 105
Petit, Philippe 33
Phelps, Sarah 127, 131, 152
Pileggi, Nicholas 15, 79, 102
Pina, Álex xxvi, 16, 42, 187
Pinter, Harold 54, 108
Piper, Billie 39, 305
Pixar 105
Play for Today xxv
Poehler, Amy 49
Poirot 35
Poliakoff, Stephen xxv
Polite Society 300
Pope, Jeff 15, 39
Post, The 51
Potter, Dennis xvii, xxv, 304
Power, Ben 39
Prebble, Lucy 39, 89, 273, 305
Presley, Priscilla 29
Price, Nathaniel xxvii
Price, Richard 150
Pride 36
Prima Facie 55, 86
Prime Suspect xviii
Priscilla 29
Puttnam, David xvii
Puzo, Mario xxiii–xxiv, 36, 64, 139, 155, 189, 216
Pye, Shaun 213

Queen & Slim 53
Quiz 14–15

Red Rose 235
Reed, Dan 33
Reich, Allon xviii
Rescue, The 28–32, 124
Reservoir Dogs 59
Responder, The 46

Reunion 235
Road, The 12, 35, 53
Rocketman 65
Rocks xxvii, 235
Rocky 51
Romita, John, Jr. 272
Room 36, 83–4, 189
Room 104 29
Rooney, Sally 16, 131, 215
Rosenthal, Jack xxv, 36
Rothwell, Jerry 32
Rowlands, Claire 141–4
Royal Television Society 265
Rudd, Paul 49
Rye Lane 35, 50, 86

Safdie, Josh and Benny 126, 135
St Johnston, Joshua 36
Salisbury Poisonings, The 16
Sally Head Productions xxiv
Sandler, Adam 51–2, 135
Saulnier, Jeremy 36
Save the Cat 110
Savile, Jimmy 144–5
Saving Private Ryan 36
Schumacher, Tony 46
Schumann, Howard xxv
Scorsese, Martin 79, 102
Scott, Ridley 53
Scott Pilgrim vs. the World 272
Scottish Screenwriters 266
Screen One xxv
Screen Two xxv
Screen Yorkshire 266
Screenwipe 9
Scrubs 36
Searching for Sugar Man 28–9, 121–2
Second City Firsts xxv
Segal, Erich 50, 79
Sellers, Peter 139
Shahmoon, Lily 251
Shaun of the Dead 54
Shawshank Redemption, The 36, 136, 214
She Said 42, 50–1
She Will 235
Shelton, Lynn 215
Sherwood 15, 36, 153
Shortcomings 215, 272
Showalter, Michael 49
Silence of the Lambs, The 79
Simmons, J. K. 145–6
Singer, Josh 51
Six Feet Under 36, 91
Sixth Commandment, The 127, 131, 152
Sky 13, 255

INDEX OF NAMES AND TITLES 321

Small Island 39
Snakes on a Plane 213
Snedden, Alice 49
Social Network, The 9
Solon, Laura 213
Somebody Somewhere 12
Somerville, Patrick 12
Sophie's Choice 128
Sorkin, Aaron 9, 185
Spacey, Kevin 102
Spencer, Melanie 45
Spencer, Si 30, 272
Spielberg, Steven xxiv, 36, 51
Spoiled 237
Spotlight 51
Springsteen, Bruce 7, 25–6
Square, The 124
Squeeze 26
Ssemuyaba, Anna xxvii
Staged 75
Stand By Me 35
Standing Up 187
Starstruck 49
Station Eleven 12
Statsky, Jen 146, 160, 163
Steadman, Alison 30
Steve Jobs 9
Stibbe, Nina 7–8
Storer, Christopher 37–8, 153, 155
Studio21 220, 254
Succession xxvi, 38–9, 152, 155, 178–80
Symon, Anna xxvi–xxvii, 217, 235, 237–8
Syndicate, The 91

Tactical Questioning 184
Taken 36
Talking Heads 56
Tarantino, Quentin 6, 9, 59, 214
Taylor, Nicole xx, 7
Tessema, Beru 153
Thelma & Louise 53
There She Goes 213
They Came Together 49
Thirteen Lives 31, 124
Thirtysomething xxvi

This Is England 7, 10, 304
This is Going to Hurt 14, 104, 162
Thorne, Jack xx, xxvi–xvii, 10, 159–60, 273, 300
Three Billboards Outside Ebbing, Missouri 66
Three Girls xx
Thunder Road 271
Thureen, Paul 12
Time 36, 87, 136, 304
Tinder Swindler, The 45
Tomalin, Paul 30, 272
Tomine, Adrian 215, 272
Tourist, The 93
Tribute 55
Trier, Joachim 187
Triet, Justine 103
Truby, John 110
True Grit xxv
Truman Show, The 136
Trying 64
Turner & Hooch 154
Twenty Twelve 183–4
Twohey, Megan 50

Uncut Gems 135
Unforgotten 153
Unlikely Pilgrimage of Harold Fry, The 135
Up 105
Upright 53
Usden, Adam 235

Vasarhelyi, Elizabeth Chai 28–32, 124
Vaughn, Matthew 272
Vertigo 19
Very Expensive Poison, A 39
Vice 29
Virtues, The 159–60, 304
Vogt, Eskil 187

W1A 183
Wain, David 49
Wainwright, Sally xxv–xxvii, 8, 38, 81–2, 104, 117, 127, 135, 146, 153, 157–9, 161, 217, 229, 232, 304

Waithe, Lena 53
Waking the Dead 63
Walking Dead, The 272
Waller-Bridge, Phoebe 103–4, 213, 217
Waugh, Evelyn 175–6
Way Back, The (2010) 216
Way Back, The (2020) 216
Way Way Back, The 216
Wayne, John xxiv–xxv
We Are Lady Parts 300
Webb, Robert 215
Wednesday Play, The xxv
Weiner, Matthew 304
Weinstein, Harvey 42, 50–1
Weisberg, Joe 153
Wells, Tom 5
Wenders, Wim 35
West Wing, The 9
What If 215
When Harry Met Sally 35, 50, 154
Whiplash 35, 145–6, 152, 159
White, Mike 69
White Lotus, The 69
Whitehill, Camilla 235
Who Wants to Be a Millionaire? 14–15
Wild Rose 7
Wilder, Billy 50
Williams, Harry 93
Williams, Jack 93
Wireless Theatre 270
Wizard of Oz, The 54
Wolton, Andy 64
Worst Person in the World, The 187
Wright, Edgar 272
Writers' Guild of Great Britain 266, 286–7

Yellowjackets 46, 217
Yorke, John 252
Young Ones, The 263

Zaillian, Steven 150
Zero Chill 235
Zodiac 51
Zone of Interest, The 187
Zwick, Edward xxvi

Index of Subjects

active/passive 72–4, 138, 166, 182
actors xvii, xix, 30, 89, 148, 185, 201–2, 209–10, 231–2, 256, 263, 267, 295
acts 77, 83, 110–16, 123, 226, 299
agents xvii, 5–6, 219, 224–5, 226, 235, 236, 245, 250, 259, 264–7, 279, 283–9, 316
animals 154, 167, 170
antagonists 127, 131, 134, 152–3, 158–9, 161, 226, 315; *see also* character *and* protagonists
articulacy and inarticulacy 9, 42–3, 48, 69, 132–3, 139, 147–9, 166, 178–80, 183, 185, 190, 198
awards and prizes 254–5, 270

backstory 61–2, 103, 117, 157, 159, 173, 299, 315
beat sheets 218–20, 239–40, 315, 317
beats 76, 110, 113, 115, 188, 298–9, 318
beginnings and endings xxvi, 11–12, 26, 43, 48, 50, 56, 64, 69, 75–9, 85–6, 88, 92, 95–7, 99–100, 105–9, 112–13, 116–17, 123, 125, 139, 147, 149, 153, 157, 165, 181–2, 189, 200, 210, 230, 299
blogs 251, 262, 272–3

callbacks 85–6, 315
'calling card' scripts, *see* 'spec' scripts
captions 52, 100, 106, 315
character 126–74, 183–5, 191–4, 204, 228
character action 96–7, 128, 163, 189, 191, 194, 203, 231; *see also* directions

character arcs 127, 139–40, 315
character biographies 233
character checklists 166–71
character choices 127–8, 163
character description 141, 147, 199–203, 231–2
character-driven xxiii, 36, 47–8, 67, 93, 113, 128; *see also* plot-driven
character exercises 22–4, 147, 149, 166–74
character 'intelligence' 66, 133–5, 156
character introduction xxvi, 74, 89, 125, 151, 181–2, 198–9, 233
character journeys 35, 129; *see also* character arcs
character names 175–6, 208–9, 212, 215
character observation 22–4, 29, 66, 95–6, 130, 140–7, 161, 172, 193, 194
choreography 30
circularity 85–6, 112
class 8, 15, 70, 185
clichés 31–2, 60, 69–71, 78, 134, 140, 189, 263, 315; *see also* tropes
collaboration xix, 18, 201, 202, 246, 264, 281, 291–4, 297
comedy xxvi, 7, 9, 41, 47–50, 53–4, 66, 74, 75, 91, 104, 122, 138, 154–5, 161, 183–4, 188, 192, 213, 231, 238, 241–2, 263; *see also* romcom *and* sitcom
comedy horror 53–4
communities, *see* society and communities
conflict 11, 15, 23, 44, 50, 73, 77, 112, 151–2, 154, 156, 180, 191, 316; *see also* internal conflict

context 48, 65, 72, 78–9, 86, 90, 98–100, 153, 227, 233, 238; *see also* settings
copyright 25, 224–6
counterpoint 65–6, 73, 102, 132–3, 163, 176, 180, 315
courses and training xx–xxi, xxvi–xxvii, 4–5, 37–8, 45, 140–4, 219–20, 227, 235, 248–60, 263, 270, 272, 279, 281, 289, 293
crime dramas 4, 33, 35–6, 41, 42–3, 46, 63, 93, 98, 100, 150, 154–5; *see also* legal dramas *and* police dramas
cuts and cutting 20, 26–7, 33, 45–6, 55, 69, 73, 75–7, 99, 106–7, 116, 181–2, 210–11, 241, 316; *see also* montage *and* transitions
CVs 255–7, 258, 287, 290

dance, *see* choreography
deus ex machina, *see* random events
development, *see* script development
dialect and idiolect 183–6
dialogue 6, 9, 22, 48, 59–61, 65, 72–7, 94, 96, 115, 118, 152, 163, 174, 175–94, 196, 198, 200–1, 206–10, 230, 317, 318
diegetic music 201, 316
direct address 82, 103–4, 190
directions 94, 163, 188, 196–8, 201–8; *see also* character action
documentaries 28–33, 45, 65, 121–2, 124, 248, 273, 316
dramatic propositions 42–8, 77, 114, 125, 316
dreams and dreaming 17–21, 73

INDEX OF SUBJECTS 323

eccentricity 130, 168
economy 72, 75, 105, 112, 177–8, 185, 190, 192, 196–7, 204–5, 207, 211, 232, 237, 239
empathy 7, 82, 93, 97, 126–8, 146, 158–9, 160
excluding/including 69, 71–2, 77, 91, 115, 117, 169, 207, 210
exercises 14, 17–18, 20–1, 22–4, 37, 53, 122, 147, 149, 166–74, 230–1, 301, 304
exposition 43, 49, 52, 59–62, 74–5, 95–104, 106, 132–3, 149, 157, 176–7, 181, 188–9, 194, 208–9, 212, 316; *see also* plots

family 10, 34, 36–8, 84–5, 95–6, 131, 139, 151–7, 164–5, 171, 213
feedback, *see* notes and feedback
flashbacks 82–3, 102–4, 157, 316
fonts 196, 230–1
football, *see* sport
foreign languages 186–8
form 13–14, 24, 54–6, 59, 84, 104, 110, 112, 114, 118–21, 124, 219, 316; *see also* genre *and* structure

games 30, 120–1, 164; *see also* sport
gaps 19, 80–1, 131–3, 145, 147–8, 191–2; *see also* time
gender politics 215
general meetings 225, 259, 264–5, 279–83, 316
genre 4, 10, 13, 21, 32, 48–54, 76, 79, 112, 124, 136, 138, 154–5, 181, 215, 226, 229, 304, 316; *see also* tone
graphic novels 30, 272

hooks 43, 62–3, 64, 101, 114, 123, 125, 191, 228, 316
hospitals xxvi, 36, 64, 83, 90, 120, 154, 317; *see also* medical dramas
humour 8, 49, 66, 69, 91, 96, 130, 167, 216; *see also* comedy

internal conflict xxvi, 19, 89, 112, 129, 130–3, 141, 149, 162–5
interviews (fictional) 29, 50, 61, 77, 101, 136; (professional) 4–5, 223, 225, 258–60, 285

journalism, *see* newspapers and journalism
journeys 18–20, 29, 32, 34–5, 45, 55, 71–2, 88, 95–6, 118, 128–31, 139, 149, 159–60, 165, 172, 197, 241, 315; *see also* character arc

legal dramas 4, 35, 154–5, 317; *see also* crime dramas *and* police dramas
loglines 11, 13–14, 40–1, 44–5, 229, 233–4, 316

medical dramas xviii, 4, 13–14, 36, 118, 154–5, 295; *see also* hospitals
metaphors 23, 27, 35, 55, 78, 87–8, 97
mockumentaries 104, 316
monologue 54–6, 103–4, 118, 141, 174, 190, 262, 269
montage 51, 105–7, 316
motifs 87, 316
movement 73, 88–9, 115, 204–5
music xxiv, xxv, xxvi, 7, 21, 24, 28, 159, 172, 201, 316; *see also* diegetic music
musicals 28, 53
mythology 28

networking 221, 246, 261–3, 274–7
newspapers and journalism xxiii, 14–16, 28, 35, 37, 50–1, 53, 58, 121–2, 146–7, 156, 170, 199, 248, 272
notes and feedback xix, 189, 212, 220, 252, 258, 261, 276, 278, 282, 286, 291–300, 316
novels and short stories 7–8, 12, 28, 39, 121, 122, 131, 135, 136, 175–6, 199, 204, 215, 248, 272; *see also* graphic novels

off screen/on screen 59–64, 71, 75, 81, 102, 117, 157, 188, 192, 200, 202–4, 207
one-sentence pitches 11, 14, 281; *see also* pitches and pitching
opera 28, 148–9
optioning 5, 225, 317
outlines 11, 96, 166, 218–20, 236, 239–42, 298–9, 317

parentheticals 209–10
passive/active, *see* active/passive
pay-offs, *see* set-ups and pay-offs
phones 50, 73–5, 91, 96, 101, 188
pilot episodes xxvi, 42–3, 114, 117, 124–5, 241–2, 252, 289, 317
pitch decks 231–2, 317; *see also* pitches and pitching
pitches and pitching 11–13, 15, 18, 20, 38, 47, 96, 218–40, 246, 256, 262, 281, 286, 289, 297, 299, 316, 317; *see also* loglines
plays, *see* theatre

plot-driven 93, 113
plots 22–3, 32, 51, 62, 80–1, 91, 93, 101, 110–13, 126, 128, 134, 158, 227–8, 233, 298–300; *see also* exposition *and* subplots
podcasts 29, 43, 248, 269
poems and poetry 25–8, 87, 96, 121, 122, 189, 199, 232, 273
point of view 16, 30–1, 36, 42, 81–5, 99, 102–3, 127, 192
police dramas xxvi, 13, 16, 36, 39, 61, 70, 77, 81, 90, 100–1, 136, 138, 153, 181, 255–6, 317
political correctness 190
politics xx, xxvi, 7–9, 11, 13–16, 38, 46–7, 55, 92, 146, 190, 237–8, 256
POV, *see* point of view
pre-laps 200, 317
precincts, *see* settings
presentation 195–217, 232, 238, 260; *see also* pitches and pitching
prisons xxvi, 36, 82–3, 107, 109, 118, 120, 136, 154
props 73, 97, 154, 172, 189, 205
protagonists 78, 87, 102, 109, 118, 134, 137–8, 153, 158–9, 161, 163–5, 200, 226, 317; *see also* antagonists *and* character

radio 29, 177, 270–1
random events 20, 24, 90–2, 315
real people 15, 21–3, 29, 38–9, 84, 140–7
real time 13–14, 54, 65, 108, 118; *see also* time
research (creative) xviii, 16, 21, 29, 32, 51, 57–9, 71, 113, 124, 183, 237, 300; (professional) 228–9, 239, 251, 254, 257, 260, 268, 281–2, 285, 287
rhythm 76–7, 118, 121, 182–6
risk, *see* stakes
road movies 35, 53
romantic comedy, *see* romcom
romcom 48–50, 53, 138, 154, 216, 316

scene headings 203, 206–8, 317
scene-by-scenes, *see* beat sheet
script development xvii–xix, xxi, 5–6, 11, 31, 34–5, 38–9, 44, 111–14, 218–25, 233–4, 239–40, 258–9, 264–7, 280, 286, 295–8, 315, 316–18
self-awareness 130, 147–9, 161, 163

INDEX OF SUBJECTS

sequences xxiv, 43, 51, 69, 71–2, 81, 83–4, 88, 96, 103, 105, 107, 110–11, 115, 116, 120, 189–90, 230, 241, 316, 317; *see also* montage
series bible 239–40, 317
set-ups and pay-offs 51, 62–3, 72, 74, 77, 83, 85–6, 90–2, 112, 114, 125, 165, 188, 192, 230, 316
settings xxvi, 9–10, 43, 33, 38, 40, 52, 54, 57–8, 61, 81, 87, 90, 94, 112, 119–20, 125, 135–6, 138, 164, 171, 191, 205, 210–11, 227–8, 317, 318; *see also* context
sex xxiv, 45, 70, 168, 170, 173
shots 20, 54, 76, 115, 200
signposts 86–7, 192
sitcom 14, 104
situation comedy, *see* sitcom
sluglines, *see* scene headings
social media 267, 274–6
society and communities xxvii, 8–9, 11–12, 36, 84, 119, 121, 153–5, 318
software 197, 316
songs 21, 25–8, 65, 76, 121, 122, 273
'spec' scripts 3–5, 13, 79, 219, 234, 236, 247, 250, 267, 271, 279, 285, 289, 315, 318
specificity 7, 10, 16, 26, 95–6, 154, 164, 189

sport 41, 51–2, 118, 120–1, 134, 156, 167
stakes 16, 20, 30–2, 37–8, 44, 46, 61–2, 78–9, 125, 137–8, 153, 155, 158
starting points 4, 11–12, 14, 19, 23–4, 29–30, 49–50, 53, 111, 140, 165, 173, 304; *see also* beginnings and endings
status 38, 62, 78, 96, 139, 151–2, 163, 168, 185, 242
status quo 38, 72, 77, 117, 139, 193, 318
stereotypes 156
story beats, *see* beats
story gaps, *see* gaps
story ideas 11–39, 40, 44, 49–50, 58, 140, 219, 229, 230, 318
story premise, *see* story ideas
story worlds, *see* context *and* settings
structure xviii, 27, 53, 54, 58, 77, 80, 83, 105, 109–24, 181–2, 194, 219–20, 252, 298–9, 316; *see also* form
subplots 30–2, 80; *see also* plots
subtext 19, 65–6, 73, 132–3, 147, 176, 178–81, 188, 192, 318
subtitles 186–8
suspense 64, 316

taglines, *see* hooks
TED talks 29

texting and messaging 188
theatre xvii, xxv, xxvii, 14–15, 28, 39, 54, 55, 86, 103, 108, 124, 153, 175–6, 184–5, 248, 265, 269–70, 273, 289, 316
time xxiii, 31, 45–6, 55, 80, 88, 94, 100, 105, 106–11, 116, 118, 193, 206, 210–11; *see also* gaps *and* real time
titles 27, 121, 128, 131, 213–17
tone 10, 40, 53–4, 79, 90–2, 96–9, 101, 103–4, 138, 186–7, 213–14, 219, 226–9, 232–3, 241, 300, 318
transitions 75–6, 84, 210–11; *see also* cuts and cutting *and* montage
treatments 96, 218–19, 233, 239–40, 245, 318
tropes 48–50, 52, 69–71, 96, 100–1, 105, 140, 318
true crime 41–3; *see also* crime dramas

voice 3, 6–10, 17, 24, 39, 53, 111, 163, 174, 183–5, 196, 233, 238, 272–3; *see also* tone
voice-over 42–4, 95, 101–4, 177, 190, 316, 318

writers' rooms 18, 296–7, 318

Zoom 74–5, 264–5, 267, 279